GREAT PREACHING ON
THE
DEITY OF CHRIST

GREAT PREACHING ON

THE
DEITY OF CHRIST

COMPILED BY
CURTIS HUTSON

SWORD of the LORD
PUBLISHERS
P.O.BOX 1099, MURFREESBORO, TN 37133

ISBN 0-87398-321-1

This Second Printing: July, 1988

Printed and Bound in the United States of America

Preface

When one considers that for nineteen hundred years the deity of Christ has been the cornerstone of the Christian church, it may seem strange that we need to consider at this time the question: **Was Christ God, or just a man?** But even a casual glance through the pages of the religious press—not to speak of the secular press—will convince one that the issue between these two views of the Saviour is a very vital one today.

Many church members—even ministers— openly reject orthodox teachings regarding Christ's personality. In recent times some have come to regard Christ as merely a good man and great teacher. They explain that He was divine in the sense in which all men have something of a divine spark in them. When one departs from his belief in Deity, there is no logical stopping place until he reaches an entire repudiation of Christ as a supernatural Being.

If Christ be not God, then salvation through His blood is only a longed-for fantasy, hope for this life is a mockery, and Heaven is only a beautiful dream.

BUT—Jesus IS God; and these seventeen messages, chosen as the best on the subject, unmask, dethrone and denounce those who blatantly deny the basic teachings of Jesus Christ. They prove from Scripture Christ's saving, supernatural nature; they clearly show how Jesus fulfilled literally hundreds of items of prophecy in His miraculous virgin birth, His life, His atoning death. Most of all, they demonstrate that Christ was raised bodily from the dead and has ascended to a place of intercession, and equality with God Himself! This evidence every preacher needs to strengthen sermons; every witness can use to win souls; every Christian requires to refute unbelievers. In a day of great departure from the fundamentals of the Faith, it behooves us as children of God to be "ready always to give an answer to every man that asketh you a reason of the hope that is in you."

Fundamental Bible believers will thrill at the convincing manner in which each author "shuts the mouths of the gainsayers." The fire and zeal of these giants of the Faith are evident in these impassioned messages dealing with this cardinal doctrine. Those who desire to be well-fortified in the fundamental doctrine of a divine Christ would do well to give this book a thorough study.

Curtis Hutson
Editor, SWORD OF THE LORD

Table of Contents

HONORABLE CLINTON N. HOWARD
1868-1955

ABOUT THE MAN:

Mr. Howard was editor of *Progress* magazine, general superintendent of the International Reform Federation, Washington, D. C., and was for five years chairman of the World Peace Commission. He had a wide hearing as a Bible lecturer; was a staunch defender of the Faith, a temperance and peace advocate.

William Jennings Bryan said, "I have never heard his equal."

One of his famous messages was, "Pearls of Paradise." At a world's fair he saw a Mohammedan counting his pearl beads, each representing a name for his Mohammedan god. He had memorized the names and challenged Mr. Howard to find 98 names for his Christian God. This great Christian undertook to find all the names for Jesus Christ in the Bible. He was thrilled and gave this marvelous lecture on 208 wonderful names for our wonderful Lord over the whole land.

I.

Was Jesus the Son of Joseph, or the Son of God?

HONORABLE CLINTON N. HOWARD

(An address given at a union evangelistic service of ten churches, Rochester, NY, January 9, 1924, in reply to Rev. Wallace Rose, Dr. Algernon Crapsey and others who denied the virgin birth of our Lord Jesus Christ as recorded in the Gospels.)

I take for my text the words of Jesus to the Jews, "What think ye of the Christ? whose son is he?"

Is Jesus the son of Joseph, begotten of man by human procreation; or is He the Son of God, begotten of God through the Holy Spirit by extraordinary and divine generation?

I affirm the virgin birth of our divine Lord according to the Scriptures while Rev. Rose and those of like mind deny it. The Bible is the only Book in the world that says anything about it. It states it by prophecy before His birth and by two of the biographers of Jesus after His birth, in language which cannot be misunderstood; is supported by Mary, by the conduct of Joseph who "before they came together" found Mary "with child of the Holy Ghost, and knew her not till she had brought forth her first born son"; and by the testimony of the Angel Gabriel who replied to Mary's question, "How shall this be, seeing I know not a man?" by saying, "The Holy Ghost shall come upon thee, and the power of the Highest shall overshadow thee: therefore that holy thing which shall be born unto thee shall be called the Son of God."

Mr. Rose and other modernists deny this and contend that Jesus was begotten of Joseph and that Joseph was the father of Jesus. There are nearly one hundred names and designations of our divine Lord in the New Testament. They leave us in no doubt as to "whose son is he?"

Jesus Not Called the Son of Joseph
in the Bible

He is called the Son of Mary; He is called the Son of David; He is called the Son of Man; He is called the Son of God. He is called the Only Begotten Son; He is called the Son of the Highest; but when, where and by whom was He called the son of Joseph?

When the Pharisees were offended in Him because He said, "I came down from heaven" and, "I came forth from God," they, His enemies, said, 'Is not this Jesus, the son of Joseph?'

But His disciples, the four evangelists, the apostles, the prophets, and Jehovah called Him again and again, more frequently than by any other name, "The Son of God."

Matthew, who was chosen to write the Gospel of Matthew and is believed to have written it within a few years after the ascension of our Lord, says, "Now the birth of Jesus Christ was on this wise," and goes into detail about the virgin birth. Luke, the physician, devotes two whole chapters to the miraculous birth of both Jesus and John, the one being born of a virgin and the other of a married barren wife "who hath also conceived a son in her old age," the Angel Gabriel said. Do barren women of old age bear children without divine intervention? Must we reject this miracle also?

These men do not recognize the significance of the fact that the one chosen of God to tell in detail the story of the virgin birth "in violation of biological law" is the beloved physican, Dr. Luke, the one of all men who knew Jesus who would be most likely to reject it. They would doubtless have made a point of it had it been related alone by the publican Matthew or the fisherman John, but God chose His witnesses with discriminating care and delegated that part of the life of His divine Son to the physician Luke, the one least likely to be deceived or inclined to accept it. They are rejecting the testimony of the most competent witness. If the story told by Dr. Luke is founded upon falsehood and is a literary fable, as Dr. Crapsey says, the most beautiful story in the life of Christ falls to the ground.

Sufficient Number of Witnesses Proves
Virgin Birth

Those who deny the virgin birth contend that there are not a sufficient number of witnesses. How many witnesses does God require to prove His Word? The silence of the others is constructed by Mr. Rose, as reported in his sermon of two weeks ago, "as not denying directly but by implication and by every rule of logic" the testimony of the other two. By the rule of "logic" one could destroy the authenticity and truthfulness of almost every statement in the New Testament concerning the life and deeds of Jesus.

If we must reject all truth concerning which one or more of the disciples are silent, you have destroyed the life and personality of Jesus Christ— human and divine. If two witnesses are not enough to establish His virgin birth, then the story of the ascension, told alone by Luke and Mark, and the resurrection of Lazarus, told alone by John, falls to the ground. Then there was no star of the East, no innocent babies slain by Herod, no heavenly host proclaiming 'peace on earth good will toward men,' as told by Luke and pronounced "the most beautiful story ever written."

The story of His virgin birth is no more wonderful as a miracle than the story of His life, His death, His resurrection, and His ascension, all of which rest upon the testimony of eyewitnesses or inspired biographers. The silence of the others about any one fact, on the contrary, proves that they accepted it.

Jesus is said never once to have referred to His virgin birth. We do not know all that Jesus said. John declares, "There are also many other things which Jesus did, the which, if they should be written every one, I suppose that even the world itself could not contain the books that should be written" (John 21:25).

We are told that after His resurrection and while on the way to Emmaus with two of His disciples, whom Rev. Rose says were silent in their discussion about the virgin birth, Jesus, "beginning at Moses and all the prophets, expounded unto them in ALL the scriptures the things concerning himself." If that is a statement of fact, it is unlikely that Jesus omitted Isaiah's prophesy, "Behold, a virgin shall be with child, and shall bring forth a son, and they shall call his name Emmanuel, which being interpreted is, God with us." Doubtless also he quoted Isaiah 49:1 and Jeremiah 1:5, both of which foretell His virgin birth.

We are told that Mark's Gospel says nothing about the virgin birth. It is not surprising that Mark should not tell as much in sixteen chapters as Luke tells in twenty-four and Matthew tells in twenty-eight. Mark, writing for the Gentiles, obviously begins his story with the manhood ministry of Jesus, but in the absence of specific denial confirms it in his first paragraph, "The beginning of the gospel of Jesus Christ, the Son of God."

It is said that John makes no reference to the virgin birth. Neither does John tell of the transfiguration, though he was one of the three disciples who Matthew, Mark and Luke say was there. More than any other one of the disciples John refers to Jesus as "the only begotten Son of God."

Does he mean begotten of Joseph or begotten of God? The word "begotten" is defined in the Century Dictionary: "to generate, to procreate, to bring into existence." And this disciple who leaned on His bosom at the Last Supper, repeatedly called Jesus "the only begotten Son of God."

But how about Paul? Mr. Rose said in his sermon as reported two weeks ago, "Paul never heard of the virgin birth, or hearing it, placed no credence in it."

That is a most amazing statement when one remembers that Luke, who wrote the gospel commonly called "Paul's Gospel," was the faithful companion of Paul for years on his missionary journeys, going with him into Asia, Macedonia and Rome. Nearly all we know about Paul and the early history of the church was written by Luke.

Luke, who wrote in detail the story of the virgin birth, was the secretary and physician to Paul and covered in the Acts of the Apostles, which he wrote, the life of Paul for a period of nearly thirty years. It is incredible that these two disciples, each of them giving their lives to the work of founding the church of Christ, had not talked over the events in the life of Christ or that Paul would doubt the testimony of Luke.

If Luke cannot qualify as a truthful witness for our Lord, he cannot qualify as a truthful witness for Paul; and you would have to cut out Paul's thirty years of missionary activity and all his marvelous miracles, even to the restoring of life to the dead Eutychus who fell down from the third loft, and the miracle of his own recovery when stoned and left for dead, and the handkerchiefs and aprons carried from the person of Paul that restored the sick, related by Luke. All must go with the virgin birth if Luke is a fabricator.

Luke wrote his Gospel in connection with the missionary ministry of Paul. If you destroy the value of his testimony, supported by Matthew, about the virgin birth, you destroy the value of his testimony about the life and miracles of Paul.

If he cannot, as a truthful historian and capable physician, be relied upon for the one, he cannot be relied upon for the other. Who wrote the story of Paul's miraculous conversion? Who reported his travels, his shipwreck, his marvelous speeches before kings and commoners at Athens and at Ephesus? Luke, the biographer of Paul and Jesus!

Think you for one moment that Paul would have chosen him for his companion, his physician and his biographer if he could not rely upon his testimony, and disbelieved the story he wrote of the life of the Lord? Such a supposition is beyond human credulity.

No doubt Luke was with Paul when he wrote it, as the time of his Gospel is fixed about A. D. 60, when Paul was in the midst of his activity. It is a highly significant fact that God chose the same evangelist to write the book of Luke with the story of the virgin birth and the book of the Acts of the Apostles. No such signal honor came to any other one of the evangelists.

It is a further significant fact that both books are addressed to the same Christian nobleman, Theophilus, a man of intelligence and distinction. It is hardly possible that Luke would attempt to confirm the claims of Christ by the invention of such an incredible tale as the virgin birth if it were not founded upon fact.

Introducing his Gospel, Luke writes,

"It seemed good to me also, having had perfect understanding of all things from the very first, to write unto thee in order, most excellent Theophilus, That thou mightest know the certainty of those things, wherein thou hast been instructed."

Writing to the same person at a later date he begins,

"The former treatise have I made, O Theophilus, of all that Jesus began both to do and to teach, Until the day in which he was taken up."

My friends, to throw out the testimony of Luke is to destroy the New Testament and lose your Christ!

Writing to Timothy, Paul says, "All scripture is given by inspiration of God." Undoubtedly he referred to Luke's Gospel, the Acts of the Apostles and his own epistles, confirming all that Luke wrote concerning the virgin birth, the Wise Men, the star and the angelic host.

Those who deny the virgin birth do not seem to realize that they are denying the power of Almighty God, the Creator of all human life, to generate an only begotten Son without the intervention of man. They have not yet discovered the father or mother of Adam, neither of whom, evidently, had a biological birth.

If God could bring human life into the world without the cooperation of either father or mother, He doubtless could without father alone.

Anticipating the denial of the virgin birth, the Angel Gabriel said to Mary who had asked, "How shall this be, seeing I know not a man?" "With God nothing shall be impossible."

"Seed of David" Does Not Disprove Virgin Birth

Reverend Rose challenges me to answer a question about the first three verses of Paul's letter to the Romans, "Concerning his Son Jesus Christ our Lord, which was made of the seed of David according to the flesh." I see no difficulty in that whatever.

Mary, the virgin mother, was of the seed of David through the line of Nathan, his eldest son, as told by Luke, as Joseph was "of the seed of David, according to the flesh."

That is evident from Paul's letter to the Galatians to whom he writes, "When the fulness of the time was come, God sent forth his Son, made of a woman." He says nothing about the "biological" part which Joseph played in the birth of Christ, according to modernists.

In the beginning of his epistle to the Hebrews, the Apostle Paul writes,

"For unto which of the angels said he at any time, Thou art my Son, this day have I begotten thee? And again, I will be to him a Father, and he shall be to me a Son?"

Are we to understand that quotation from the second Psalm, repeated also by Luke in the Acts of the Apostles, as meaning a begotten son of God in the same sense in which those who deny the virgin birth of Jesus are begotten sons of God?

Matthew and Luke Confirm Virgin Birth

Finally, Mr. Rose appeals to the genealogies of Matthew and Luke as destroying faith in the virgin birth. In support of his interpretation of Paul, he says, "This is no more than Matthew and Luke admit in their genealogies." They make no such admission; they confirm the virgin birth.

Matthew begins with Abraham and moves forward saying from beginning to end, "Abraham begat Isaac; and Isaac begat Jacob," and so on down until he comes to the last two before Christ, when he concludes,

"And Jacob begat Joseph the husband of Mary, of whom was born Jesus, who is called Christ."

He does not say that Joseph begat Jesus. He does say that Joseph was "the husband of Mary, of whom was born Jesus."

But why does Mr. Rose accept Matthew's genealogy to prove his case when he immediately rejects his account of the virgin birth which follows? What right has one to accept only that part of one's testimony which supports his interpretation and his denial of another part? You cannot prove that a witness is false in one instance by establishing his veracity in another. It is a species of mental gymnastics to accept only that part of one's testimony which supports one's denial of another part. As for Luke, he specifically denies the fatherhood of Joseph in his genealogy.

Luke begins at Joseph and goes backward to Adam, saying, "And Jesus himself began to be about thirty years of age, being (as was supposed) the son of Joseph."

Whose Son Was Jesus?

Whose Son then was Jesus who is called Christ? It is not irreverent to say, "He is of age; ask Him."

When the young man whose eyes He had opened had been cast from the Temple by the enraged Pharisees, Jesus found him and said, "Dost thou believe on the Son of God?" He answered, "Who is he, Lord, that I might believe on him? And Jesus said unto him, Thou hast both seen him, and it is he that talketh with thee."

He asked of His disciples, "Whom do men say that I the Son of man am?" When they had answered, "One of the prophets," He asked, "Whom say ye that I am?" Peter said, "Thou art the Christ, the Son of the living God." Jesus did not rebuke him; rather, He commended him, saying, "Blessed art thou, Simon . . . for flesh and blood hath not revealed it unto thee, but my Father which is in heaven."

When the high priest said at the trial of Jesus, "I adjure thee by the living God, that thou tell us whether thou be the Christ, the Son of God," He answered, 'I am.' Both at His baptism and at His transfiguration God acknowledged Him in a voice from Heaven saying, "This is my beloved Son, in whom I am well pleased."

Rev. Rose, in his sermon denying the virgin birth, quoted the answer of Jesus to the young man who addressed Him as Good Master, "Why callest thou me good? there is none good but one, that is, God." These words were quoted as a denial by Christ of His own deity. "He disclaims deity," the preacher said, "and rebukes the young man who called him 'Good Master.' " On the contrary, Jesus confirmed His deity when He said, "There is none good but God," for either He was God—or He was not good.

If Jesus were not born of a virgin, then Mary was not a good woman; for Joseph found Mary "great with child" and "before they came together." What a fearful imputation to put upon the virgin Mary! I resent this assault upon the character of the mother of Jesus.

The Case Plainly Stated

To state the case plainly—if Jesus were not begotten of God and conceived by the power of the Holy Ghost, then He was begotten by ordinary generation, by two unmarried and immoral people who invented the most extraordinary story of the virgin conception, as Elbert Hubbard says, "to cover up their sin," and put it over on Matthew and Luke and the church, Catholic, Greek and Protestant, for two thousand years. What a horrible conception of the birth of the Son of God!

If that be true, then Christianity is founded upon a colossal fraud. BUT IT IS FALSE!

The most supernatural thing claimed for Christ was His extraordinary and divine generation. Take that away and you destroy the God-Man of the Holy Bible.

My friends, those calling themselves modernists were not the first to make this sacrilegious charge. It is evident that the story of the virgin birth was denied by His enemies in the day of our Lord.

In the 8th chapter of John there is a running fire of controversy between Jesus and the Pharisees. Driven into a corner they said to Him, "We be not born of fornication; we have one Father, even God." Jesus indignantly answered the shameful imputation, saying, "I proceeded forth and came from God . . . . Ye are of your father the devil." A little later to the same group of scoffers who rebuked Him for saying, "Abraham rejoiced to see my day," He replied, "Before Abraham was, I AM."

Was Joseph the father of that Son who was before Abraham? Jesus said NO!

When? In His reply to His mother who said, "Thy father and I have sought thee sorrowing," He replied, "Wist ye not that I must be about MY Father's business?" Did He mean Joseph?

Matthew says NO; Mark says NO; John says NO; Peter says NO; Paul says NO; the prophets say NO; God says NO:—Rev. Rose says **yes!**

The burden of proof rests with those who say yes; and they make a sorry mess of it when they attempt to disprove it by the Bible, using one part which they accept to disprove another part which they reject.

Jesus was never accused of being the son of Joseph except by His enemies; it is a late day for so-called Christian ministers to side with them as against the testimony of the disciples who were chosen of God to write the story of His life, as Jehovah "hath spoken by the mouth of all his holy prophets since the world began."

Peter says, "We have not followed cunningly devised fables, when we made known unto you the power and coming of our Lord Jesus Christ" (II Pet. 1:16).

Belief in the Virgin Birth Important

Some say that belief in the virgin birth is not important. But it is. If this attack upon His cradle is allowed to go unchallenged, they will attack His tomb next, and end their attack upon His cross.

If they are allowed to deny the miracle of His birth and we keep silent, they will attack the miracle of His resurrection and the miracle of His incarnation; and we will soon be asked to deny the very person of Christ.

These great facts in the life of our Lord are all bound together in one Life and one Book and stand on the testimony of the four Gospels divinely inspired and divinely preserved through the centuries from the attacks of men.

Their hammers break! God's anvil stands!

> Last night I paused outside a blacksmith's door,
>   And heard the anvil ring the vesper chime,
> And, looking in, I saw upon the floor,
>   Old hammers worn with beating years of time.
>
> "Good Sir," said I, "how many anvils have you had
>   To wear and batter all those hammers so?"
> "Just one," said he,
>   The anvil wears the hammers out, you know."
>
> And so, methought, the anvil of God's Word,
>   For ages, skeptic blows have beat upon.
> The ANVIL still remains,
>   The HAMMERS—gone!

R. A. TORREY
1856-1928

ABOUT THE MAN:

Torrey grew up in a wealthy home, attended Yale University and Divinity School, and studied abroad. During his early student days at Yale, young Torrey became an agnostic and a heavy drinker. But even during the days of his "wild life," he was strangely aware of a conviction that some day he was to preach the Gospel. At the end of his senior year in college, he was saved.

While at Yale Divinity School, he came under the influence of D. L. Moody. Little did Moody know the mighty forces he was setting in motion in stirring young R. A. Torrey to service!

After Moody died, Torrey took on the world-girdling revival campaigns in Australia, New Zealand, England and America.

Like many another giant for God, Torrey shone best, furthest and brightest as a personal soul winner. This one man led 100,000 to Christ in a revival that circled the globe!

Dr. Torrey's education was obtained in the best schools and universities of higher learning. Fearless, quick, imaginative and scholarly, he was a tough opponent to meet in debate. He was recognized as a great scholar, yet his ministry was marked by simplicity.

It was because of his outstanding scholastic ability and evangelistic fervor that Moody handpicked Torrey to become superintendent of his infant Moody Bible Institute. In 1912, Torrey became dean of BIOLA, where he served until 1924, pastoring the Church of the Open Door in Los Angeles from 1915-1924.

Torrey's books have probably reached more people indirectly and helped more people to understand the Bible and to have power to win souls, than the writings of any other man since the Apostle Paul, with the possible exceptions of Spurgeon and Rice. Torrey was a great Bible teacher, but most of all he was filled with the Holy Spirit.

He greatly influenced the life of Dr. John R. Rice.

II.

Jesus Is the Christ, the Son of God

R. A. TORREY

"These are written, that ye might believe that Jesus is the Christ, the Son of God; and that believing ye might have life through his name." — John 20:31.

Our text declares that Jesus is the Christ, the Son of God, and that everyone who really believes that fact obtains eternal life by so believing.

I. HOW DO WE KNOW THAT JESUS IS THE CHRIST, THE SON OF GOD?

1. We know that by a careful and candid study of the Gospel of John.

John says, "These *are written*, that ye might believe that Jesus is the Christ, the Son of God; and that believing ye might have life through his name." In other words, John in his Gospel presents the evidence that Jesus is the Christ, the Son of God. We have no time to take up that evidence in detail tonight, nor do we need to. Any of you may take it up for yourselves; and if you will read the evidence as John presents it candidly, that is, read it with a sincere desire to know the truth and with an earnest determination to obey the truth when discovered, you will know to a certainty, before you get through the Gospel, that Jesus is the Christ, the Son of God.

I have seen men try it again and again, many who were skeptics or even thoroughgoing agnostics when they began; and in every case where any man has pursued that study with a mind eager to know the truth and a willingness to obey the truth at any cost, that man has become a believer that Jesus is the Christ, the Son of God, and by believing in Him as such, has obtained eternal life. I suppose I could stand here by the hour and tell you of specific instances that have come under my own personal observation. Let me give you only one.

When I was holding meetings in Wellington, New Zealand, I spoke at the noon hour in one of the theaters to business and professional men. At the close of one of these meetings, a prominent traveling man came to me—he was said to be the most prominent traveling man in New Zealand. He said to me, "Charlie George [that is one of the proprietors of the leading department store in the city] thinks I ought to have a talk with you, but you can't help me."

I said, "What is the trouble?"

He replied, "I am an agnostic and you can't help me."

"Well," I said, "I have helped a good many agnostics, and perhaps I can help you." Then I continued, "What do you believe anyhow?"

"I don't believe anything."

"Do you not believe that there is an absolute difference between right and wrong?"

"Oh, yes," he said, "I do believe that."

"Well, you do believe something after all. That is all that I believed to begin with, and that is enough for anyone to believe to begin with." Then I said to him, "If you have some of anything and want more, what do you do?"

"Why," he said, "I use what I have."

I said, "That is right. If you have some muscle and want more muscle, what do you do?"

"I use the muscle I have."

"If you have some memory and want a better memory, what do you do?"

"I use the memory I have."

"If you have some money and want more money, what do you do?"

"I use the money I have."

"All right," I said, "you have some faith. You believe there is an absolute difference between right and wrong. You want more. Will you use what you have? You say you believe that there is an absolute difference between right and wrong. Will you use that faith? Will you take your stand upon the right to follow it wherever it carries you, at any cost?"

With a little hesitation, he said, "Yes, I will do that, but you can't help me. You are just wasting your time."

"Now," I said, "do you know that there is no God?"

"No," he said, "I don't know there is no God. I don't know anything about it."

"Well," I said, "I know that there is a God, but that won't do you any good. Do you know that God does not answer prayer?"

"No," he said, "I don't know that God doesn't answer prayer. I don't believe that He does, but I don't know that He doesn't."

"Well," I said, "I know that He does, but that won't do you any good. But you know the method of modern science. The method of modern science is this—that whenever you find a possible clue to knowledge you follow that clue out to find out what there may be in it. You don't have to know that there is anything in it. You simply follow it out to find out what there may be in it."

"Yes," he said, "that is right."

"Well, now, are you willing to apply this method of modern science to religious investigation? You admit that there may be a God and it may be He answers prayer. Here then is a possible clue to knowledge. Will you follow it out to find out what there may be in it? Will you pray this prayer—'O God, if there be any God, show me if Jesus Christ is Thy Son or not, and if Thou showest me that He is, I promise to accept Him as my Saviour and confess Him as such before the world'?"

"Yes," he said in a half laughing way, "I'll do that, too, but it won't do any good; you can't help me. You are just wasting your time."

"Well," I replied, "I have helped a good many and perhaps I can help you. Now, just one thing more. John says in John 20:31, 'These are written, that ye might believe that Jesus is the Christ, the Son of God; and that believing ye might have life through his name.'' Now John presents you in his Gospel the evidence that Jesus is the Christ, the Son of God. Will you take the evidence and read it? I don't ask you to believe it; I don't want you even to try to believe it; I simply want you to be willing to be convinced. Will you take the Gospel and read it with an open mind?"

"Oh," he said, "I have read it."

"Yes," I said, "but I want you to read it a new way. Begin at the first chapter and the first verse and read on verse after verse until you finish the Gospel. Don't read too many verses at any one time. Pay careful attention to what you read; and each time before you read, offer this prayer—'O God, if there be any God, show me what of truth there is in these verses I am about to read; and what Thou showest me to be true, I promise to take my stand upon.' "

Rather languidly and wearily he said, "Yes, I will do that, too, but it won't do any good."

Then I went over what he had agreed to do and got him to promise me he would write me the result.

Several weeks passed. I left Wellington and had gone to Christ Church and from Christ Church to Dunedin. After I had been a few days in Dunedin, a lady called at the house where I was stopping and asked to see me. When I entered the reception room, she arose and walked toward me with a letter in her hand, which she held out to me. She said, "I have a letter from my husband, and it is the queerest letter I ever received. I don't understand it, but he said I could show it to you." She handed me the letter, and I took it and read it. It was from this man. It began:

> My Dear Wife:
>
> I think I have been converted. I am not sure yet, and I don't wish to tell anyone until I am sure, but you can show this letter to your pastor and to Dr. Torrey; for it was he who spoke to me in Wellington.

That man came out clear cut as a Christian, as a believer in Jesus as the Christ, the Son of God, and in the Bible as the Word of God; and when we got to England, his mother, who was a very prominent woman in public life in England, wrote to Mr. Alexander to thank us for what we had done for her son in New Zealand.

Any one of you can try it for yourself. The result always has been and always will be the same. There has never been an exception.

2. We know that Jesus is the Christ, the Son of God, because that is what Jesus Himself claimed to be; and God set the stamp of His endorsement on Jesus Christ's claim by raising Him from the dead.

That Jesus claimed to be the Christ, the Son of God, the Son of God in an entirely unique sense, in a sense that no other man who ever walked this earth was the Son of God, admits of no honest question. In Mark 12:6 our Lord Jesus draws a contrast between Himself and all the prophets of the old dispensation, even the greatest, and says that while they were servants and merely servants, He was the Son, the one and only Son of God. In John 10:30 Jesus went so far as to say, "I and my Father are one." In John 14:9, He even dared to say, "He that hath seen me hath seen the Father." In John 5:23, He goes so far as to say, "all men should honour the Son, *even as they honour the Father.*" Such was Jesus' oft-repeated claim.

This was a stupendous claim to make. If the claim were not true, it was an utterly and shamefully blasphemous claim. The Jews put Jesus Christ to death on a charge of blasphemy for making this claim. And if this claim of Jesus were not true, if Jesus were not the Christ, the Son of God, the Son of God in a sense that no other is the Son of God, then the Jews did right, according to their own God-given law, in putting Him to death on the charge of blasphemy, only they should have put Him to death by stoning and not by crucifixion.

You cannot deny the deity of Jesus without thereby justifying the Jews in putting Him to death. If you are a Unitarian, and are also logical, you must justify the putting to death of Jesus Christ.

But before the Jewish authorities put Him to death, Jesus said to them that God would set the stamp of His endorsement upon His claim for which they were putting Him to death, by raising Him from the dead.

Put Him to death they did; lay Him in Joseph's sepulchre they did; seal the stone with the Roman seal, which to break was death, they did. But when the appointed hour came, just as Jesus had foretold, the quickening breath of God swept through that sleeping clay; and God raised Him triumphant over death and the grave, and so proclaimed to all coming generations, and to us, more clearly than if He should proclaim it from the open heavens above Los Angeles tonight, "This Man is what He claimed to be; He is the Christ; He is the Son of God; He is very God of very God; all men should honor Him even as they honor Me, the Father."

I have proved time and time again from this platform that the resurrection of Jesus from the dead is the best proven fact of history; and the absolutely certain resurrection of the Lord Jesus Christ proves to a demonstration that He is the Christ, the Son of God, very God of very God.

3. We know that Jesus is the Christ, the Son of God, by His influence upon all subsequent history.

That Jesus Christ claimed to be the Christ, the Son of God, in an entirely unique sense, admits, as we have already seen, of no honest question; but that Jesus claimed to be the Christ, the Son of God, a divine Person to be honored and worshiped, even as God the Father is honored and worshiped, does not prove that He really was so. But it does prove that He either was the Son of God in an entirely unique sense, as He claimed to be, or else that He was the most daring and blasphemous and outrageous impostor that ever walked this earth, or else that He was one of the most hopeless lunatics that ever disgraced humanity by His mental imbecility.

The modern Unitarian position, the position also of some preachers who do not call themselves Unitarians, but orthodox and evangelical, that Jesus was not a divine Person, very God of very God, that He was the Son of God only in the sense that we are all sons of God, but that He was a good man, perhaps the best man who ever lived on this earth, is the very acme of irrationality and intellectual absurdity. Whatever Jesus was, He was not good if He was only a man; that is to say, if He were not God as He claimed to be, He was not good, but one of the most hopeless lunatics that ever walked this earth.

Now let me put to each of you a question. Was the influence of Jesus of Nazareth upon subsequent history the influence of a lunatic? Only a lunatic would venture to assert it. Here then we are—not a lunatic, not an impostor, then beyond question, the Christ, the Son of God, God manifest in the flesh.

4. We know that Jesus is the Christ, the Son of God, by the divine power that He displays.

Jesus displayed divine power when He was here on earth. He displayed divine power when He stilled the tempest and calmed the waves by His words, "Peace, be still." He displayed divine power when He called Lazarus, who had been four days dead, from the grave; and Lazarus came forth. He displayed divine power when He turned water into wine. He displayed divine power when He fed five thousand men, besides women and children with five small loaves and two small fishes and had more left over when He was through than when He began, which was a creative act. Over and over again He displayed divine power when He was here on earth.

But we do not need to go way back into the history of His life here upon earth, nearly 1,900 years ago, to find Him displaying divine power. He displays divine power today. He raises the dead today. He raises men and women who are dead in trespasses and sins into spiritual life and power and victory. He does something far more wonderful than turning water into wine. He turns outrageous sinners into glorious saints.

He turned Jerry McAuley, a miserable, contemptible, low-down river thief, an inmate of Sing-Sing State Prison, into Jerry McAuley, the apostle of life to the outcasts of New York; so honored when he came to die in the very city where he had been a water thief, that the best people of New York gathered by the thousands at his funeral to do honor to his blessed memory.

He turned Sam Hadley, a fugitive from justice, with 138 counts of forgery out against him, and a hopeless barrel house bum, into Sam Hadley, one of the most lovable and self-sacrificing lovers of his fellow men I ever knew, and whom I once met in Washington as the honored guest in the home of the Postmaster General of the United States of America.

Jesus turned William S. Jacoby, a drunkard at nine, a tough at fifteen, a criminal at nineteen, and a companion of thugs, a desperado in Omaha, twice dishonorably discharged from the regular army, invited to join the Jesse James gang, unanimously chosen chief of a gang of desperados in the Leavenworth Federal Prison, riding through the streets of Omaha firing his revolver out of the window of a cab at everything he passed, into the Rev. William S. Jacoby, the most loved man in Chicago, the dearest and truest friend I ever had, and the most truly Christlike man I ever knew.

Yes, and God changed me. I will not tell you from what; but at least from hopeless bondage to glorious liberty, and from awful death to exultant life. Yes, Jesus is surely the Christ, the Son of God, very God of very God. There is no possibility of honest and intelligent doubt of that.

II. THE RESULT OF BELIEVING THAT JESUS IS THE CHRIST, THE SON OF GOD

If one believes that Jesus is the Christ, the Son of God, what will be the result? Listen to my text again—"These are written, that ye might believe that Jesus is the Christ, the Son of God; and that believing ye might have life through his name."

1. The result will be that the one who believes that Jesus is the Christ, the Son of God, will obtain eternal life.

All that anyone needs to do to obtain eternal life, that greatest of all gifts, a gift in comparison with which all the wealth and splendor and honor and glory and pleasure of this world are as nothing, the gift of eternal life—all that anyone has to do to obtain this wondrous gift is to believe with heart trust that Jesus is the Christ, the Son of God. Anyone in this audience may have eternal life in the twinkling of an eye by just believing with heart committal that Jesus is the Christ, the Son of God. Listen again to our text, "These are written, *that ye might believe* that Jesus is the Christ, the Son of God; *and that believing ye might have life through his name."*

Listen to another verse: John 3:16, "For God so loved the world, that he gave his only begotten Son, that *whosoever believeth in him* should not perish, but *have everlasting life."* You may be a drunkard, a thief, an embezzler; you may be a forger; you may be a man or woman disgraced by divorce and you yourself the guilty party; you may be an outrageous blasphemer; you may have a polluted imagination and a rotten heart; you may be the victim of the lowest and vilest passions that ever cursed a man or woman; you may be anybody or anything— but BELIEVE WITH HONEST HEART THAT JESUS IS THE CHRIST, THE SON OF GOD, AND ETERNAL LIFE IS INSTANTLY YOURS. Oh, how often I have seen men and women of all kinds and conditions and nationalities get eternal life in an instant by simply believing that Jesus is the Christ, the Son of God.

2. But, of course, it must be real faith.

The faith that John here speaks of is not a mere intellectual opinion; John never uses *"faith"* in that sense. No man ever obtained eternal life by merely having an orthodox opinion about Jesus. When Jesus Himself was here on earth, the demons held a perfectly orthodox opinion about Him. They cried out (even before men saw it and confessed it), "I know thee, who thou art, *the Holy One of God."* The Devil himself holds a perfectly orthodox opinion about Christ. He knows, and only too well for his own comfort, that Jesus is the Christ, the Son of God. He does not teach it, but he knows it.

He gets men to teach that Jesus is not the Christ, the Son of God, very God of very God, because "he is a liar, and the father of it." He gets men to teach that Jesus is a good man, a great example, but that He is not divine, that He does not save by the shedding of His blood, but by His example and His teaching; for the Devil is, as I say, a liar, and the father of it. But all the time the Devil knows who Jesus is. He knows that some day he will himself be forced to bow his knee to Jesus and "confess that Jesus Christ is Lord to the glory of God, the Father." Yes, the Devil believes in that sense that Jesus is the Christ, the Son of God; but that belief does not save him from going to the everlasting fire prepared for him and his angels.

No, the faith that saves is real faith, a faith with the heart. As Paul puts it in Romans 10:9,10:

"If thou shalt confess with thy mouth the Lord Jesus, and shalt believe

in thine heart that God hath raised him from the dead, thou shalt be saved. For with the heart man believeth unto righteousness; and with the mouth confession is made unto salvation."

If you believe with your heart that Jesus is the Christ, the Son of God, you will accept Him as your divine Saviour who purchased forgiveness for you by dying in your place on the cross, for that is what He said He did (Matt. 20:28), and your risen Saviour who, by His resurrection power, can set you free from the power of sin today, for that is what He Himself offers to do (John 8:34-36).

(From the book, *The Gospel for Today.* Revell Publishers.)

B. R. LAKIN
1901-1984

ABOUT THE MAN:

On June 5, 1901, a baby boy was born to Mr. and Mrs. Richard Lakin in a farmhouse on Big Hurricane Creek in the hill country of Wayne County, West Virginia. Mrs. Lakin had prayed for a "preacher man" and had dedicated this baby to the Lord even before he was born.

Lakin was converted in a revival meeting at age 18. Following his conversion, he became a Baptist preacher. With a mule for transportation, he preached in small country churches in the mountains and hills of West Virginia and Kentucky. The transportation changed as well as the size of his congregations.

In 1939, he became associate pastor of Cadle Tabernacle, Indianapolis, and upon the death of Founder Cadle, became pastor of that once great edifice of evangelism that seated 10,000, and had a choir loft of 1,400. Lakin preached to over 5,000 on Sunday mornings and half that many on Sunday nights.

Cadle Tabernacle had no memberships. It was a radio-preaching center broadcasting from coast to coast. In those fourteen years there, Ray Lakin became a household word across America.

In 1952, he entered full-time evangelism. His ministry carried him around the world, resulting in an estimated 100,000 conversions, and legion the number entering the ministry.

He was the preacher's friend, the church's helper, the common man's leader, and for sixty-five years, God's mighty messenger.

He was one of the most sought-after gospel preachers in America. On March 15, 1984, the last of the old-time evangelists took off for Glory. He would soon have been 83.

III.

I Know Jesus Is God

B. R. LAKIN

(Recorded live from Landmark Baptist Temple, Cincinnati, Ohio.)

"But these are written, that ye might believe that Jesus is the Christ, the Son of God; and that believing ye might have life through his name."—John 20:31.

If Jesus Christ was not the Son of God as He claimed He was, then He is the greatest impostor of all time and the Christian Faith is nothing but meaningless sham and must be discarded upon the rubbish heap of false religion.

We are facing a most important question tonight and that is, How may I know that Jesus is the Son of God? The whole weight of the Christian teaching hangs by this one thread. If it cannot stand the test of truth, then all of the alleged verities of the centuries come tumbling down.

We do not hope to convince anyone by logical argument that Jesus is the Christ. We do not arrive at this conviction by mere human reasoning; the knowledge that Jesus is the Christ must and will come by means of divine revelation.

When Jesus asked the disciples, "Whom do men say that I the Son of man am?" Peter gave his inspired answer, "Thou art the Christ, the Son of the living God." And Jesus immediately informed Peter that his answer was a revelation. He said Peter was incapable of arriving at this conclusion by the process of his own reasoning; his mind was too limited to fathom such an infinite truth, and so He said, "Flesh and blood hath not revealed it unto thee, but my Father which is in heaven." He was saying, "Peter, you didn't get this merely at the college or seminary but by divine revelation." It was not, Jesus said, a discovered truth but a revelation.

And it is our purpose in this discussion to lead some confused souls to the threshold of revelation and prepare their hearts for the dawning of the glorious truth that Jesus Christ is verily the Son of God. And if I didn't believe that, I would quit the ministry out of self-respect and common decency. A man who does not believe that Jesus is God and that the Bible is God's Word ought to cease preaching and sailing under false colors, because we could indict and convict him before a jury of honest people of taking money under false pretenses.

Hundreds of years before Jesus came into this world, Job said, "I know that my redeemer liveth, and that he shall stand at the latter day upon the earth" (Job 19:25). Paul, who wrote several years after Jesus' ascension into Heaven, could say, "I know whom I have believed, and am persuaded that he is able to keep that which I have committed unto him against that day" (II Tim. 1:12). Even the Devil said, "I know thee who thou art, the Holy One of God" (Mark 1:24).

If these could know Him, it would not seem unreasonable to believe that we for whom Christ died should be able to know Him personally, positively, intimately. The disciples of Jesus entertained no doubt, after the resurrection, that Jesus was the Son of God. The writers with one harmonious voice declare Him to be God's Son, the Saviour of the world. And John, in concluding His Gospel, said that "this is the disciple which testifieth of these things, and wrote these things: and we know that his testimony is true" (John 21:24).

We offer for your consideration several infallible proofs of the Sonship; and if you do not know Him as Lord and Saviour, our prayer is that through hearing these truths you may come to know Him as your personal Saviour. I know Jesus the Son of God personally.

Jesus Was the Son of God Because He Fulfilled Prophecies Concerning God's Son

No other man born of woman could possibly lay claim to the exact fulfillment of Bible prophecy concerning the Son of God as did Jesus. False christs have risen across the centuries, but none answered to the description given of Him in the Old Testament in any detail. The birth, the life, the death, the resurrection of Christ fulfilled every detail of the prophecy of the Old Testament.

Back in Genesis, chapter 3, verse 15, is a preview of the life of Jesus; and the ministry of Him was given cryptic, though it seemed it was an exact description of the unique birth and unusual ministry of Christ. The prophecy was this: "And I will put enmity between thee and the woman [between Satan and the woman], and between thy seed and her seed; it shall bruise thy head, and thou shalt bruise his heel." He said, "You may bruise His heel, but Jesus will get your head!"

There are two books in the Bible that liberal seminaries and colleges hate: the book of Genesis and the book of Revelation. I do not wonder that Satan hates these books, because in the book of Genesis he is condemned, and in the book of Revelation he is executed. Therefore, he would seek to bring these two books out of the Bible.

Notice the prophecy does not say "the seed of man" but the seed of the woman. This is the first glimpse we have of the virgin birth of our Lord. As Jesus hung upon the cross on Golgotha, He looked at John and said, "Behold thy mother!" And then looking at Mary, He said, "Woman, behold thy son!" Satan at that moment was being bruised by Jesus, and He in turn was being bruised. Isaiah said, ". . . he was bruised for our iniquities" (53:5). Jesus' death on the cross was the end of Satan's power over the souls of men. It was on the cross that He bruised Satan's head.

Isaiah also prophesied that He would be born of a virgin: "Therefore the Lord himself shall give you a sign; Behold a virgin shall conceive, and bear a son, and shall call his name Immanuel" (7:14). I believe He was born of a virgin without a man in it, my friend. Some have said that was a biological impossibility. I do not think it was. I think he was born of a virgin, not of a "young woman" as the Revised Standard Version says. She could have been a young woman and not have been a virgin, or she could have been a virgin and not have been a young woman, but I believe He was born OF A VIRGIN.

A person said to me, "Why, Dr. Lakin, Jesus could not have been born of a human mother without a human father." Listen, I would have you know that the first man who ever got in this world got here without either.

Let me show you something. In the New Testament in Matthew 1:18, we read that Jesus literally fulfilled this prophecy: "Now the birth of Jesus Christ was on this wise: When as his mother Mary was espoused to Joseph, before they came together, she was found with child of the Holy Ghost." Many people cannot accept the miraculous fact of the supernatural birth of our Lord. The Word says with men this is impossible but with God all things are possible. You won't have any trouble with any of the miracles of the Bible when you place God positionally where He belongs—in the beginning.

If God could make Adam without a father or mother, if God could make Eve from the rib of Adam, and if He could create the worlds from nothing, it would be a simple matter for Him to create the body of Jesus without the agency of an earthly father.

You have heard it said that Mary was the mother of God. Mary merely furnished the body in which Jesus lived for thirty-three and one-half years, the body in which He was incarnated.

John 3:16, so often quoted by Christians, carries a deep meaning in regard to this truth: "God so loved the world, that he gave his only begotten Son . . . ." "Begotten" means "to be the father of." The word not only is defined thus by the authors of the modern dictionaries, but it was used in that sense in the Holy Scriptures. We may all be sons of God by faith, but Jesus was the only begotten of the Father and in the sense that God actually begot Him in the same respect that Abraham begot Isaac.

A little girl said to me one day, "Dr. Lakin, what do you do with the 'begats' of the Bible?" I said, "I read them. What do you do with them?" She said, "I skip them." I said, "If you skip them you will miss something."

". . . and Matthan begat Jacob; And Jacob begat Joseph the husband of Mary, of whom was born Jesus, who is called Christ." Notice that the begetting stopped with Joseph. It didn't say, "And Joseph begat Jesus." Why? Because Jesus was not begotten by natural parentage and natural generation. Jesus verified this relationship to His Father in Heaven, and more than fifty times in the New Testament He refers to God as "my Father." No other person who has ever lived on this earth can lay claim to such a supernatural, physical heritage.

It was prophesied that the Messiah or the Coming One would be the Heir to the throne of David. Listen to this: "Of the increase of his government and peace there shall be no end, upon the throne of David, and upon his kingdom, to order it, and to establish it with judgment and with justice from henceforth even for ever. The zeal of the Lord of hosts will perform this" (Isa. 9:7).

A man made this statement: "There is no Scripture that says Jesus would ever occupy an earthly throne."

I said, "Is that so? He shall take the throne of His father David, and David never had anything but an earthly throne. So it will have to be an earthly throne."

The genealogy of Joseph is given in the first chapter of Matthew. And the genealogy of Mary is recorded in the third chapter of Luke. Joseph's lineage is only traced back to Abraham, but Mary's goes back to Adam and Eve that we might know that He was the Seed of the woman which was to bruise the head of the serpent.

Even the Jews did not try to contradict the fact that He was a direct descendant of David, for they knew the genealogy records were in the Temple and were open to public inspection.

When Jesus ascended into Heaven, the royal lineage of David was broken; and He is the only living heir to David's throne with an unbroken record. The Jewish royal genealogies were burned by the Roman invaders in the Temple of Herod just seventy years after Christ completed His earthly ministry. When the angel announced to Mary that she was to be the mother of the Son of God, he said, "He shall be great, and shall be called the Son of the Highest: and the Lord God shall give unto him the throne of his father David" (Luke 1:32). Such exact fulfillment of the prophecies cannot be passed off. Jesus not only fulfilled the prophecies that I have mentioned but scores of others as well.

We may know He was the Son of God because He correctly fulfilled all the requirements and all the inspired predictions concerning the Messiah, the Coming One.

Jesus Was the Son of God Because of His Godlikeness

"In whom the god of this world hath blinded the minds of them which believe not, lest the light of the glorious gospel of Christ, who is the image of God, should shine unto them."—II Cor. 4:4.

It is natural for a son to resemble a father. Jesus was the very image of the Heavenly Father. Not only are physical characteristics inherited but traits of character are also inherited. There is always a unique and interesting parallel between father and son. And we might know that Jesus is the Son of God because He is so much like we imagine God would be.

His conduct on earth was the conduct of God. His understanding was the understanding befitting to God. His wisdom, His strength, His authority were Godlike. He was, as our text says, the image of God. Therefore, Jesus Himself witnessed to this truth in the 14th chapter of John when He said, "If ye had known me, ye should have known my

Father also: and from henceforth ye know him, and have seen him."

These characteristics have been attributed to God which no other person in Heaven or earth possessed. Omnipresence, omniscience and omnipotence—Jesus possessed these Godlike traits and demonstrated them in the New Testament.

You see the omnipresence of God reflected in the life and ministry of Jesus when Saul was stricken on the Damascus road. He asked, "Who art thou, Lord?" The Lord answered, "I am Jesus." And at the same moment Christ appeared to Ananias in Damascus and instructed him to meet Saul at the house of Judas. Ananias then said to Saul, "Brother Saul, the Lord, even Jesus, that appeared unto thee in the way as thou camest, hath sent me, that thou mightest receive thy sight." Here we see Jesus demonstrating the omnipresence of God by being in two places at the same time. He also appeared simultaneously to Peter and Cornelius at Joppa and Caesarea, once again demonstrating His omnipresence.

In Jesus' last talk with the eleven disciples, He commissioned them to preach the Gospel and assured each that He would be present with them, even though they be scattered to the ends of the earth. "Lo, I am with you alway, even unto the end of the world" (Matt. 28:20).

In a physical body, Jesus was limited in His ministry; He could not be everywhere at the same time. But in His present glorified state He is unlimited, omnipresent, like His Heavenly Father.

His omniscience was demonstrated on numerous occasions—for example, His talk with the Samaritan woman at Jacob's Well; and when Peter came to Jesus with the problem of taxes. There is nothing hid from the sight of the Lord. He is still the omniscient One. He knows the thoughts, the sins, the lusts, the vain imagination of each life.

His omnipotence is all powerful, like the omnipotence of God. He has power over disease. Infection, infirmities and affliction could not exist in the mighty presence of the Saviour. He is the Physician who never lost a case. He had power over the elements. The wind and the waves obeyed His voice. When He spoke to the howling winds, softly whining, they fell submissive and subdued at the Master's feet. When He spoke to the angry waves they ceased their fury and lapped peacefully at the sides of His boat. The devils snapped to attention at the voice of authority; and they departed at His command, leaving a tranquil joy and calm in the hearts of those whom they had possessed.

His words were full of authority and power. Even His enemies and the Pharisees said, "Never man spake like this man." And the reason—He was not a man but the omniscient, omnipresent and omnipotent Son of God. He is truly the image of God!

Jesus Was the Son of God Because of His Influence

There is no other way to account for the tremendous influence of Jesus of Nazareth upon the conduct, the epics and the history of the world but to confess that He was the Son of God. Born of a lowly mother, without an earthly or human father; reared in meekness in a remote town of Nazareth; without credentials from the religious leaders of His time; with no accredited education from the schools of His day; hated by the religious leaders; followed by the poor, the illiterate and the downtrodden; gathered twelve men from the lower class of His disciples; called a son of the Devil because of His unorthodox birth; falsely accused of blasphemy by the hierarchy; mocked by the crowds which had pursued Him in the days of His prosperity; His death demanded by the angry mob, the multitude; condemned to die by crucifixion; buried in a borrowed tomb.

It would seem the world had heard the last of Him—but, no! The pages of history are besmirched with the blood of those who died for Him. Wars have been fought, thrones have been abdicated because of Him. Throughout the centuries His name has been above every name. His life, His teaching and His ethics have changed, altered and transformed individuals, communities, cities, nations and continents. That is the Saviour I speak about tonight.

"I am the light of the world: he that followeth me shall not walk in darkness, but shall have the light of life" (John 8:12). Not only individuals but nations have found Him the Light of life. By following Him who is the Light of the world, the shadows of superstition, slavery and serfdom have been dispelled from the land where His light has been permitted to shine.

Listen! Prostitution, political corruption and poverty have fled before His presence as naturally as night flees from day. Sin, sorrow and sensuality cannot exist in the presence of His gospel light.

He never wrote a book, but hundreds of thousands of volumes have been written about Him. His words have been translated into more than one thousand languages and dialects.

He composed no music, yet thousands of songs have been written about and acclaiming Him as Lord. The world's greatest musicians have blended their skill in lauding Him as the Saviour of the world.

He built no sanctuary; but millions of churches, chapels and cathedrals have been built in which to worship Him.

He built no hospitals; but His followers through the agency of the Christian church have, the world over, erected institutions of healing, of mercy, to care for the sick, the needy and the dying!

He raised no army, but those who would fight for His truth and principles the world over can be numbered into the millions.

The influence of Jesus has been aptly expressed by a little poem called

THE MARCHING CHRIST

He walked the shores of Galilee,
And taught His truth sublime;
But Calvary did not stop the Christ,
He walks the shores of Time.

He marches through the corridors
Of Medieval years;
The footprints of His wounded feet
Are damp with suppliants' tears.

He marches as the centuries roll,
Naught can deter His goal;
He stirs the consciences of men,
And heals the sin-sick soul.

He walks on through the history books,
And makes His Presence known;
To beggars in the marketplace,
To kings upon their throne.

Though wars may come, and wars may go,
This Jesus marches on;
And, "Onward, Christian Soldiers" is
His glorious battle song.

He walks the halls where nation's meet,
Where solons cry, "lend-lease!"
And with His pierced hands outstretched
He offers them His peace.

Though men may spurn His voice Divine,
As others did of yore;
He marches on, nor never slacks;
He lives forevermore!

—Lee C. Fisher

The influence of Jesus goes on like an eternal river through the centuries, somehow or other etching its way upon the hearts of men, leaving in its wake the transformed lives of thousands through salvation, the illumination of a lightless world.

Jesus Is God Because of His Atoning Death

Jesus not only lived and worked and walked like a God, but He died like a God. His life provided us with the paramount example; His death gave us complete redemption.

The cross as related to the Son of God is one of the most significant in the whole scope of Christian thinking. Not a mere ornament to be worn as a piece of jewelry around the neck, nor merely an architectural ornament to adorn the steeples of churches—not that, my friend. Perhaps there is no particular wrong in these uses of the cross, if we properly understand the deeper meaning. The cross itself is powerless to save, but it symbolizes the finished work of Christ on the cross for the sins of the world. Because of this, it has been hallowed, respected and honored by men and nations as the greatest and most important act of the centuries.

The cross tells me Jesus was the Son of God. If He was the manifestation, it was the manifestation of God's love: "For when we were yet without strength, in due time Christ died for the ungodly," for those who were unlike God, for those who had been wrung out of shape and made unlike God.

We speak of the love of God as manifest in nature. And we see it in the glorious sunset, a ruby rose, a vivid rainbow, or a babbling brook.

It is true that God's love is manifest in the beauties of this physical universe we live in; but to really see God's love perfectly manifested, go to Calvary! Look with grateful heart into the crimson pool at the foot of the cross of Jesus and see the blood, pure and guileless, pouring from His hands and side. See His tear-stained cheeks swollen by the blows inflicted by the drunken Roman soldiers. See His back scarred and lacerated by the heartless scourging of a vulgar mob. What do you see? The expression of human cruelty, unfairness and beastlike heartlessness.

Look closer and you will see more—a triumphant expression of the love of God's Son for the world. No mere man could die like this. This was the triumphant death of Deity. It was surely the Son of God, as the Roman proclaimed Him.

My friends, if you want to see the love of God, you may look up at the stars and see His glory; you may look at the ocean and see His power; you may look at the flowers and see His wisdom; but when you look at Calvary, you see really the uncovering of the heart of God, because the cross was central in His life.

Jesus was fully aware of His chief mission in the world. Little by little He revealed to His disciples and followers that He must die vicariously for the sins of the world. There is only one means by which man could be saved, and Jesus reconciled man to God by making atonement for man's sin.

But the skeptics ask, "How could the death of Christ, the death of one Man, exonerate man from guilt?" This is a good question and it is the very heart of the Gospel. True, my friends. If one man, Adam, could bring death to the race, then why could not one Man, Christ, bring life everlasting? If one man could bring condemnation to the race, should it seem strange that one Man, Christ, should bring freedom from condemnation?

The cross of Christ, with its upright and crossbeams, pointed upward to the Heavenly Father, the Author of the plan of salvation; it pointed outward to the reaches of earth for lost men, beckoning them to come from every nation and plunge beneath the crimson fountain; it pointed downward to the burning Hell, decreeing that the sending of men to Hell should be cancelled for those who trust Christ.

I know Jesus is the Son of God because of the cross of Calvary! I know He is the Son of God because of the power to change men's lives! The acid test of religion is discovered in the test tube of human experience. The Gospel of Christ is different than other religions of the world. As a matter of fact, the Christian Faith should not be classified with other religions of the world.

I could go on and on tonight and tell you of multitudes who have been transformed marvelously by His power, Simon Peter being one of them. But I want to say this: The great question of this hour is not, "What shall we do about atomic energy?" or "What shall we do about world peace?" but, "What think ye of Christ?" Upon the correct answer to this simple question hangs your eternal destiny.

And as He hung yonder upon the cross, round and round the cycle of suffering—until at last He dropped His chin upon a pulseless chest while bloody drops dripped in His eyes and spattered, and He cried out between parched and swollen lips, "It is finished!"

How I thank God for those words! I think the blood dropped down to His beard and on down to the ground, into the sand, and the drop of blood whispered to the grain of sand, "It is finished!" The grain of sand whispered to the roots of the grass, "It is finished!" Then the roots whispered to the tiny green blades of grass, "It is finished!" And they waved their fingers to the boughs of the tree and the branches and said, "It is finished!" And the branches whispered to the little birds, "It is finished!" Then the birds took off for the fleecy, floating clouds above and said, "It is finished!" And they gathered it up and carried it to the gates of Heaven and resounded it down the streets of Glory, "It is finished!"

It is finished! Salvation is complete! Salvation is finished! Salvation is for you!

I KNOW JESUS CHRIST WAS GOD'S SON because He saved me, because He offered that fountain open for sin and for uncleanness.

TOM MALONE
1915-

ABOUT THE MAN:

Tom Malone was converted and called to preach at the same moment! At an old-fashioned bench, the preacher took his tear-stained Bible and showed Tom Malone how to be saved. He accepted Christ then and there. Arising from his knees in the Isbell Methodist Church near Russellville, Alabama, he shook the circuit pastor's hand; and this bashful nineteen-year-old farm boy announced: "I know the Lord wants me to be a preacher."

Backward, bashful and broke, yet Tom borrowed five dollars, took what he could in a cardboard suitcase and left for Cleveland, Tennessee. Immediately upon arrival at Bob Jones College, Malone heard a truth that totally dominated his life and labors for the Lord ever after—soul winning!

That day he won his first soul! The green-as-grass Tom, a new convert himself, knew nothing of soul-winning approaches or techniques. He simply asked the sinner, "Are you a Christian?" "No." In a few minutes that young man became Malone's first convert.

Since that day, countless have been his experiences in personal evangelism.

Mark it down: Malone began soul winning his first week in Bible college. And he has never lost *the thirst* for it, *the thrill* in it, nor *the task* of it since. Pastoring churches, administrating schools, preaching across the nation have not deterred Tom Malone from this mainline ministry.

It is doubtful if young Malone ever dreamed of becoming the man he is today. He is now Doctor Tom Malone, is renowned in fundamental circles for his wise leadership and great preaching, is pastor of the large Emmanuel Baptist Church of Pontiac, Michigan, Founder and President of Midwestern Baptist Schools, and is eagerly sought as speaker in large Bible conferences from coast to coast.

Dr. John R. Rice often said that Dr. Tom Malone may be the greatest gospel preacher in all the world today!

IV.

How I Know Jesus Christ Is the Son of God

TOM MALONE

(Message at 50th annual Fundamental Baptist Fellowship.)

"And we believe and are sure that thou art that Christ, the Son of the living God." —John 6:69.

Matthew 16:13-18 and John 6:60-71 should be discussed together because of their similarities. In both passages Jesus asks the disciples a question. In both passages the same man, Simon Peter, comes forth with a thrilling answer.

In Matthew, Jesus asks: "Whom do men say that I the Son of man am?" Simon Peter replies: "Thou art the Christ, the Son of the living God."

In that passage in John, Jesus asks this question: "Will ye also go away?" The multitudes had heard who He was and what He came to do; then they had turned and walked away. Now Jesus asks, "Will ye also go away?" Once again the same Simon Peter answers: "Lord, to whom shall we go? thou hast the words of eternal life." Then Peter adds: "And we believe and are sure that thou art that Christ, the Son of the living God."

Thus from the lips of Simon Peter come probably the two greatest statements found in the Bible as to the testimony of who Jesus Christ is.

I want to deal with the subject, "Who Jesus Christ Is," or, "How I Know Jesus Christ Is the Son of God."

How do we know that Jesus Christ is deity? I refrain from using "divine" because it is misused. People in our day make up a concoction and call it divinity fudge. One person sees another and says, "Oh, isn't she divine!" or, "Isn't he just divine!" So I dispose of that word and talk about the deity of Christ, or why I know that He is the Son of God—just as much God as if He had never been a man.

We need to distinguish three things when discussing His deity. I am not talking primarily about the virgin birth which was prophesied many times in the Old Testament, such as, "Behold, a virgin shall conceive, and bear a son, and shall call his name Immanuel" (Isa. 7:14). The Bible tells us Jesus would be virgin born, but I am not discussing primarily the virgin birth.

On that night of the annunciation, the angel of God appeared to Mary, saying, "The Holy Ghost shall come upon thee, and the power of the Highest shall overshadow thee: therefore also that holy thing which shall be born of thee shall be called the Son of God" (Luke 1:35).

Neither am I discussing that which is often referred to as the incarnation, which is also taught in Scripture. For instance, John 1:14 says, "And the Word was made flesh, and dwelt among us, (and we beheld his glory, the glory as of the only begotten of the Father,) full of grace and truth." And Paul says in I Timothy 3:16, "And without controversy great is the mystery of godliness: God was manifest in the flesh . . . ." That is the incarnation, that is, both God and man dwelt in one body and walked physically among men for thirty-three years. We must distinguish between His virgin birth and the incarnation and deity of Christ.

I am talking about why I know Jesus is God. When we talk about His deity, one of the great problems confronting the mind is the same problem that causes many to doubt the Bible. You see, the Bible has both divine and human authors.

Now the Bible is a divine Book, a Book inspired of God, the Word of God. But the Lord spoke to thirty-eight or forty men over a space of fifteen hundred years, on three continents: "Write what I tell you to write." In II Peter 1:21, we read, ". . . but holy men of God spake as they were moved [borne along, carried along] by the Holy Ghost." God told these men, "Write what I tell you." So we have the Bible which has both human and divine authorship, although the Book is divine.

Had God not used man to write it, perhaps people would not doubt that this Book comes from God.

Take the Holy Bible—the written Word; take Jesus Christ—the living Word; the same is true of Him. The mind of the natural man says, "How can a man with a human body, and subject to all the limitations of that body, be God Himself?"

So the human-divine Jesus causes many to doubt His deity.

But Mary was a human being; Jesus was born of the Holy Ghost. Now we have man (or human) plus God—a God-Man. That is the Christ of the Bible, the Christ of my heart, the Christ of Calvary, the Christ who conquered death and walked out of the grave.

Jesus was the divine Son of God and just as much God as God the Father or God the Holy Spirit.

How do I know that Jesus was deity? A number of ways. First, I believe what the Bible says. I am not one who goes off in some other direction, digs up a piece of stone and says archeology proves the Bible. This Bible doesn't have to have archeology to prove it. No one need go outside the Bible to find proof that Jesus is the Son of God.

Peter said, "And we believe and are sure . . ." (John 6:69). That is just the opposite of how the average person wants to approach this subject. He says, "You make us certain that Jesus is the Son of God, then we will believe." Peter said, "And we believe and are sure . . . ."

What I preach comes right out of the Bible. I believe that Jesus is the Son of God. And we can make it plain and clear to any open-minded man that Jesus Christ is deity.

"And we believe and are sure that thou art that Christ, the Son of the living God."

I. BY POSSESSION AND MANIFESTATION OF ALL THE ATTRIBUTES OF DEITY

Jesus possessed and manifested every attribute that God has. Colossians 2:9 is a blessed verse: "For in him [Jesus] dwelleth all the fulness of the Godhead bodily." Some Greek scholars say "fulness" can be translated "attribute"—not "attributes" because "fulness" is singular. So read that verse this way: "in him dwelleth all the attribute of God."

The Bible says Jesus has every attribute or characteristic that the Father has. The attributes of God the Father are those distinguishing characteristics of the nature of God which are inseparable from the idea of deity and which constitute the basis and grounds for His various manifestations to His creatures. That is why Jesus was able to say, ". . . he that hath seen me hath seen the Father" (John 14:9).

Don't be persuaded into believing the liberals who say, "Yes, we will consent that Jesus was a great teacher; we will consent to the fact that Jesus was a great man and lived a great life." What foolish talk! If Jesus is not God, He is not good, for He claimed to be God. If Jesus is not God, the Bible is not true, for it says that He has every distinguishing characteristic that is related to the idea of God Himself and to deity. So Jesus has every attribute that God has.

Now what are the attributes? If you ask people what God's greatest attribute is, many may say, "That He is omnipotent," that is, all-powerful. He stood on the morning of creation and flung from His omnipotent fingers countless worlds into space; He is the omnipotent God. Many Bible believers would tell us that the greatest attribute of God is His omnipotence, that is, that God is all-powerful; and He is, but that is not His greatest attribute.

If you ask uninstructed people and those who do not know the Bible well and do not believe the Bible, such as the liberals and modernists, "What is God's greatest attribute?" they might answer, "Love." They paint a picture of a God of love who cannot possibly punish sin, who never condemns anyone to the fires of Hell; but neither of these things are true.

1. The Attribute of God's Holiness

According to the Bible, the greatest attribute is God's holiness, God's purity. Jesus Christ was the holy Son of God. We read in Psalm 145:17, "The Lord is righteous in all his ways, and holy in all his works."

To talk about holiness means the self-affirming purity of God. I could say about a good man that he is a holy man. First, he is robed in the righteousness of Christ; he is clad in the garments of salvation; he is washed in the blood of the Son of God; he is indwelt by the Holy Ghost, and he is in the process of being made like his Lord. But that holiness he has is not naturally his own; he must get it from another. It is an imputed righteousness. But the holiness of God is a self-affirming purity that is inherent with God, a part of God. That was true also of Jesus Christ.

My friends, "righteous in all his ways, and holy in all his works" could never be said about any earthly person.

When Isaiah got that glorious illuminating vision of God and saw the Lord lifted up, he saw Him as I wish all of us could see Him: "Holy, holy, holy, is the Lord of hosts: the whole earth is full of his glory" (Isa. 6:3). Holy in His person, holy in His ways, holy in His works. So Jesus Christ has this attribute of God called holiness or purity.

Speaking of Jesus, Hebrews 7:26 says, "For such an high priest became us, who is holy, harmless, undefiled, separate from sinners, and made higher than the heavens." The Bible says Jesus had this first, this primary, this all-important attribute of God: He was holy.

We read many times in the Old Testament this expression: "without blemish and without spot."

Exodus 12:5 says, "Your lamb shall be without blemish . . . ."

Then we get an amplification of that in Peter's epistles: "Forasmuch as ye know that ye were not redeemed with corruptible things, as silver and gold, from your vain conversation received by tradition from your fathers; But with the precious blood of Christ, as of a lamb without blemish and without spot" (I Pet. 1:18,19).

So every lamb of the Old Testament which typified Jesus Christ and pointed toward the Lamb of God who would take away the sin of the world was "without blemish." No blind eye, no crooked limb, no torn flank, no twisted ear, no distorted feature—no lamb could ever be sacrificed upon the altar that had a blemish, because it pointed forward to One in whom there is no blemish. So Peter spoke of Him as one "without blemish and without spot."

A blemish is a defect in the original. Buy a new suit, look at it; and if you find the lining twisted and torn, you know it came from the factory in that condition. That is called a blemish. But if you buy it and on your way home drop it in a mud puddle and get some dirt on it, that is called a spot.

Jesus had no blemish, no spot. He has always been pre-existent with God and as perfect as He was when He said, "Which of you convinceth me of sin?" (John 8:46).

While walking thirty-three years—from the cradle in Bethlehem's lowly manger to that hour when He died robed in blood and crowned with thorns upon the hill called Calvary—He picked up not one spot, not one. Thank God, today we have a Saviour who is without spot, without blemish! Standing one day facing His enemies, Jesus could say what no human being could ever say—"Who convinceth me of sin?" "Convinceth" is synonomous with "convict." So what He said was, "Who convicteth me of sin?" Thank God, no one!

When He died, a centurion said, "Truly, this was the Son of God" (Matt. 27:54). When He died, a thief said, ". . . this man hath done nothing amiss" (Luke 23:41).

I want it on record that I believe I have a perfect Saviour, the divine Son of God, who possessed and manifested all the attributes of God.

2. The Attribute of God's Justice

Theologians say that the second great attribute of God is that of justice. Today justice is often not defined as it was in the Bible: "the certainty of the punishment for wrongdoing." As God is holy, it necessarily demands that God must punish anything unholy. God the Father possessed the attribute of justice.

Ezekiel 18:4 and repeated in verse 20 says, "The soul that sinneth, it shall die . . . ." When it speaks of death, it speaks of separation. Physical death is separation of soul from body; spiritual death is separation of one's soul from God.

Have you ever sinned in word, thought or deed? If so, 'The soul that sinneth shall surely die.' And Romans 3:26 says, "To declare, I say, at this time his righteousness: that he might be just, and the justifier of him which believeth in Jesus."

I speak reverently when I say this: God faced the greatest dilemma that anyone could ever face. Here is a holy, righteous God who cannot look upon sin. Everyone, without one single exception—from the original die cast in Adam, down to this very hour, to the youngest babe—is born in sin. ". . . for there is no difference: For all have sinned, and come short of the glory of God" (Rom. 3:22,23). Now God faces a dilemma. If He is just and He said the soul that sinneth shall surely die, then how is that man going to get to that God and ever be one in Him? That is the dilemma. The book of Romans teaches that God has bridged that gulf fixed between the righteousness of God and unrighteous man, and that bridge is Jesus Christ.

That is why Jesus said, "I am the way . . . ." He didn't say, "I will point you to the way," nor, "I will show you the way," but, "I am the way to God." He is the bridge that spans that chasm; and by believing, man comes out of the area of unrighteousness to a God of righteousness personified. So Jesus possessed the attribute of justice.

I wish to say that the justice of God is inexorable, implacable, impartial. No person, no family, no nation, no generation, has ever escaped the justice of God. Neither will you. The Bible says, ". . . be sure your sin will find you out" (Num. 32:23). Jesus had that wonderful attribute of justice.

3. The Attribute of Mercy

The third great attribute of God, according to theologians, is His mercy.

When I come to speak of this, how tender my heart is! Thank God for His mercy!

That is what Jesus taught when two men in Luke 18 came to the Temple to pray. The Pharisee prayed, 'God, I thank thee, that I am not as other men are . . . I tithe, I fast, I pray'; while the publican prayed, "God be merciful to me a sinner."

God has the attribute of mercy; so does Jesus. Men have tried to prove that Jesus would not be merciful. One of the greatest examples of this, and one of the most beautiful passages in the Bible and sweetest story of someone getting saved, is when Jesus was in the Temple and the woman taken in the very act of adultery was brought to Him, recorded in John 8. These men were more the enemies of Jesus than they were of the woman. Since this sin was regularly committed in a multiplicity of ways and by many people, what cared they about one little woman! They themselves were not that righteous and holy, but they hated Jesus and wanted to place Him upon the horns of a dilemma. So they brought her, this woman taken in adultery, to Jesus, flung her at His feet, then said, "Moses in the law commanded us, that such should be stoned: but what sayest thou?"

What would you say if that were presented to you? I would have to say, "Do what the Bible says." But they were talking to the One who wrote the Bible!

What did Jesus do? He stooped down and wrote something in the sand of that outer court of the Temple with His finger, as if to say: "Don't you remember that the Old Testament says the Decalog given to Moses was written with the finger of God?" (Exod. 31:18).

That is the finger that wrote it!

There that woman stands, weeping, lost, ashamed, embarrassed, while she hears these carping critics, these enemies of the Lord, say, 'The law of Moses demands she be stoned to death. What do You say?' Jesus answers, "He that is without sin among you, let him first cast a stone at her." The Bible says from the eldest to the youngest walked out, leaving her quivering at the feet of the Son of God.

Now Jesus asks, "Woman, where are those thine accusers? hath no man condemned thee?" In other words, "Are there none left to condemn you?" She answered Him, "No man, Lord."

How sweet are these words: "Neither do I condemn thee . . . ." Before you say that that is compromise, listen to His next words: ". . . go, and sin no more."

Thus He is just and merciful, and none of the attributes of God conflict one with the other. Friends, He will be merciful to you, as He was to me who, just short of twenty years of age, was without God and without hope, ever conscious of my sin, like David was who said, ". . . my sin is ever before me" (Ps. 51:3). I knelt at an old-fashioned altar and asked Jesus to save me. And that beautiful attribute of God, deep as the deepest sea, high as the highest sky, broader than the east is from the west, saved me!

Jesus possesses and manifests all the attributes of God.

4. The Attribute of Love

Says I John 4:8, "God is love." So is Jesus Christ: "For God so loved the world, that he gave his only begotten Son, that whosoever believeth in him should not perish, but have everlasting life" (John 3:16).

Dr. Harry Rimmer told one of the most wonderful stories I have ever heard.

Just before the bombing of Pearl Harbor, December 7, 1941, the Gideons' Association had given white New Testaments to each one in the Pacific Fleet of the United States Navy. Someone had also given one to Dr. Rimmer. Inside the cover was written:

TO THE PACIFIC FLEET OF THE U. S. NAVY.

Dr. Rimmer always carried that New Testament in his pocket.

The Japanese bombed Pearl Harbor, killing many people and sinking our ships. Thus began World War II.

While preaching one day, the war still fresh on minds, Dr. Rimmer held up that Testament and said, "I have here in my hand a white Testament, given by the Gideons to all our boys in the Pacific Fleet in the Navy."

After the service a man came forward with a sad expression. He stood by, waiting while others talked to Dr. Rimmer. After they had gone, this man came up to Dr. Rimmer, pulled out a white Testament from his pocket, just like the one Dr. Rimmer had held up—only there was one difference. There were the unmistakable brown stains upon that white Testament. This man fondled it in his hands as if it were his most prized possession as he said to Dr. Rimmer, "My boy was at Pearl Harbor and had this in his pocket. He stood at his post until his body was riddled with many bullets. When all his personal effects were gathered and his body was shipped back for burial, in his belongings was this Testament, just like yours, stained with the blood of my son." Then he added, "Preacher, this is my most valued possession, this book stained with the blood of my son."

Moved by the story, Dr. Rimmer paused a moment, then said, as he held out his Testament, "And that one was stained with the blood of God's Son."

There they stood with two Testaments. One man said, "Stained with the blood of my son"; the other, "Stained with the blood of God's Son."

I hold in my hand a Book that tells me that Jesus died in love and mercy and pity for you and wants to save you. You are dealing with God, for Jesus is God—the deity of Jesus Christ.

5. The Attribute of Truth

Jesus said in John 14:6, "I am the way, the truth, and the life: no man cometh unto the Father, but by me."

It is impossible to associate falsehood or deceit or error with the character of God. One of His attributes is truth; Jesus also had that attribute. In fact, He said, "I am the truth."

Someone could ask the question that Pilate asked, "What is truth?" The Bible has the answer, as it does to all others essential to the salvation of your soul. Jesus has the attribute of truth.

Many things I could say about this attribute. Mark this down: Everything that He ever said is absolute truth. Jesus said that He saves people, and He does. Jesus said that He could keep people, and He does. Jesus said that we are to be raised with Him, that He is resurrection; and He is. Jesus said that someday we are to be with Him, and we shall be. Jesus said that someday we will be like Him, and we will be.

These are five moral attributes of God, all of which Jesus had.

6. The Attributes of Omniscience, Omnipotence and Omnipresence

Then there are three attributes of God which we might call physical; that is: God is omniscient, omnipotent and omnipresent. He knows all, is all-powerful, and is everywhere at the same time. Jesus also possessed these three physical attributes.

He was omniscient. The closing verse of the second chapter of John reads: ". . . for he knew what was in man" (vs. 25). Jesus knows all things. Seven miles away from Nathanael who was sitting under a fig tree, Jesus said, ". . . when thou wast under the fig tree, I saw thee" (John 1:48). When Nathanael realized that seven miles away, on the other side of a hill, through all that granite and soil, Jesus looked and saw him, Nathanael said, ". . . thou art the Son of God" (vs. 49). The omniscience of Christ made Nathanael know that it was God to whom he was speaking.

Then there is the omnipotence of the Son of God. Matthew 28:18 says, "All power is given unto me in heaven and in earth." Jesus Christ is all-powerful.

Jesus is omnipresent, everywhere at the same time. He said, "For where two or three are gathered together in my name, there am I in the midst of them" (Matt. 18:20).

I read of a teacher trying to teach on the omnipresence of the Lord. She was saying, "The Lord can be everywhere at the same time. He is with us here in our Sunday school class."

A little boy spoke up: "Is He with the Methodists over on the other side of town?"

"Yes, He is with the Methodists."

This little skeptic asked, "Is the Lord back home in my house?"

"Yes, He is there and here, too."

Again he spoke: "We have a big barn; is He in our barn?"

"Yes, He is in your barn. The Lord is omnipresent. He can be everywhere."

The skeptical little guy couldn't understand that; and he thought, as many modernists and liberals do, that if he couldn't understand it, he ought not believe it. So he continued his query: "Is the Lord in our cellar?"

"Yes, the Lord is in your cellar, too."

"Uh huh, I thought so! We ain't got no cellar; so what you are saying is not true!"

Nevertheless, the Lord is omnipresent. He can be everywhere at the same time.

So the burden of the message on the deity of Christ was that He possesses all the attributes that God the Father and God the Spirit possess.

II. HIS DEITY PROVEN BY HIS RESURRECTION

One of the great statements of the book of Romans is Romans 1:4. The thing I have mentioned is set forth here, as it is in many places in the Bible. In verse 3 we read these words concerning His Son, Jesus

Christ, our Lord: ". . . which was made of the seed of David according to the flesh." Now verse 4, which speaks of His deity: "And declared to be the Son of God with power, according to the spirit of holiness, by the resurrection from the dead."

I mentioned earlier that some people cannot understand how the Bible can be the Word of God because it had human and divine authorship. Some people cannot understand the deity of Jesus because He was both God and man—just as much God as if He had never been man, and just as much man as if He had never been God. Verse 4 says that the resurrection of Christ proves that He is deity, that He is God. Let us see a wonderful example of this.

Here is the Apostle Paul, a bigoted Jew who did not believe that Jesus was the Son of God, did not believe He was divine or that He was deity or that He was God. Paul went about to kill everyone who did, and he opposed those who believed that this Christ was the promised Messiah of the Old Testament.

One day after Jesus came, died, went back to Heaven and the Holy Spirit came on the day of Pentecost, that bigoted young rabbi was riding along the Damascus Road about twelve o'clock, the noon hour, when a light from Heaven shined upon him and a voice spoke: "Saul, Saul, why persecutest thou me?"

Paul said, "Who art thou, Lord?"

He heard the answer, "I am Jesus whom thou persecutest."

Paul said, "Lord, what wilt thou have me to do?"

The Lord told him, "Go into the city, and it shall be told thee what thou must do."

Paul was saved by a living, resurrected Jesus.

Acts 9 gives a record of his testimony. Immediately Paul began preaching. What did he preach? "And straightway he preached Christ in the synagogues, that he is the Son of God." Why did he preach it? He had heard from Heaven, had seen the light of His Shekinah glory that day on the Damascus Road. The first thing he preached was that Jesus is the Son of God.

It is wonderful to read about His resurrection in Matthew 28 and in Matthew 27 just before His entombment. After Christ had died upon the cross, we read what was said to Pilate by the chief priests and Pharisees: "Sir, we remember that that deceiver said, while he was yet alive, After three days I will rise again" (27:63).

They got rather scared. I don't blame them. If you had watched someone die like Jesus died, you, too, would begin to doubt whether you were right in rejecting Him and denying His deity. So they became frightened. Pilate said, "Ye have a watch: go your way, make it as sure as ye can" (27:65). We read in verse 66, "So they went, and made the sepulchre sure, sealing the stone, and setting a watch." They put a Roman seal over that stone, set a Roman guard at that tomb with the instruction, "See that this man never comes out of that grave."

Listen! The Devil would give all if he could keep Jesus from coming out of the tomb. Even he knew that when Christ arose, He would conquer death and prove once and for all time the deity of the Son of God.

After three days, the stone rolled away and Jesus walked out. Those who watched Him die, even His enemies, had to say, "Truly, this was the Son of God" (Matt. 27:54). So the resurrection proves the deity of Jesus Christ.

III. HIS DEITY IS PROVEN BY HIS ASSERTIONS

Think of some things that Jesus asserted.

I read where a man was preaching on the deity of Christ. He catalogued all his information under three headings: "First, He claimed to be; second, He seemed to be; third, He proved to be."

I would like for you to see how He not only claimed to be, not only seemed to be, but, bless God forever, how He proved to be the Son of God!

In John 10:30 Jesus said, "I and my Father are one." Immediately His enemies took up stones to stone Him because He claimed equality with God. They have never quit stoning Him for that assertion. Men today hurl their stones of liberalism, intellectualism and rationalism at the Son of God because He said, "I and my Father are one." Then in John 14:9 Jesus said, ". . . he that hath seen me hath seen the Father."

Now Jesus claimed to be God. He seemed to be God. He proved to be God. Let us notice some of His assertions.

1. Jesus Claimed He Was Worthy of Worship

When they sought to worship the Apostle Paul, he absolutely forbade it. When in the Bible there were attempts on some occasions to worship angels, even they wouldn't accept it. But Jesus did. Jesus claimed that He was worthy of worship and accepted it on many occasions.

I read in Matthew 2:11 that the Wise Men "fell down, and worshipped him." Here He is not a babe in a manger, because chapter 2 of Matthew does not deal with Jesus' birth. He is now a child when the Wise Men come. ". . . they presented unto him gifts; gold, and frankincense, and myrrh." These potentates from other nations fell down before a little child, two years old or less, and recognized in Him deity and worshiped the Son of God.

The next thing you read in that passage is that the Wise Men went home "another way" because God had warned them. Had they been doing wrong by worshiping the Son of God, even in His infancy, would God have warned them, "If you go back the way you came, you will be killed"? God in a revelation warned these good men because they were doing right to worship the Christ child. Jesus accepted their worship.

I read again in Matthew 8:2, "And, behold, there came a leper and worshipped him, saying, Lord, if thou wilt, thou canst make me clean."

I read again in Matthew 9:18, ". . . there came a certain ruler, and worshipped him."

Matthew 14:33 says, "Then they that were in the ship came and worshipped him, saying, Of a truth thou art the Son of God."

So if Jesus is not deity, He is the greatest imposter the world has ever known. He is deity. And for anyone to say, "Well, I don't believe that He is deity, but I do believe He was a good man," is the most foolish thing anyone could ever say.

A man came to me at the Sea of Galilee, saying, "I agree with you that Jesus was a great teacher," and these were his very words: "He was really sharp. He really must have been a good man."

I said, "That won't do. That can't be. Jesus claimed to be God. He claimed equality with the Father. He accepted worship. If He was not the Son of God, then He was not good. You must come down to this sober decision: either to accept Him as deity or brand Him as demon."

With all my heart, soul, body, mind and strength I will worship Him like these in the Bible did. He proved His deity by His assertions.

2. Jesus Claimed to Forgive Sin

You find again in the Bible many times where He claimed to forgive sin. He said to that paralytic brought of four, "Son, be of good cheer; thy sins be forgiven thee" (Matt. 9:2). Four neighbors brought this man who could not come by himself, and laid him at the feet of Jesus through much trouble. When Jesus saw their faith, we read His words: "Son, be of good cheer; thy sins be forgiven thee."

I read in Luke 7:48 where they criticized Him there. Here comes this woman with a bad reputation, for a Pharisee said, 'If you were the Son of God, you would have known that this woman is a sinner.' What does Jesus say to her? "Thy sins are forgiven."

Thank God, He forgave mine also! When I was nearly twenty, I labored with sin. I would think of it every night. I would get out of bed, kneel and pray, "O God, let me see the light of another day. O God, don't take me now. I am not ready to go." I had an awful burden of sin. My heart was as heavy as lead.

Then in August of 1935 I believed what Jesus said: "All that the Father giveth me shall come to me; and him that cometh to me I will in no wise cast out" (John 6:37). I gave myself to Christ, and that day my sins were gone! Gone forever! They are removed as far as the east is from the west. They are buried in the depths of the sea. They are put behind the back of God and buried in divine forgetfulness, and God will remember them against me no more forever!

He proved His deity by His assertion. He said He was worthy of worship.

3. Jesus Claimed to Answer Prayer

He goes further. Listen! The divine audacity you will find here—how beautiful and wonderful! Jesus said that you get prayers answered through Him. Only God can do that. John 14:13,14 says: "And whatsoever ye shall ask in my name, that will I do, that the Father may be glorified in the Son. If ye shall ask any thing in my name, I will do it." The Bible says that there is one God and one mediator between God and men—the man Christ Jesus.

Have you ever tried it? I have asked Jesus to answer my prayers. I have asked Him to do many things. I have heard the bells of Heaven ring as my High Priest yonder the Holy of Holies ministered for me, advocated my cause. I can testify that Jesus answers prayer. Hallelujah!

Yes, He defied the laws of nature by His own assertions, by His own deeds, by His own miracles. He walked on the water; He calmed the storm. Jesus Christ proved His deity by His assertion.

IV. HIS DEITY PROVED BY UNERRING PREDICTION OF THE FUTURE

Jesus told the people of His day some things that would happen.

In fact, He said some things would happen through the course of these two thousand years; and these came to pass exactly as He predicted.

It has been my privilege to visit Capernaum several times. It used to be a commercial, thriving, bustling city at the north end of the Sea of Galilee, a crossroad of commerce and tourism even in Jesus' day. One day Jesus said, "Thou, Capernaum, which art exalted unto heaven, shalt be brought down to hell: for if the mighty works, which have been done in thee, had been done in Sodom, it would have remained until this day" (Matt. 11:23)

Capernaum was a great city, a strong city, a thickly populated city, a commercial center. Jesus wrought seventeen miracles in and around Capernaum. Right on its site He walked on water. Since Capernaum didn't repent, Jesus said the city would be brought down to Hell. Today every stone is a mute reminder of a city that God cursed. Just what Jesus said would happen, happened to Capernaum.

Here was Solomon's beautiful Temple which had been the glory of the people of God. Some came to Jesus and began to ask questions. "When shall these things be?" and, 'What sign will there be of thy coming?' Jesus said, "These things which ye behold, the days will come, in the which there shall not be left one stone upon another" (Luke 21:6). They were real stones weighing hundreds of tons, forty-five feet by twenty-two by fifteen—a miracle that they could have ever been placed there in those days. They must have asked, "By what unknown power, by what unusual power, can such stones as these be removed from their places?"

But thirty-five years later, in A.D. 70 when Titus, the Roman militarist, came against Jerusalem, he leveled the Temple, leaving not one stone upon another. Then he sowed the fields with salt so neither tree nor grass could grow for many decades.

The words of Jesus came to pass exactly as He said.

Jesus said in the same chapter of Luke: "But woe unto them that are with child, and to them that give suck, in those days!" (vs. 23). Women were ripped up. He said people would die by the sword. It is said that at that siege of Jerusalem under Titus in A.D. 70 trees were cut down to make crosses on which they nailed Jews, until no trees were left. The words of Jesus came to pass.

Listen to Jesus talking about His own death. He even told who would kill Him. In Matthew 16:21, He said that He must go to Jerusalem and suffer many things of the chief priests and scribes and elders and be killed.

Jesus told of His own death, of His own resurrection, of His own ascension. He told of His own betrayal—"One of you shall betray me." No one could believe those words. Those closest to Him, twelve in all, one day were told that one of them wasn't saved; one of them was a demon; one of them wasn't clean; one of them would betray Him.

Thomas asked, "Lord, is it I?" James asked, "Lord, is it I?" John asked, "Lord, is it I?" They didn't know who it was, but Jesus knew. The night before His death on the cross of Calvary, sitting at the Last Supper—the darkest hour of human history—Jesus said, 'He who dips with his hand in the dish, it is he that will betray me.' Judas knew who it was.

Jeanne Dixon claims that seventy percent of her predictions are accurate; God is one hundred percent right all the time.

A sweet verse to me is Isaiah 34:16, "Seek ye out of the book of the Lord, and read: no one of these shall fail, none shall want her mate: for my mouth it hath commanded, and his spirit it hath gathered them." Not one. Not one. If anyone could ever show me one error in that Bible, I wouldn't believe a word of it. But thank God, the Bible is as impeccable as Jesus Himself. It is without spot or blemish, just like He is. It is without error, without contradiction, just like Jesus is. Everything that Jesus said came to pass just exactly like He said it would. He proved His deity by His knowledge of the future.

V. HIS DEITY PROVEN BY HIS IMMUTABILITY

Immutability is not just a big word; it is a Bible word. We read in Hebrews 13:8, "Jesus Christ the same yesterday, and to day, and for ever." Jesus never changes. He is absolutely immutable. He is unchanging, just like God the Father is.

I read about the immutability of Jesus Christ in Hebrews 6:18: "That by two immutable things, in which it was impossible for God to lie, we might have a strong consolation, who have fled for refuge to lay hold upon the hope set before us."

In that passage the Lord wants to affirm His Word. It says when He swore to Abraham, "because he could swear by no greater, he swore by himself," that is, by His person, for His person is immutable. He swore, as it were, that His Word was as unchanging as His person.

Hallelujah for an unchanging Saviour!

A beautiful passage is Psalm 102:26,27: "They shall perish, but thou shalt endure: yea, all of them shall wax old like a garment; as a vesture shalt thou change them, and they shall be changed. But thou art the same, and thy years shall have no end."

Hallelujah for a Saviour who never changes! He is immutable. Only God is unchanging.

Malachi 3:6 says, "For I am the Lord, I change not; therefore ye sons of Jacob are not consumed." I noticed something in that verse that I had never thought about before, though I have read it many times. There are two great statements here: "I am the Lord, I change not," and ". . . therefore ye sons of Jacob are not consumed." Now Israel is the burning bush that was not consumed, and here the Lord says, "I am the Lord, I change not; therefore ye sons of Jacob [Jews] are not consumed [shall never be destroyed]." They never have been; they never will be.

It is said Hitler destroyed some six million Jews. But he caused them to multiply, to flee back home. He helped fulfill Bible prophecy. They are not consumed. Why? That verse tells us why: "For I am the Lord, I change not; therefore ye sons of Jacob are not consumed." They are not consumed because of the immutability of God. The Jews will live on forever. The Lord never changes.

All of us have heard an expression: "As solid as the Rock of Gibraltar." All my life I had wanted to see the Rock of Gibraltar. So one day I had it pointed out to me—the rock jutting out of the waters, the rock created by God out in His vast, expansive ocean. There it stood. I was so awed by it.

I read one day that the Rock of Gibraltar started crumbling away. Afraid it might begin to disappear beneath the water's surface, men began hauling in large boatloads of concrete to patch up the rock, like a dentist patches a tooth to keep it from rotting and decaying and crumbling away.

Thank God, I know one Rock that never changes!

> **Rock of Ages, cleft for me,**
> **Let me hide myself in Thee;**
> **Let the water and the blood,**
> **From Thy riven side which flowed,**
> **Be of sin the double cure,**
> **Save me from its guilt and power.**

I stand on a Rock that is immutable, unchanging! Jesus proved His deity by His immutability.

"Jesus Christ the same yesterday, and to day, and for ever."—Heb. 13:8.

"Thou art the Christ, the Son of the living God."—Matt. 16:16.

"And we believe and are sure that thou art that Christ, the Son of the living God." —John 6:69.

R. L. MOYER
1886-1944

ABOUT THE MAN:

Dr. R. L. Moyer was an evangelist from 1915-1920, then became pastor of the United Brethren Church in Minneapolis. Later Dr. W. B. Riley invited him to become his assistant at First Baptist Church in the same city.

When Dr. Riley retired from the pastorate in 1942, Moyer then became pastor and served in that capacity until his death.

Dr. H. A. Ironside said about him: *"Few men have the winsomeness and tenderness, combined with sound scriptural teaching that characterizes the ministry of my esteemed friend and fellow-laborer, Dr. Robert L. Moyer."*

Dr. Moyer was long dean of Northwestern Bible School and the author of several books. He went to be with the Lord in 1944.

V.

Son of Mary, Son of God

R. L. MOYER

"His mother." "My Son."—Matt. 2:13-15.

The incarnation is fundamental truth. It is initial. All truth that follows grows out of this. "Incarnation," a Latin word meaning literally "enflesh-ment," is the account of God's assuming a living, bodily form. Too many times, in thinking of the entrance of Christ into the world, men consider merely the birth of a baby. We need to remember that we are not talking merely about the birth of a baby, but about the incarnation by way of the virgin birth.

"His Mother"

When an angel of the Lord instructed Joseph to go into Egypt, he did not say, "Take *your* wife," but rather, "Take *the* young child and *his* mother." This expression is found four times in Matthew 2:13-21, and proves that Joseph had nothing to do with the begetting of the Child.

The testimony of Scripture is very clear as to the virginity of Mary and her discovered motherhood before her marriage to Joseph. "Now the birth of Jesus Christ was on this wise: When as his mother Mary was espoused to Joseph, before they came together, she was found with child of the Holy Ghost" (Matt. 1:18).

Mary was espoused to Joseph. The tie of betrothal was, in the eye of the Jew, as sacred as marriage. The hand of God was evident in this betrothal, or marriage. God had covenanted with David that he should never lack a son to sit upon his throne in Jerusalem, and now God was moving to bring this about.

Mary was espoused to Joseph, but the marriage had not been consummated. She was still in the home of her parents; the bridegroom had not taken the bride home, but they were both looking forward to the nuptials. Then, after the espousal and before the marriage, "she was found with child of the Holy Ghost."

I suppose no greater trial ever came to a betrothed couple than came to Mary and Joseph. Bishop Ryle says, "It brought with it, no doubt, at a distant date, great honor; but it brought with it for the present no small danger to Mary's reputation, and no small trial to Mary's faith."

"And when she saw him [the angel of the Lord], *she was troubled at his saying."*—Luke 1:29.

Mary was espoused to Joseph, but now there arose what must have seemed an impassable barrier between them. Mary knew the secret; Joseph did not. Who can imagine the feelings of Mary in those days? She was to have the highest grace that the Lord could bestow upon a woman—to be the mother of the Christ; but she had to undergo a trial most painful, a shame most terrible to a pure, human soul.

Who would believe her story? Who did? Undoubtedly, very few. Undoubtedly Mary was looked upon as a sinful girl. That is what those Jews meant when they cast this into the face of the Lord Jesus: "We be not born of fornication" (John 8:41). And when this story came to Joseph—may it be that Mary whispered it to him one day?—it seemed strange, incredible, impossible. Joseph could not believe it. His suspicions were natural, excusable; but how cruelly they must have wounded the tender heart of Mary.

But the Child of Mary was of the Holy Ghost. The power of the Highest overshadowed her. Through the power of the Holy Spirit that body was formed within her—a body that partook of the sin of neither man nor woman. She was indeed favored among women. Some have exalted her beyond measure, but others have neglected her. She was born in sin, like every other descendant of Adam; and she needed the sacrifice of the Son of God, to whom she gave birth, for her salvation! But the mother of our Lord must have been a beautiful and noble character. Someone has given her the beautiful title, "Moss-Rose of Palestine." This girl God chose for His incarnation.

When Mary visited Elizabeth, she said, "My soul doth magnify the Lord, And my spirit hath rejoiced in God my Saviour." These are not the words of a woman who had conceived out of wedlock, in sin and shame. Such a woman never shouts for joy and never magnifies God.

A little sidelight on the incarnation is seen in the visit of the Wise Men. These Wise Men were taught of God and led by God. The star led them to the home of the Child. The record declares that when they came to the Child, they "fell down, and worshipped him."

It is worthy of note that they did not worship Mary. Certainly this worship on the part of the Wise Men was impossible apart from their belief in the incarnation. Men, who had been taught and led of God as they had been, could not have worshiped a son of Joseph and Mary.

We might consider for a moment the objection to the incarnation that having one human parent did not guarantee sinlessness, so that it would be of no advantage to be born in that way. A sinful nature could be contracted from one parent just as well as two. We do not contend that having one human parent guarantees sinlessness, but we do contend that the fact that the conception was to be under the power of the Holy Spirit guaranteed sinlessness. "The Holy Ghost shall come upon thee, and the power of the Highest shall overshadow thee: THEREFORE also that holy thing which shall be born of thee shall be called the Son of God." The generation of our Lord was pure and holy and untainted because it was sanctified by the Holy Spirit.

There are some who object to the virgin birth on the ground that it is not scientific. How do they know that this is not the *only* scientific way in which God could become incarnate? To the one who complains that this birth is out of the ordinary, we reply that the first Adam did not come through natural generation, and neither did the second. We refuse to rule out the supernatural.

So far as that is concerned, all birth is supernatural, for the reproduction of the young in the human family is an unfathomable mystery. Certainly if God created the first man in the beginning from the dust of the earth, He could create the second man in the womb of the woman. The Creator is not subject to limitation. The incarnation was the method by which an uncreated divine being, who had pre-existence, took unto union with His own divine personality a human nature. The first man Adam had neither father nor mother nor previous existence. But He who was born of the Virgin Mary was the pre-existent Lord who became incarnate through His supernatural birth.

The God who brought a motherless woman from the body of a man brought a fatherless man from the body of a woman.

His mother was Mary.

"His Father"

In the Scripture in which we have four times the expression, "the young child and his mother," we have the mention of His Father—in the quotation from prophecy, "Out of Egypt have I called MY son." Compare these words—"His mother" and "MY Son."

It is true that in some places in Scripture Joseph is called the father of the Lord Jesus. But by whom? By the people of Nazareth and Capernaum who did not believe in Him, who believed Him to be begotten in illegitimacy, who flung into His face the charge that He was begotten of fornication. It is true that once Mary spoke of Joseph as the father of the Lord Jesus. This was in the Temple when she found Him after He had been lost for three days. She said, "Thy father and I have sought thee." Did He rebuke her when He said, "Wist ye not that I must be about my Father's business?" She spoke of Joseph as His father. He spoke of God as His Father.

But even with the knowledge of the virgin birth, would it not be natural of her to speak so of her husband? Christ was born in Joseph's house. He stood in legal relation as the son of Joseph. That is, while He was not the child of Joseph, He was the son of Joseph according to Jewish legal reckoning. He was under Joseph's protection. It was but natural that Mary should so speak.

More than one person has had in the home a child who was not born in the home, but who yet called the members of that home father and mother. Our Lord Jesus never spoke of Joseph as His father. Neither does the narrative of Scripture except to give the words of others. When our Lord spoke of His Father's house, He surely did not refer to the carpenter's home in Nazareth.

It is worthy of note that in the genealogy in Matthew 1:1-17, which runs from Abraham down to Joseph, we find the word "begat" thirty-nine times. We are told that "Abraham begat Isaac"; "Isaac begat Jacob"; "Jacob begat Judas"; etc. But when we come to verse 16, note carefully the omission of the word "begat." That verse reads, "Jacob begat Joseph, the husband of Mary, of whom was born Jesus." It does not say that Joseph begat Jesus as it does in every other instance of the thirty-nine sons. There is no statement of Christ's having been begotten of Joseph. Instead of that, verse 18 distinctly declares that Mary was with child of the Holy Ghost.

Joseph's attitude in the matter also makes plain the fact that he was not the father of the Lord Jesus. Joseph is espoused to Mary. Before marriage she was found to be with child. Joseph was convinced of Mary's impurity and immorality just as any other man would be under the circumstances today. Joseph was a just man, that is, a man who desired to obey God's law. He wanted to do right in the sight of God. Only three things could Joseph do. The first two he considered; he gave no thought to the third. What Joseph took into consideration was whether he should make Mary a public example, that is, declare her guilt, or give her a private bill of divorce. Both of these were provided for in the law. The first meant that he would expose her to public shame. Under the law, this would necessitate her being stoned to death (Deut. 22:21; John 8:5).

There was another provision, however, whereby a man might put away a woman privily, that is, divorce her secretly by putting a bill of divorcement into her hands, as we have it in Deuteronomy 24:1.

Joseph thought of these things and finally made up his mind that he would put her away privately. The only other thing that Joseph could do was to take Mary to wife and so legitimize the birth of the Child in the eyes of the Jewish law. This was the thing that was brought to pass by the intervention of God.

Remember, Joseph was not considering this last possibility. He had made up his mind to put Mary away privily. Do you think that God would permit this? Absolutely not! And so there came an angel of the Lord who gave instruction to Joseph which he, being a man of faith, was to follow. Joseph was to assume paternity of the Child. Therefore, he took Mary; and under his care, she brought forth a Son—not Joseph's son, but a Son for a time entrusted to Joseph's care. So Mary's first-born became the possessor of a legal father. Jesus Christ had two fathers, one by nature, and one by law.

The very first promise and prophecy of the Saviour in Scripture magnifies the virgin birth. Christ is spoken of there as the One in all the millions of earth who stands out as such a seed. It is not the seed of Adam, but the Seed of the woman. Human fatherhood does not enter into it at all.

Harry Rimmer has written:

> You know as well as I that there is no such thing as "seed of a woman." There is no life in any but the male seed. So well is this fact established that in all modern races a child takes the name of his father, because his life comes through the male parent . . . .

But here is a statement made that when the promised Redeemer comes, He will be "seed of a woman." That will be a biological miracle, as He will have no earthly father. To have a child born which could be scientifically spoken of as the seed of its mother would be contrary to the known laws and facts of biology.

The difficulty of a man being born without a human father is met in the incarnation. Jesus Christ has the unique distinction of being born into the human race of the seed of a woman. Someone has said that it would be very remarkable if the birth of Jesus had not been unique. "In a person so supernatural the virgin birth was natural." There is no question but that our Lord's sinless life testifies to His sinless birth.

Dr. Tiffany says:

If the birth of Jesus was natural, who was His father? If I deny His virgin birth, my logic would force me to stand with the gossips of Nazareth and believe Joseph a vile seducer who begot Jesus out of wedlock, or that Mary was a harlot, worthy of death by stoning, but who imposed upon the pious simplicity of her fascinated betrothed. In either of these cases Jesus would be a bastard, and His reputed father and mother guilty of the grossest and most revolting licentiousness.

My Lord was not thus born. Joseph disclaimed himself the father of Jesus. Logic forces me to face the alternative that Jesus was born of the Holy Spirit, or conceived out of wedlock.

Jesus Christ implied the virgin birth when He claimed God as His Father in a sense not true of any other man (John 5:17,18). Paul refers to the Lord Jesus as being "made of a woman" instead of begotten of man. There is no question concerning the attitude of the New Testament writers to the virgin birth.

His Father Was God

In conclusion, we answer the statement sometimes made that "it makes no difference whose son He was." But it does make a difference. If Jesus Christ was the son of Joseph, then the Jews were right when they laid the charge of blasphemy against Him and demanded His death; then Jesus Christ died for His own sins, but not for ours. You could no more be saved by a son of Joseph nailed to a tree than you could by a murderer hanged on the gallows.

It does make a difference whose son He was—all the difference between Heaven and Hell. Only divine birth could provide divine Sonship, and only divine Sonship could achieve divine redemption. We close with a quotation from the late Dr. I. M. Haldeman:

If God the Father did not stoop down from Heaven and, in prime accord with the Son as His verbal and eternal expression, and through the co-ordinate and covenant operation of the Holy Spirit, take hold on a cell or seed of the Virgin Mary, creating a new and distinct human nature which the Son of God took into union with Himself, becoming a unique being with two natures, human and divine, in one body and with one personality forever, then the whole foundation and fabric of Christianity is completely overthrown.

The men who deny the virgin birth; who do so that they may the more easily be delivered from carrying the baggage of the miraculous; who shift the fatherhood of Jesus from the eternal God to the act of some unknown and sinful man, are paying a dear price for their jaunty endeavor to accommodate the supernaturalism of Christianity to the poverty-smitten weakness of their own faith, and the noisy clamor of an unbelieving, spiritually ignorant and scoffing world.

No angel could His place have taken,
Highest of the high tho' He,
The loved One, on the cross forsaken:
Was One of the Godhead three!

Will you surrender to this Saviour?
To His scepter humbly bow?
You, too, shall come to know His favor;
He will save you, save you now.

I. M. HALDEMAN
1845-1933

ABOUT THE MAN:

Dr. Haldeman was long pastor of First Baptist Church, New York, and one of the foremost of Bible expositors.

His best-known work was *The Tabernacle Priesthood and Offerings.* With great wealth of detail, he shows how the framework, the coverings, the curtains, the hangings, the priesthood, the robes and the offerings of the Tabernacle in the wilderness prefigured the Person, the work and the glory of Christ.

Another well-known volume was *How to Study the Bible.* Dr. Haldeman believed that the New Testament is a fulfillment of the Old, that each book of the entire Bible finds place and value by the law of growth—and by a moral and spiritual logic.

In *Christian Science in the Light of Holy Scripture,* Dr. Haldeman states his case with legal exactness—first, calling as witness the words of the Scientists, then calling as witness the words of the Bible. The reader must act as jury and decide whether the witnesses agree or whether they are flatly contradictory. It shows the naked deformity of Christian Science.

Other books by this great Bible scholar include: *The Coming of Christ; Ten Sermons on the Second Coming; Christ, Christianity and the Bible; Can the Dead Communicate With the Living,* etc.

VI.

Virgin-Born — or Bastard?

I. M. HALDEMAN

*"Now the birth of Jesus Christ was on this wise: When as his mother
Mary was espoused to Joseph, before they came together, she was found
with child of the Holy Ghost. Then Joseph her husband, being a just
man, and not willing to make her a publick example, was minded to
put her away privily. But while he thought on these things, behold, the
angel of the Lord appeared unto him in a dream, saying, Joseph, thou
son of David, fear not to take unto thee Mary thy wife: for that which
is conceived in her is of the Holy Ghost. And she shall bring forth a
son, and thou shalt call his name JESUS: for he shall save his people
from their sins. Now all this was done, that it might be fulfilled which
was spoken of the Lord by the prophet, saying, Behold, a virgin shall
be with child, and shall bring forth a son, and they shall call his name
Emmanuel, which being interpreted is, God with us. Then Joseph being raised from sleep did as the angel of the Lord had bidden him, and
took unto him his wife: And knew her not till she had brought forth
her firstborn son: and he called his name JESUS."* —Matt. 1:18-25.

A large number of people, professing Christians among them, think
it of no importance whether or not one believes in the virgin birth. They
look upon it, so they say, as altogether a matter of theological interpretation, having nothing whatever to do with what they are pleased
to call the "vital" side of Christianity.

I affirm it makes a great difference, a difference so great, so radical,
that should the church consent to cut it out of the doctrine of Christianity, Christianity would have no decent, moral or intellectual basis
on which to stand. I ask you to consider:

I. THE EFFECT ON THE NAME, THE CHARACTER AND REPUTATION OF MARY, THE MOTHER OF JESUS, IF HE WERE NOT VIRGIN BORN

Mary was espoused to Joseph. Espousal in that day was something more than lip-service. The parties to espousal must come before the elders of the congregation and pledge their vows. In making her vow, the woman committed herself to and assumed all the responsibility of a wife. Before the marriage ceremony was performed, she was looked upon by the elders, the congregation, and the neighborhood, as a wife.

When the angel would comfort Joseph concerning Mary's condition with child, even though they had not yet come together, he said: "Fear not to take unto thee Mary *thy wife*" (Matt. 1:20). In the eyes of God and man, Mary had all the reputation and responsibility of a wife to maintain.

That Joseph was not the father of Mary's child ought to be self-evident to every logical, intellectual and decent mind. When he discovered she was about to become a mother, he determined to divorce her. Divorce in Israel was both solemn and serious. The parties to divorce must present themselves to the elders in open meeting. The case would be fully and searchingly tried. If the woman were found guilty, she would be taken out to a public place or field. The whole populace would surround her, and under the command of the elders, without mercy, they would stone her to death.

Joseph knew this would be the doom appointed to Mary if he sought publicly to divorce her. He was not willing to do that. He believed she had proven false to him, but he still loved her. He therefore determined to put her away privately. He would put in the claim of annulment against his own vows, and set her aside, having henceforth no more to do with her. This is what the Scripture means when it says: "Then Joseph her husband [mark, even before the marriage he is recognized as "husband," as she is as "wife"], being a just man, and not willing to make her a *publick example*, was minded to put her away privily" (Matt. 1:19).

But the living God never allows us to be in doubt about the truth. After the angel had spoken to Joseph and had bidden him without fear to take Mary to himself, we read in Matthew that he "took unto him his wife: And knew her not till she had brought forth her firstborn son: and he called his name JESUS" (1:24,25).

This is the plain statement that marriage between Joseph and Mary had not been consummated before he brought her home; that it was not consummated till after Jesus was born. What more would you have? What more need you have to prove, at the least, that Joseph was not the father of Jesus?

Since, then, Joseph was not the father of Jesus, behold where it places Mary if Jesus were not virgin-born. It brings her into the light as Joseph's accredited wife, and mother of a child of whom he was not the father. As his wife, it makes her guilty of breaking wedlock. It makes her guilty of fornication. It makes her guilty of adultery.

Deny the virgin birth, and this is the category in which by inexorable logic you are under bonds to put Mary, the mother of Christ, a stain, a shame, that all the waters of all the seven seas can never wash out. Think you a light matter to put this indelible stain upon the mother of our Lord? Deny the virgin birth and this is what you do.

Consider, I pray you,

II. THE EFFECT THIS DENIAL OF THE VIRGIN BIRTH MUST HAVE UPON THE NAME AND REPUTATION OF JESUS HIMSELF

If some man other than Joseph were the father of Jesus, and He were begotten and conceived out of wedlock, then He was an illegitimate child, a child who had no legal right to come into the world. This is what you must face: Jesus Christ, an illegitimate son. But that is not all.

Deny the virgin birth, make Mary a faithless wife, guilty of breaking wedlock, and you make her son something more than illegitimate. It is plain enough what that something more is. It is just this: If some other man than Joseph were the father of Jesus, we have to reckon this— **that man was not known.** He was not known in that day. He has not been known any day since. He is not known now. No man can put his finger upon his identity and name, and say, "This is the man who betrayed Joseph and begot Mary's illegitimate son."

There can be no question about it. He was and is unknown. It follows, therefore, if Jesus had an earthly father, and that father was not known, we have to say that Jesus was the son of an unknown father. And what is the name in all languages you give to the son of an unknown father? There is but one name and title, and that is "a bastard." It is an ugly name. It looks ugly. It sounds ugly.

Would you know what God thinks of a bastard? Hear what He says: "A bastard shall not enter into the congregation of the Lord; even to his tenth generation shall he not enter into the congregation of the Lord" (Deut. 23:2). A bastard could not enter into the congregation of the Lord. The posterity of a bastard could not enter into or partake of the privileges of the congregation of the Lord for ten generations, that is, *three hundred years.*

This tells you what God thinks of an unmarried woman who gives birth to a child. This tells you what God thinks of a married woman who gives birth to a child by another than her own husband. This tells you what God thinks of the bastard himself.

Bastardy is a shame to the mother. It is a double shame to the son. He must carry his mother's shame and advertise it wherever he goes; and he must bear his own shame, shamed of God. Illegitimacy and bastardy are two millstones heavy enough to hang about the neck of any son. What think you is the weight of these millstones about the neck of Him whom we seek to call the Son of God?

Consider,

III. THE EFFECT THE DENIAL OF THE VIRGIN BIRTH MUST HAVE UPON THE ESSENTIAL BEING OF JESUS HIMSELF

If He were not virgin-born, then of course He had a human father. If He had a human father, He inherited the nature of that father. As that father had a nature of sin, He inherited his nature of sin. If he had a nature of sin, He would be under the penalty of all who are born in sin. He would be under the penalty of death.

When, therefore, He claimed that no one could take His life from Him, that He had power over His own life, He did not tell the truth. Being born in sin *(if He had a human father),* He was, as all others, doomed to die. He was therefore a lost sinner. As a lost sinner, He needed a Saviour. He needed a Saviour to save Him from death. According to His own legislation, He needed to be born again; He needed a new nature.

It is terrific—but it is inexorable logic. If Jesus Christ were not virgin-born; if He had a sinful human father, He was as much in need of regeneration and sacrificial redemption as any other begotten of a human father.

Deny the virgin birth and you paralyze the whole scheme of redemption by Jesus Christ. What claim or right of claim has any man to be the Redeemer and Saviour of men who Himself is born in sin, under the doom and penalty of sin, needing regeneration? But that is not the only consequence of having a human father. Mark it well. If He had a human father, and as that father had a finite personality, then He inherited a finite personality. If He had a finite personality, of course, we are bound to say He did not have an infinite personality. He was not an infinite Person. If He were not infinite, He was not God. If He were not God, then He was not the second Person of Eternal Trinity. If He were not the second Person of the Trinity, then none was. If none was, there is no triunity of God. If there be no triunity of the Godhead, we are landed at the front door of Unitarianism, that bloodless, emotionless, soulless system which substitutes intellect for the spirit, and reason for faith. Prating about God, it knows Him not.

Deny the virgin birth, and as absolutely as two and two make four, as inexorably as the arrow to the mark, you deny and reject the Trinity of God.

Do you think it a light and inconsequential thing to deny the virgin birth, or that it is something that matters little one way or another?

Behold what takes place when you deny the Trinity. You deny and must cut out of the Bible this tremendous Scripture: ". . . who through the eternal Spirit offered himself without spot to God" (Heb. 9:14). It is, indeed, an immense Scripture. It means the whole Godhead was engaged in the sacrifice of the cross—the whole Godhead in the fullness of personality was engaged in the act of redemption. The Father, the Son, the Holy Spirit, each of them an infinite Person subsisting in the indivisible Being of God. The Lord Jesus Christ as the Son of the Father offered Himself unto God as the Father. He offered Himself through the eternal, personal Spirit. As an infinite Person, He offered Himself through the infinite personality of the Spirit to the infinite personality of God the Father: even the God and Father who through the Spirit gave Him out of His bosom that He might make this offering.

Deny the Trinity of God and you deny and make impossible that Scripture. Deny and reject that Scripture, you deny and reject the sacrificial death of Christ; you deny it in relation to the everlasting covenant and the pledge and honor of the whole Godhead. When you do that, you sweep away the foundation of Christianity as set forth in Holy Scripture from Genesis to Revelation. You deny that Scripture when you deny the Trinity. You deny the Trinity when you deny the virgin birth.

To deny the virgin birth, and to talk about the ethical value of Christianity is worse than childish. There are no ethics left. Instead of ethics, the whole system is buried in a moral ruin, out of whose chaos there looks the face of one illegitimate, bastard-born, a helpless sinner like the rest of us, and like the rest of us bereft of any hoped-for Saviour.

Without the virgin birth, for us there is only a Christianity whose beginning is a fiction and whose ending is the substitution of an ethical for a sacrificial Christ, a substitution that bears the stamp of its own reason; and in every promise it makes, mocks the hope of our soul both for time and eternity.

Without the virgin birth, Christianity has no authority, neither as an ethical or doctrinal system. Without the virgin birth, I repeat, Christianity has no decent, moral, spiritual, or intellectual basis on which to stand.

He who denies the virgin birth denies Bible Christianity, smites the mother of our Lord with shame, snatches the crown of deity from His brow, strips Him of His sinless humanity, makes His cross a blood-stained failure and bids us face eternity with no light in the darkness.

R. E. NEIGHBOUR
1873-1949

ABOUT THE MAN:

Dr. Neighbour was noted as a Bible teacher, missionary and founder of a number of large churches, including one which was reputed to have the most attended regular church prayer meeting existing. He served in far separated areas such as the British Isles, Israel, Brazil, as well as India where he traveled widely. His work in Brazil was especially amazing. He went far into the interior where white men had never gone, and he took the first printing press into Brazil. He translated the Scripture and printed page by page the first Brazilian Bibles.

He was the outstanding author of about ninety-nine books, three of which were poetry and two of songs, and some of which were written as early as age twenty-one. He authored *The New Daily Devotional Volume* about which H. A. Ironside said, "Not since Spurgeon's *Morning and Evening Readings* have I seen as delightful a volume . . ." Other books by him include: *WHAT ABOUT Separation? Sanctification? and Spirit Filling?*, *The Epistle of James*, *The Baptism of the Holy Ghost*, *Jonah*, *Song of Songs*.

VII.

15 Unanswerable Proofs of the Virgin Birth

R. E. NEIGHBOUR

(Preached at Chicago Gospel Tabernacle in the 1930's, and broadcast over radio.)

Some may question whether this is a very vital theme. Most of us fully believe that Jesus Christ was born of the Virgin and, therefore, was incarnate in the flesh, very God of very God. I say I consider this the most important theme that could possibly be preached at this hour, because there are many who are stalking over the land denying the virgin birth, denouncing that Jesus Christ was begotten of the Holy Ghost.

Remember, beloved, that on His Holy Ghost conception is based every vital of the Faith. If Jesus Christ was not born of the Virgin, if He was not God manifest in the flesh, everything else that we hold dear has collapsed. He must be born of the Virgin or He could not be the Son of God, neither could He have been called Saviour nor could He be the anointed of the Father. So we are going to show you several unanswerable proofs that Jesus Christ must have been born of the Virgin.

We will consider certain proofs in the opening chapters of the Gospel of Matthew first; then, second, the proofs in the opening chapters of the Gospel of Luke. In each case we will find that Jesus Christ must have been born of a virgin. We are not going out of the scenes connected directly with His babyhood. Our testimony will include Elisabeth, Zacharias and those who gathered around the manger in Bethlehem and around the subsequent circumcision of the infant Christ in the Temple of Jerusalem.

Proof 1—The Matthew Genealogy

First of all, in the book of Matthew we will observe the genealogy of Jesus Christ beginning with Abraham and running down to Joseph. There is something very striking that you may have overlooked as you read it: the word "begat" occurs thirty-nine times, because there are that many generations mentioned. It starts, "Abraham *begat* Isaac; and Isaac *begat* Jacob; and Jacob *begat* Judas." You read through these thirty-nine generations until you come to the 16th verse, then it says—mark it carefully—"Jacob begat Joseph the husband of Mary, of whom was *born* Jesus."

It does not say that Joseph *begat* Jesus. It does say, in *every other* instance, that each son was begotten of his father. When you come to the occasion of the birth of Jesus, the word "begat" is dropped; and it says, "Joseph the husband of Mary, of whom was *born* Jesus."

There is no statement of Christ's having been begotten of Joseph. The query naturally comes to the mind, how then was Jesus begotten, if He was not begotten of Joseph?

The answer is given in the 18th verse: "Now the birth of Jesus Christ was on this wise." No explanation had to be given of the birth of Abraham or of Isaac or of Jacob or of Judah or of any of the rest, because their generation was by natural begetting. There is a particular statement, however, concerning the birth of Jesus Christ:

Proof 2—Joseph's Attitude

"Now the birth of Jesus Christ was on this wise: When as his mother Mary was espoused to Joseph, before they came together, she was found with child of the Holy Ghost."

When Joseph found his espoused wife with child, the Bible says, "Joseph her husband, being a just man, and not willing to make her a publick example, was minded to put her away privily."

The testimony concerning the man who became the husband of Mary, and thereby the legal father of Jesus Christ, is that he was a *just* man. He was not the kind of a man who would have been untrue to his be-trothed wife. Therefore, Joseph, her husband, was minded to put her away privately:

"But while he thought on these things [now mark what the angel said], behold, the angel of the Lord appeared unto him in a dream, saying, Joseph, thou son of David, fear not to take unto thee Mary thy wife: for that which is conceived in her is of the Holy Ghost. And she shall bring forth a son, and thou shalt call his name JESUS: for he shall save

his people from their sins. Now all this was done, that it might be fulfilled which was spoken of the Lord by the prophet, saying [this was accomplished that it might be brought to pass which has been written by the prophet], *Behold, a virgin shall be with child, and shall bring forth a son, and they shall call his name Emmanuel, which being interpreted is, God with us. Then Joseph being raised from sleep did as the angel of the Lord had bidden him, and took unto him his wife: And knew her not till she had brought forth her firstborn son: and he called his name JESUS.*"

In all of this there are two proofs of the virgin conception and birth. First, Joseph's trouble and anxiety over the discovery of Mary's delicate condition is proof positive that he was not, himself, the father of the child. Second, the fact that Joseph took unto him Mary his wife is proof positive that Joseph accepted the angel's explanation that that which was conceived in her was of the Holy Ghost. Joseph cast away from him forever the unjust fear that some man was the father of the child.

Proof 3—The Testimony of the Wise Men

In the second chapter of Matthew you have another great proof which we present, and that is, the testimony of the Wise Men:

"Now when Jesus was born in Bethlehem of Judea in the days of Herod the king, behold, there came wise men from the east to Jerusalem, Saying, Where is he that is born King of the Jews? for we have seen his star in the east, and are come to worship him."

These Wise Men of the East had not come seeking a son of Joseph; they had not come seeking a mere man. They knew the prophecies of the Old Testament Scriptures; and when they saw His star in the East, they began their journey to seek One born of the Virgin—the Son of God. The very fact that this star of this constellation of the heavens, moved along, marking out the road faithfully, like signposts on the way, guiding the Wise Men to the manger of Christ in Bethlehem, was enough to show them that there was something marvelous and wonderful about the birth of Jesus Christ. Thus they saw His star in the East and followed it. After seeing Herod,

". . . they departed; and, lo, the star, which they saw in the east, went before them, till it came and stood over where the young child was. When they saw the star, they rejoiced with exceeding great joy."

You know, there will be constellations marking the second coming of our Lord Jesus Christ. The Bible says there shall be signs in the sun and moon and stars. When He came the first time, the very stars of Heaven gave obeisance and honor to the little Babe at Bethlehem—the Holy One of God. He was dedicated unto God far back before the world was. His birth had been promised in the Garden of Eden and reiterated through the prophets.

What a wonderful hour it was when the star appeared and announced that after four thousand years of waiting, the holy Babe had been born. The Son of God had come to the earth. Isaiah's prophecy, "Unto us a child is born, unto us a son is given," was fulfilled. Thus when the Wise Men saw this little Babe, they did the unusual thing: they fell down before the little Babe and worshiped Him.

Proof 4—The Babe, Not Mary, an Object of Worship

Mark this carefully: it does not say that they fell down and adored Mary. We love the memory of Mary, the mother of the Lord Jesus Christ. We consider her the most highly favored of any woman who has ever been born. We would not take from her one iota of the glory which belongs to her, for the Lord God marked her out and chose her as the mother, the virgin mother, of the Son of God.

However, the Wise Men did not *worship* her, neither should we. We worship Mary's Son. Mary was the channel through which God brought into the earth the little body in which the Son of God was destined to dwell. Thus, while we honor Mary and revere her name, we will not render to her Divine worship. We cannot do that.

"When they . . . saw the young child with Mary his mother, [they] fell down, and worshipped him: and when they had opened their treasures, they presented unto him gifts; gold, and frankincense, and myrrh."

It is impossible to consider this *"worship* of the Babe" on the part of the Wise Men apart from belief in the Virgin birth. Men taught of God might have brought gifts to a son of Joseph and Mary, but men taught of God would not have *worshiped* the son of Joseph and Mary, nor the son of any other human pair. Such an act was positively prohibited by God—"Thou shalt worship the Lord thy God, and him only shalt thou serve." Thus the *worship* of the Wise Men and the star that marked where the Child lay both attest the Virgin birth.

Proof 5 —"The Young Child and His Mother"

Matthew next discloses how God interposed in behalf of His holy Child. If that little Babe, born of Mary, had not been the Son of God, He would not have been honored of God by the warning which God, by the angel, gave to Joseph. "And [Joseph] being warned of God . . . took the young child and his mother by night, and departed into Egypt."

There is, however, a special thing here. Four times this expression is given: "The young child and his mother." The angel did not say to Joseph, "Take *your* young child and your wife." The angel said, "Take the young child and his mother, and flee into Egypt . . . . he took the young child and his mother by night, and departed into Egypt."

Why did not the angel recognize Joseph's parenthood? The next verse tells us: "and [Joseph] was there until the death of Herod: that it might be fulfilled which was spoken of the Lord by the prophet, saying, Out of Egypt have I called my son."

There you have it, "Out of Egypt *have I called my son.*" Mark the words: "The young child and *his mother,*" and, *"my son."* Jesus Christ was the Son of God, begotten of the Holy Ghost. Verse 21 reads of the return:

"He arose, and took the young child and his mother, and came into the land of Israel."

Proof 6 —The Things Most Surely Believed Among Us

There are some who deny the virgin birth, saying that in the Gospels of Mark and of John you find nothing of the virgin birth; therefore, they say, you must not believe in Matthew's and Luke's account.

We answer that Mark in his first chapter definitely designates Jesus Christ as the Son of God. Besides, John, in his Gospel, opens his message with: "In the beginning was the Word, and the Word was with God, and the Word was God. . . . And the Word was made flesh." From the first verse right on through all of his twenty-one chapters, he designates everywhere that Jesus Christ was the Son of God. Neither Mark nor John say anything directly about the details of the virgin birth. I will tell you why. Luke, in his first chapter, first verse, says: "Forasmuch as many have taken in hand to set forth in order a declaration of those things which are most surely believed among us."

What is Luke writing? The things that were most surely believed among the apostles. Now where did Luke get this testimony? "Well," you say, "he got it from God." Yes, but read verse 2: "Even as they delivered them unto us, which from the beginning were eyewitnesses, and ministers of the word."

Jesus Christ was the Word made flesh. Who were the eyewitnesses of that Word? In John's First Epistle, he says of Christ, "That which was from the beginning, which we have heard, which we have seen with our eyes, which we have looked upon, and our hands have handled, of the Word of life."

Luke says, "We received this testimony from the men who were eyewitnesses." John himself was not led of the Spirit to record the details of the virgin birth because the Holy Spirit gave through Luke exactly what John (and others) most surely believed and which he had himself delivered unto Luke. Why should we demand that Mark and John also write the details? Luke plainly records that the others most surely believed, and most surely taught, what he, by the Spirit penned.

Men and women, there was no doubt of the virgin birth in the mind of any of the early apostles and the early disciples. Luke said:

"It seemed good to me also, having had perfect understanding of all things from the very first, to write unto thee in order, most excellent Theophilus, That thou mightest know the certainty of those things, wherein thou hast been instructed."

When your children come home from college, perhaps with doubts instilled into their minds, you can say, "Children, come to me. I want to open up to you in the Word of God the things most surely believed among the early fathers. I want to show you how the virgin birth was most surely taught by the apostles."

Proof 7—The Annunication to Zacharias

That annunciation made to Zacharias by an angel is important to our theme. "There was in the days of Herod, the king of Judea, a certain priest named Zacharias, of the course of Abia: and his wife was of the daughters of Aaron, and her name was Elisabeth."

Zacharias was priest and his wife was born of the lineage of the priests. If any couple on earth were worthy to have a son who would be the forerunner of Jesus Christ, it was this man of the course of Abia, and this woman of the daughters of Aaron. They "were both righteous before God."

The angel of the Lord appeared unto Zacharias and said unto him:

"Fear not, Zacharias: for thy prayer is heard; and thy wife Elisabeth shall bear thee a son, and thou shalt call his name John. And thou shalt have joy and gladness; and many shall rejoice at his birth."

Of course, John was born of natural generation.

"For he shall be great in the sight of the Lord, and shall be filled with the Holy Ghost, even from his mother's womb."

Then the record goes on:

"And he shall go before him in the spirit and power of Elias, to turn the hearts of the fathers to the children, and . . . to make ready a people prepared for the Lord."

Now, let us sum up the whole message of the angel. Zacharias was to have a baby born in his home. He was to call his name John. When he became grown, he would preach, giving testimony concerning the Lord, who was to be born of Elisabeth's cousin, Mary. John was to be born prior to the birth of Jesus, and His message would center in the announcement of his successor.

In the Epistle of Hebrews we read that the words spoken by angels are sure and steadfast; and there is no doubt that the angel acclaimed to Zacharias that his son, John, was to herald One who was more than a son of any man. John was to herald the coming of the Lord.

Zacharias understood this, as his magnificat, which we consider shortly, demonstrates. John, his son, also understood this in after years, for he bore witness, saying, "This is the Son of God."

Proof 8 – The Annunciation to Mary

Six months after the angel had come to Zacharias, he came to Nazareth unto

". . . a virgin espoused to a man whose name was Joseph, of the house of David; and the virgin's name was Mary. And the angel came in unto her, and said, Hail, thou that art highly favoured, the Lord is with thee."

No woman with child out of wedlock is highly favored of the Lord. His dark anathemas are against all sin and all impurity. When anyone dares to deny the virgin birth, he makes God evil in His approval of Mary. For the Bible declares that a messenger came from God to Mary and acclaimed her the most highly favored of women, the most honored, the most loved of Heaven. That is the testimony of the angel. The next statement presents Mary's query: "Then said Mary unto the angel, How shall this be, seeing I know not a man?"

Then the angel said unto her: "The Holy Ghost shall come upon thee, and the power of the Highest shall overshadow thee: therefore also that holy thing which shall be born of thee shall be called the Son of God."

This angelic testimony is final. Remember, Gabriel came from the presence of God. To impeach his word is to impeach God. Gabriel discounted in his words to Mary, must be Gabriel discounted in his words to Daniel—yet Gabriel said to Daniel, "I am come to give thee skill and understanding," and he opened up to Daniel the Word of Truth.

Now listen: "Mary arose in those days, and went into the hill country with haste, into a city of Juda; And entered into the house of Zacharias, and saluted Elisabeth."

Proof 9—The Magnificat of Elisabeth

As soon as Elisabeth saw Mary, did she cry out in anguish and say, "O Mary, this is an awful shame that has come upon us. Here you are betrothed to Joseph, and your conception proves you a sinner, as vile as any 'dog of a Gentile' "? Did she bewail Mary? Not at all. Remember that Elisabeth was a just woman, a daughter of the line of Aaron. Such an one could not condone impurity. Yet what did she do? "Elisabeth . . . spake out with a loud voice, and said, Blessed art thou among women."

If Jesus Christ were not God-begotten and virgin-born, even a sinner of the street would not have uttered such words as Elisabeth used. How then could this true woman, this righteous woman, this woman honored and owned of God, shout for joy? Listen to Elisabeth: "And whence is this to me, that the mother of my Lord should come to me?"

Elisabeth did not only praise God for Mary, but she acknowledged that she was not worthy for the mother of her Lord to visit her. These words of Elisabeth remind you of what her son, John the Baptist, said thirty years later, in speaking of Christ: 'I am not worthy to stoop down and unloose the latchet of his shoes.' Elisabeth felt unworthy that the mother of her Lord should come to her.

You see, the angel had informed Zacharias of the birth of the Lord and that John should be His forerunner. Zacharias, doubtless, and his wife also, knew of the 40th chapter of Isaiah and how it prophesied that one should come to "prepare . . . the way of the Lord," and to "make straight in the desert a highway for our God." Thus they were doubly assured that Jesus, Mary's Son-to-be, was the Lord, Jehovah God.

What else did Elisabeth say?

"Lo, as soon as the voice of thy salutation sounded in mine ears, the babe leaped in my womb for joy. And blessed is she [Mary] that believed: for there shall be a performance of those things which were told her from the Lord."

Elisabeth not only commended Mary for believing, but she also believed. What stronger proof of the virgin birth do you want than the attitude of Elisabeth toward her cousin and her magnificat on the occasion of Mary's visit to her? God pity the one who does not believe.

Proof 10—The Magnificat of Mary

The most wonderful thing to me in all the record of the conception and birth of Christ is the magnificat of Mary. Mary was not only a blessed woman, favored of God; but she was a literary woman of high attainment; her rhetoric was sublime; her mastery of language was superb. Besides all of this, her knowledge of the Old Testament Scriptures was established. As we read her great magnificat, let us ponder her words: "My soul doth magnify the Lord, And my spirit hath rejoiced in God my Saviour."

A woman who had conceived a son in sin and in shame could never have shouted for joy and magnified her God as did Mary. The most hellish thing, the most damnable thing that any man can do is to decry the virgin birth of the Son of God. To deny it is to denounce His mother, Mary, and to put her beneath the woman of the street. To deny it is to acclaim that her Son was begotten out of wedlock, a bastard; and to make Jesus Christ, instead of the holy One begotten of the Holy Ghost, a Babe conceived in sin and a sinner unworthy of trust. To deny it is to make it impossible for Jesus to be the Saviour of men.

Let us give heed as this beautiful woman continues to rejoice in God her Saviour. "For he hath regarded the low estate of his handmaiden."

Mary was not a woman of Belial, not a servant of the Devil, impure in heart and life. In verse 38, Mary said to the angel Gabriel, "Behold the handmaiden of the Lord; be it unto me according to thy word."

In her magnificat she said: "For he hath regarded the low estate of his handmaiden: for, behold, from henceforth all generations shall call me blessed."

Mary, with the eye of a prophet, looked down to this very hour and knew that she would be called blessed, the handmaiden of the Lord. Blessed because of her virginity, blessed because of her purity, blessed because she was chosen of God. Let us give honor to whom honor is due.

"All generations shall call me blessed. For he that is mighty hath done to me great things; and holy is his name. And his mercy is on them that fear him from generation to generation."

The Lord God could not have honored Mary had she, as a woman of impurity, made claim that God, in an unholy conception, had done great things for her. God cannot look on sin with favor, neither can He approve one who sins.

Mary must have conceived by the Holy Ghost or else Mary herself would not have dared to voice such praise to God, as the One who had done great things for her.

Notice next how Mary knew the Old Testament Scriptures (vs. 55): "As he spake to our fathers, to Abraham, and to his seed for ever."

Mary knew her seed was prophecy's fulfillment.

After Mary's magnificat, it briefly says: "Mary abode with her [Elisabeth] about three months, and returned to her own house."

It was, upon her return, when she was three months with child, doubtless, that the scene as related in Matthew occurred: How Joseph came around to see her, as had been his custom of yore and observed her condition; how that night he wept before the Lord; how he rolled upon his bed, and made up his mind to put her away. Then it was the angel said to Joseph, "Fear not to take unto thee Mary thy wife: for that which is conceived in her is of the Holy Ghost."

Mary's delicate condition was in fulfillment of the prophet's words, 'Behold, a *virgin* shall be with child, and shall bring forth a son, and they shall call his name *Immanuel,* which being interpreted is, God with us.' Then Joseph took unto him his wife, and knew her not until Christ was born.

Proof 11—The Magnificat of Zacharias

Shortly after Mary had returned to her own house, John the Baptist was born. At his birth all the friends and kinfolk gathered around and asked what he should be called. Elisabeth said he should be called "John." The friends demurred, "Why, Elisabeth, you have no member of your family named John. You should call him Zacharias after his father." She said, "No, his name is John." Then the friends went over to Zacharias, whom the angel had struck dumb. They made signs unto him asking, "What do you want to call the baby?" Zacharias called for a tablet and wrote, "His name is John." Then suddenly his mouth was opened and he spake his magnificat. They had some hallelujah meetings about this birth of John, did they not? Zacharias was filled with the Holy Ghost and prophesied, saying, "Blessed be the Lord God of Israel; for he hath visited and redeemed his people, And hath raised up an horn of salvation for us in the house of his servant David."

Then he spake on, declaring the ministry of his son, John, until he gave his prophecy (vs. 76): "And thou, child, shalt be called the prophet of the Highest."

Christ was not yet born when Zacharias called his little baby the "prophet of the Highest," and said, "Thou shalt go before the face of the Lord to prepare his ways."

Zacharias may not at first have believed Gabriel's message to him announcing the birth of John; but, when John was born, all unbelief left him, and he fully announced the future ministry of his son; and in his announcement he established his faith in the deity of the Lord, Mary's Son, who was about to be born.

Proof 12 — The Magnificat of the Angels

Let us see what happened when this little Babe was born to Mary: "She brought forth her firstborn son, and wrapped him in swaddling clothes, and laid him in a manger."

If Jesus were an illegitimate child, do you think all Heaven would break out with praise? If you wondered that Elisabeth could make such wonderful music and shout such beautiful poetry as she saw Mary, and if you wondered that Mary sounded such an all-glorious magnificat as she visited Elisabeth, then how you must wonder as you hear all Heaven sound their gloria. Listen to this:

"And there were in the same country shepherds abiding in the field, keeping watch over their flock by night. And, lo, the angel of the Lord came upon them, and the glory of the Lord shone round about them:

and they were sore afraid. And the angel said unto them, Fear not: for, behold, I bring you" —

Did the angel say, "Behold, I have an awful scandal to tell you. I have a shameful thing to relate: There is born unto you this day in the city of David, a child conceived out of wedlock; his mother is unclean, and his father is impure. I want you shepherds to go to Bethlehem and put a black hood upon that baby, and sackcloth upon his mother"? *Never, never, never.* Rather this: the angel burst out, saying,

"Behold, I bring you good tidings of great joy, which shall be to all people. For unto you is born this day in the city of David a Saviour, which is Christ the Lord. And this shall be a sign unto you; Ye shall find the babe wrapped in swaddling clothes, lying in a manger. And suddenly there was with the angel a multitude of the heavenly host praising God, and saying, Glory to God in the highest, and on earth peace, good will toward men."

May I ask you, my radio friends who are listening in over WHT, and may I ask you who sit before me in the audience, how many of you believe that it was possible for these angels to give their magnificat unless Jesus Christ was virgin-born? How else could they acclaim Him Christ the Lord—a Saviour? When the angels had given their message, the shepherds went to the manger and found it even as the angels had told them. Then they too rejoiced and began to praise God for what they had seen.

What did Mary do? She kept all of these things in her heart. Oh, how strangely was Mary, the mother of Christ, moved, as, from the lips of the shepherds, she heard of the message of the angel, and the magnificat of the angels!

Proof 13—The Magnificat of Simeon

Eight days passed and they carried Christ up to be circumcised.

"And, behold, there was a man in Jerusalem [where they had gone into the Temple], whose name was Simeon; and the same man was just and devout, waiting for the consolation of Israel . . . ."

He was not a libertine, or a vulgar man; he was just and devout—

". . . and the Holy Ghost was upon him. And it was revealed unto him by the Holy Ghost, that he should not see death, before he had

seen the Lord's Christ. And he came by the Spirit into the temple: and when the parents brought in the child Jesus, to do for him after the custom of the law, Then took he him up in his arms, and blessed God, and said, Lord, now lettest thou thy servant depart in peace, according to thy word: For mine eyes have seen thy salvation, Which thou hast prepared before the face of all people; A light to lighten the Gentiles, and the glory of thy people Israel. And Joseph and his mother [Why doesn't it say his father and mother? Because Joseph was not his father] *marvelled at those things which were spoken of him. And Simeon blessed them, and said unto Mary his mother, Behold, this child is set for the fall and rising again of many in Israel; and for a sign which shall be spoken against."*

Perhaps there is a man listening in over the air who saw in the paper that we would speak on the "Unanswerable Proofs of the Virgin Birth"; perhaps you did not believe that Christ was virgin-born and so you said, "I will listen in and see what that man says about the virgin birth."

Well, then, don't stop listening in until you hear this—And this shall be "for a sign which shall be spoken against." The Holy Ghost through Simeon prophesied that men would deny the virgin birth. That was the "sign that would be spoken against." Have you read Isaiah 7:14: "Therefore the Lord himself shall *give you a sign; Behold, a virgin shall conceive, and bear a son, and shall call his name Immanuel*"—"God with us"? That manger-cradle yonder in Bethlehem was not as beautiful as some of you have pictured. But the virgin mother and her Babe were God's sign to His people. And now as Simeon draws near to Mary and as he blesses her, he says that this shall be "a sign that shall be spoken against: (Yea, a sword shall pierce through thy own soul also.)"

Women do not like to be called vulgar. Women do not like to have their names cast out as mud and dirt to be trampled under the feet of men. They hold their virtue, their good name, as the most priceless pearl that God ever put into their hands. They cherish it as they do their very life. Sympathize, then, with Mary, the mother of Jesus. This shall be "a sign that shall be spoken against; (Yea, a sword shall pierce through thy own soul.)"

Do you know, men and women, that the very sons and daughters of Mary and Joseph—James and Joses and Judas, (the daughters' names are not given)—must have held Jesus at arm's length for a while. There is a passage in the 69th chapter of the Psalms which reads,

"Because for thy sake I have borne reproach; shame hath covered my face. I am become a stranger unto my brethren, and an alien unto my mother's children."

An evil story, perhaps, went out and was scattered around about the birth of Jesus; this gossip doubtless fell on the ears of James and Joses and Judas. As they went about their games with the neighbors' children, the vile report came to them. Thus, the brothers of Christ treated Him as an alien. They did not want to play with Him; they did not want to walk with Him, and the sisters held themselves aloof from Him. In all of this a sword pierced through His mother's heart.

Perhaps you think that the words, "A sword shall pierce through thy own soul also," refers to Mary's anguish at Calvary. Yes, Mary's heart was pierced through with sorrow as she clung to John at the foot of the cross; but, beloved, it was not only at Calvary that Mary groaned. At Calvary Jesus was not an alien to His mother's children, but He was during His Nazareth home experiences.

Thus, Mary paid the price of being the virgin mother of the Son of God because of the unbelief of some; but all of this gave only added and unanswerable proof to Christ's virgin birth.

Proof 14—The Magnificat of Anna

We have yet another thing. Simeon had scarcely concluded his words when Anna, a prophetess, the daughter of Phanuel of the tribe of Asher, who was of a great age, came in. If there is one thing that you can depend upon, it is that older women with an unimpeachable character will not harbor, let alone praise, an impure girl. Her righteous spirit stands aghast at evil.

Many an older lady would like to preach a moment to the girls of this generation. When they see how lax the young girls live and walk, they rebel against it and say, "When I was a girl it was not so." Well, here was a woman of great age, a true and righteous woman who came in while this little Babe, eight days old, lay in the arms of His virgin mother. "and she coming in that instant gave thanks likewise unto the Lord, and spake of him to all them that looked for redemption in Jerusalem."

Anna's words acclaim Christ as Son of God, and they attest the virginity of Mary.

No son of Mary, humanly conceived, could meet the hope of them that look for redemption in Israel. The prophets had all too plainly prophesied that Israel's Redeemer was Israel's Lord. "But now saith the Lord that created thee . . . I have redeemed thee . . . I am the Lord thy God, the Holy One of Israel, thy Saviour." "Thus saith the Lord, the King of Israel, and his redeemer, the Lord of hosts; I am the first, and I am the last; and beside me there is no God."

Thus Anna gave her proof along with the prophets of old that Jesus was God's Son, virgin-born.

Proof 15 –"Calvary" and "Upper Room" Scenes

We have seen from the records of the events that surrounded the infancy of Christ—His annunciation, His birth and the different magnificats—that Christ must have been begotten of the Holy Ghost in the womb of the virgin. Have you considered that when Jesus Christ hung on Calvary's cross, there was one who came to that scene whose name was Mary? John, the beloved disciple, who testified so faithfully to the deity of our Lord—to the Word made flesh—stood at Mary's side. Jesus looked down from the cross and said, "John, behold thy mother!"; and He said unto Mary, "Woman, behold thy son!" That scene at the foot of Calvary's cross could never have been thus if Jesus Christ had been an illegitimate son and Mary an impure woman. She stood at the foot of that cross in adoration and love and in worship of her Son, because she knew Him as the Son of God.

But I have a deeper scene. It is in the Upper Room, where one hundred and twenty were gathered together after both the resurrection and the ascension of Christ had taken place. The Bible says, "They were gathered together with the women and with Mary, the mother of Jesus." Let us speak to Mary:

"Mary, it seems to us you would have stayed at home."

Mary asks, "Why?"

"Because, Mary, you know that these women around here are a bunch of fanatics. They all surely believe that your Son was virgin-born, and that He was conceived by the Holy Ghost; and, Mary, you know better. They are all deceived. We can understand how they, hallucinated as they are, can worship Jesus as the Son of God, but why are *you* here?"

Then Mary lifts her face to ours as she seems to say to us, "These saints are not deceived. I am gathered with the men and women who believe the truth. I know it is truth for I am the woman to whom the angel came and of whom Christ was born. I am gathered together with those who accept the blood of His cross, the atonement which He made. I believe in Him just as sincerely, just as fully, just as deeply, as do any of the disciples. John, or James, Peter, or Thomas, Bartholemew, or Matthew, Thaddaeus, or Simon Zelotes—none of them have a stronger faith in the Son of God than have I. They believe He was virgin-born by testimony—I believe by experience."

WILLIAM EDWARD BIEDERWOLF
1867-1934

ABOUT THE MAN:

Presbyterians produced some of the most noteworthy evangelists of the late 1800's and early 1900's—and a notable among them was William E. Biederwolf.

After his conversion, he continued his education at Princeton, Erlangen and Berlin universities, and at the Sorbonne in Paris.

Biederwolf's first church was the Broadway Presbyterian Church of Logansport, Indiana, the state where he was born. Then he became a chaplain in the Spanish-American War and then entered evangelism —a ministry he was to serve for 35 years.

In conjunction with his evangelism, Dr. Biederwolf was associated with the world-renowned Winona Lake Bible Conference for 40 years.

In 1929, he became pastor at the storied Royal Poinciana Chapel in Palm Beach, Florida, a position he held until his death.

Biederwolf's ministry was mighty. Perhaps his greatest campaign was in Oil City, Pennsylvania, in the bitter winter of 1914. Thousands thronged the tabernacle. Twice it was enlarged. His messages were pungent and powerful.

His kind of preaching brought men and women from every walk of life coming in deep contrition for their sins—the mayor of the city, physicians, lawyers, and men from the factories, young people from the schools; and the whole city and county were mightily stirred in deep concern about the things of God.

He was the author of several books.

VIII.

God Became a Man!

WILLIAM EDWARD BIEDERWOLF

"And the Word was made flesh, and dwelt among us." —John 1:14.

The hardest proposition the infidel crowd has ever been up against is to account for Jesus Christ.

Isaiah said, "His name shall be called Wonderful." There is no better name to describe Him. He is the world's one great wonder. No one else ever approached Him. He is in a class all by Himself. He has no second.

No man ever uttered such wonderful teaching. It was so simple the common people heard Him gladly, yet so profound that no philosopher has ever sounded their depths. He never wrote a sermon, never published a book; He founded no college to perpetuate His doctrines but handed them down to a few poor and humble fishermen, yet His teaching has endured for two thousand years. It has been translated into every language under the sky, and it has so transformed human life that whole nations have been lifted out of darkness and degradation by its power. And before this humble Galilean peasant the scholarship of the world uncovers its head today, bows and says, "Never man spake like this man."

Then no man ever lived such a wonderful life. He backed up what He said by the way He lived. He was there with the goods. He never had to ask God to forgive His sins, because His character was perfect. His enemies watched Him like a hawk, and the worst thing they could say about Him was that He did good on the Sabbath and that He let a sinful woman come near enough to Him to touch the hem of His garment.

Then there never was a character so wonderful in its universality. He was born, of course, in a given race and age. He had to be. But He utterly transcended His age and His race and became the ideal of every age and every race.

Come, Mr. Infidel, how are you going to account for Jesus Christ?

If He was only a man, then by every law of evolution and progress this twentieth century ought to produce a better one, intellectually and morally.

Somebody says, "Give us a man's race, his surroundings and his epoch, and the man himself is accounted for." This is largely so. Socrates is of Greece and belonged to his age. Luther is of Germany, and the circumstances of his day had much to do with his heroic life. And so to a large extent we can account for them all—Confucius, Buddha, Sakyi-Muni, Abbas Effendi, Alexander, Napoleon and Cromwell.

But this is not altogether so. One day a tourist came to the birthplace of Robert Burns and as he looked out over the charm of the highland scenery and saw the quaint and quiet beauty of it all, he exclaimed, "Ah, no wonder Burns was a poet!" But the guide at his side said, "Sir, there have been many children born here since Robert Burns was born, but none of them was a poet."

Jesus was a Jew. But you look in vain for the intolerance, the bigotry and the intellectual narrowness of His race. The best of the Jew was in Him, but in place of these other things He combined with Himself the finer traits of the Greek, Celt, Roman, Teuton and Anglo-Saxon. Account for Him as the product of His race! No, sir, you can't do it.

No more can you account for Him by His environment or the times in which He lived. Other children were born and reared under the Syrian skies and among the Judean hills. Other young men had the same surroundings and grew up among the same influences, the same institutions, the same religious ideals, the same personalities, the same conflict of opinions and all the rest of it.

How then does it come that Christ alone among them all became the wonderful Man we see Him to be—the God-Man of the universe who walked like a giant among the pygmies of the earth?

Account for this Man, Mr. Infidel. Yes, come on, Mr. Critic, Mr. Psychologist, Mr. Evolutionist; what have you got to say?

He is the one great mystery of the universe; and the only clue to His origin you will ever find, you will have to find in this Gospel where it says, "The Holy Ghost shall come upon thee, and the power of the Highest shall overshadow thee: therefore also that holy thing which shall be born of thee shall be called the Son of God" (Luke 1:35).

Jesus Christ said, "What and if ye shall see the Son of man ascend up where he was before?" That shows His claim to pre-existence and shows us where He was before He came to this earth. He said, "O Father, glorify thou me . . . with the glory which I had with thee before the world was" (John 17:5).

And now comes the text in John:

"And the Word was made flesh, and dwelt among us."

Of course there always has been a set of critics who have had their knife out for this doctrine of the Virgin Birth. In Christ's own day they said, "Why, this is the carpenter's son!" That criticism of His divine origin has never let up. But in 1892 over in Germany it broke out anew, and we've had a pretty warm fight on our hands ever since.

A preacher over there by the name of Schrempf started it. He wouldn't use the Apostles' Creed in baptism because it said that Jesus was conceived of the Holy Ghost and born of the Virgin Mary. They gave him his walking papers—deposed him from the ministry. He might have gotten off a good deal easier if he had only lived over here; like Dr. C. F. Aked, once pastor of the First Congregational Church of San Francisco. He denied openly the Virgin Birth; and when the Presbyterian ministers demanded his resignation from the ministerial association, the San Francisco Church Federation refused to allow him to resign by a vote of 74 to 19.

OBJECTIONS OF THE INFIDEL

But let's see why it is the infidel objects.

1. They Say Nothing Is Said About It by Mark, John, or Paul

But that simply begs the question. Because they said nothing about it is no sign they didn't know it or didn't believe it. They had other purposes in writing.

Mark began with His public ministry and passed in silence over the first thirty years of His life. Don't you suppose he knew He had a birth of some kind, but he never said a word about it. John knew it because he had Matthew's and Luke's Gospels with him when he wrote, but it was not in point with his purpose. Luke was with Paul and of course told him all about it, but it's not to be expected that Paul would mention it. The whole theme of his ministry was the moral significance of Christ as based upon His public ministry, His life, His death and His resurrection.

2. You Say, "The Thing Was Impossible"

I say, "What is impossible?"

You say, "Such a birth itself."

I say, "Not with God."

Let God step in on the scene and impossibility must go way back and sit down.

Because you can't understand it is no sign it is not true. There are lots of things you can't understand, yet you must acknowledge that you believe them or acknowledge that you are a fool.

3. You Say, "It's Unthinkable"

I say, "What is unthinkable?"

You say, "The alleged result of such a birth."

I say, "What do you mean?"

You say, "The union of a divine and human nature in one person."

Well, now, let us see; because that's just exactly what the Incarnation is—the union of two natures in one person, a combination of the divine and human in Jesus Christ.

Well, if you will do a bit of real thinking it may not be as unthinkable as you now think. But if it's unthinkable to the best human thinker that operates, that is no sign it is untrue.

Can you understand the mechanical union of oxygen and nitrogen that makes air, or of hydrogen and oxygen that makes water; or the union of body and soul that makes yourself? You are a person, and if you can't understand this simpler union, don't growl about divinity and humanity uniting in one person; for it is no more incompatible than the union of matter and spirit that makes one person out of you.

You say, "If the divine in Jesus was truly divine and the human truly human, then there must have been both a divine consciousness and a human consciousness in Him"; then you add, "It can't be; one or the other of them must be sacrificed on the altar of reason."

But hold on. I know it may be hard to understand. But here is something else. If Christ was divine and united with the Father in the function of creating and sustaining the universe, how could He produce a storm on the Sea of Galilee and stop it at the same time? His divine will could not act in two opposing directions at the same time, could it?

You say, "No, but I don't believe He ever calmed the storm or did any other miracle."

But hold on. That doesn't help you out any. You have God to deal with. How could God make the iron axe head swim? Could He will, as He apparently does, that iron shall sink in water and at the same time will that it shall not, as He apparently did, without at least seeming to have a double consciousness in Him at that particular moment?

You say, "I don't believe God ever did it. Nothing doing when it comes to miracles."

But hold on. That doesn't help any. Ruling the Bible out of court doesn't get rid of the laws of nature. These are always operating against each other: life and death, growth and decay, and the two opposing forces in gravitation. We claim that these and all laws are expressions of the divine will. But whether they are or not, how are you going to explain?

Has God then got a double consciousness? I don't know; but I do know that you can't escape your philosophical difficulty by denying the divine nature to Jesus Christ, and that any argument you may bring against His double consciousness, you are compelled to bring with equal force against the Lord God in Heaven.

And I do know that this mysterious thing of a double consciousness in Jesus Christ is not any more mysterious than the metaphysical conundrum of how you can think of yourself as the subject and the object at the same time, which thing you know you do; nor any more mysterious than the fact of a spiritual union between God and man, as the result of which the man acts sometimes under God's impulse and sometimes under his own and sometimes under both at the same time, without being able to tell just where one begins and the other ends, or how they operate together at one and the same second of time.

And so the difficulty is not so great after all.

Of course, we can't fully understand it. But to avoid it, shall we be wheedled into accepting some of the weak substitutes for it; like Beyschlag's embodiment of an impersonal idea, or one who is divine only in the sense of being God-filled and thus revealing to us the spiritual capacity to which any soul may aspire and attain? God forbid. The Word was made flesh; and it was the essence of God that came into man and gave us the God-Man, and not only a Godlike man.

4. You Say, "This Doctrine of the Virgin Birth Seems Utterly Unnecessary"

You say, "When the Word was made flesh, whatever of God came

into the man Jesus could have done so without the method of conception involved in the doctrine of the Virgin Birth."

Well, in the first place, it takes an infinite amount of conceit for a little, erring mortal like you to say what was or was not necessary in such
a stupendous thing as the bringing into the world of the only begotten
Son of God. It's a pity God didn't wait till you were born and graduated
from high school before He undertook to do it.

But in the next place, it is in the Bible, and that ought to be enough.
Matthew's and Luke's accounts are genuine, The account of the virgin
birth is found in every manuscript and version of the Gospels that have
ever existed, so you can't cut them out. They are there; and, if you have
any respect for the Bible, you will put up your penknife and scissors.

And then in the next place it would *seem* necessary.

If Christ was the very Son of God made flesh, a miracle in His birth
is the very thing one would expect; and it is just this miracle in His earthly
origin that furnishes us the necessary explanation of His supernatural
person and all that goes with it. So what's the use of growling about it?

But, in the next place, it *was* necessary for two reasons.

1. *That the Scriptures might be fulfilled.*

　　(a) Isaiah prophesied, "Behold, a virgin shall conceive, and bear
a son, and shall call his name Immanuel" (7:14). That is one reason
why the Virgin Birth was necessary.

　　(b) Jeremiah distinctly said that no man of the seed of Jechonias
should sit on the throne of David (Jer. 22:30), and Joseph, the husband of Mary, was of the seed of Jechonias; and Christ therefore could
not be of the seed of Joseph and at the same time inherit the throne
of David. This is another reason why the Virgin Birth was necessary.

2. *That He might be a man and yet escape the moral taint that comes
to everyone born into the human race by natural means.* This He had
to do in order to be sinless, and sinless He had to be in order to offer
Himself a sacrifice for our sins. A sacrifice for sin had to be pure and
unblemished. If not, John the Baptist or any other good man would
have done. If Christ had inherited the moral taint of ordinary generation, He would have needed a Saviour Himself.

The fellow who denies the Virgin Birth usually ends up by denying
the virgin or sinless life of Christ. A virgin life is just as much of a miracle
anyhow in the moral world as a virgin birth is in the physical world.

Oh, you say, "Mary was sinful, and Christ would have gotten the moral
taint from her as well as from Joseph."

Well, what does the record say? It says Jesus was born of a virgin mother. Yes, but it says more than that. It says He was conceived by the Holy Ghost. It doesn't say a new person was created. It was an already existing divine person entering by this method into the human race, and the divine creative miracle wrought by the Holy Ghost precluded the possibility of any taint of sin from the earliest moment of conception.

And so, Mr. Objector, if you will just make the proper adjustment of your mental bearings, you will see your objections vanish into thin air.

WHY DID CHRIST BECOME MAN?

But now comes the most important question of all, and that is, *Why was Jesus incarnated*—the purpose of it? Well, there was more than one purpose. Let's see what the Word of God says.

1. First John 3:8 Says, "For This Purpose the Son of God Was Manifested, That He Might DESTROY the Works of the Devil"

Isn't that a piece of the most glorious news this old world has ever heard? The Bible says the Devil is a murderer. It says he is a liar and the father of lies. But there is no use to particularize. The Bible calls Him, "The Lawless One." Sin is a transgression of God's law, and the Devil is the fountainhead of lawlessness and sin, so we know what the works of the Devil are: murder, lying, lust, dishonesty, and everything else that is born in Hell.

Say, do you know the only thing I'm afraid of in God's world is sin? No man ever played with sin that sin didn't get the better of him. Don't you try to play with sin. If you must do it, then go out into the field, pick up a rattler, and let it play in your bosom. Go down to the electric railroad and play with the third rail. Reach up into the skies and play with the forked lightning. But for God's sake, don't play with sin.

Two little Italian lads of New York City were returning from a swim. They were each about fifteen years old. Pietro had picked up a piece of copper wire and thought he would have a little fun with the third rail of the New York Central track along which they were walking. He poked away around the wooden covering of the rail, but nothing happened. "That's funny," he said; "I guess I didn't touch the right spot." Then he pushed the point of his wire down underneath the covering. There was a flash of blue flame and a shriek of pain as 11,000 volts of electricity shot through the wire. In a moment and less his clothing was on fire and his hair and eyebrows were burned off. He tried to drop the wire as it hissed and sputtered at white heat, but it wouldn't let go. He tried to pull it away, but it stuck to the rail as if it were soldered there. His little friend tried to pull him away but was hurled to the ground with a terrific shock. The brave little fellow then threw his rubber coat around Pietro and pulled him loose. Pietro started to run but fainted and fell. They took him to the hospital, and the doctor said, "One chance in a thousand to recover."

The two boys said they knew there was something dangerous about that rail. They had heard older people say so, but they didn't think it would hurt to play with it a little.

And so sin scorches, burns and kills like a live third rail. People know it, yet they will trifle with sin. And there are men and women right here in this city, and maybe right here in this meeting, who have played with your passion and played with sin so long it looks to you as if your case is hopeless.

But thanks be to God, sin never took anyone so low that Jesus Christ, the God-Man, couldn't reach down a little lower and snap the fetters and set him free. That's why He was manifested—to destroy the works of the Devil.

I met my old friend John Callahan of New York City the other day. He had gone the limit in sin and had done time in Joliet penitentiary. When the day of his release came, he promised the keeper that he would let the booze alone. But he was drunk as a Bowery bum in less than twelve hours.

Then he became a bartender, struck a man in a drunken brawl and landed behind the iron bars again. The police knew him only as a criminal, a man to be watched. The only words they had for him were, "Move on."

But one night he found his way into a rescue mission. You know the rest of the story. Longing to be free from the shackles of sin, he went to the front, fell down on his knees and said, "God forgive me."

When one of his old pals asked him to drink, John said, "No, I don't want any." That was a stunner for his pal. He couldn't understand why he didn't want it. John told him that Jesus had come into his life and the desire for drink had been destroyed.

He had four photographs in the Rogues' gallery, and it troubled him. He got three of them from the Chicago police through a friend, but the one in Joliet he couldn't get. A little later he went to the Battle Creek Sanitarium with Harry Monroe who had been asked, along with John, to conduct a meeting for the guests. Among the guests were the governors of three states, including John P. Altgeld of Illinois.

My friend told what Jesus had done for him, and he told of how he had tried to get his records away from Joliet. When he had finished, the three governors came and shook hands with him. Governor Altgeld was wiping his eyes as he said, "Mr. Callahan, I'll see what I can do for you." A few weeks later my friend got a letter from the Executive Mansion at Springfield, Illinois, and it said:

> My dear Mr. Callahan:
>   It gives me pleasure to enclose your photograph from the penitentiary of Joliet and to tell you that your Bertillion records there have all been destroyed. There is no record except in your memory that you were ever there. You have the gratitude and best wishes of your friend, John P. Altgeld.

John Callahan has been down on the bowery now for years doing a great work for God. What do you think of that? It's a mighty Christ who can do a thing like that. But He was manifested to destroy the works of the Devil, and nothing the Devil has ever done is too hard for Jesus to undo.

And so I come to you with the question: What are the master forces in your life? If they are the forces of evil and you find yourself in their grip, I am here to tell you of One who was manifested two thousand years ago to destroy the works of the Devil, and who works as powerful today as he worked then. And if you will turn to Him, He will set you free; He will destroy the works of the Devil in you and give you the victory, and the days of defeat will be over.

"Well," you say, "that's mighty fine, and I need that kind of a power in my life. But I'm already burdened with a sense of guilt; I've done enough sin already to lose my soul a thousand times over; what about the past?"

Yes, that is so. But I have another piece of good news for you:

2. First John 3:5 Says, "Ye Know That He Was Manifested to Take Away Our Sins"

No Jew of that day ever heard an expression like that that he didn't think at once of the day of atonement back in the Old Testament. You know the high priest would lay his hands on the head of a goat and confess over it the sins of the people; then the goat would bear them away into the wilderness, and they would be gone forever. That goat was a type of a Lamb that was to come.

And you remember how John was baptizing in the River Jordan. Jesus came along, and John pointed Him out to the people and cried, "Behold the Lamb of God, which taketh away the sin of the world."

It is hell in a man's breast when his soul is lashed by the whips of a guilty conscience. And to the man who knows his sin and loathes it, who hates the memory of his sin, and to whose soul the consciousness of the wrong he has done is like a hideous nightmare—to this man, the sweetest song that was ever sung, the brightest message that was ever delivered, is the glad news that in some mysterious way which he can never quite fully comprehend Jesus Christ puts Himself underneath his sin, underneath all that is foul and vile in the experience of the past, lifts it up and off his soul and takes it away.

But that is just why Christ was manifested—to take away sins. God has exhausted the possibilities of human language to let you and me and every poor sinful man and woman know how completely our sins through the person and work of Christ have been put away.

You say, "My thoughts have been dirty and impure"; and the message rings out, "It's all taken away." He says, "I will remove thine iniquities from thee as far as the east is from the west."

You say, "I've cursed and blasphemed and profaned"; and the word rings back, "It's all taken away." He says, "I will cast all thy sins behind my back."

You say, "I have a virtuous wife, but I've kept a woman on the side"; and the glad news leaps out from the pages of God's Word, "It's all taken away." He says, "I will cast all thy sins into the depths of the sea."

You say, "I've been a crook, a liar and a thief"; and God's glad answer is, "It's all taken away." He says, "I will blot out thine iniquities as a thick cloud."

But you say, "I took a man's life in cold blood." Yes, and you've done something worse than that; you've crucified the Son of God. Your sin wove the crown of thorns and pressed it down on His brow. Your sin fastened Him on the cross. Your sin drove the spikes through His hands and feet. Your sin drove the spear into His side. And it was your sin that broke His heart. But I can hear the angels shouting down from

Heaven, "It's all taken away." God says, 'I will remember thine iniquity against thee no more forever.'

He was manifested to take away sins. Oh, I wish I could paint a picture of Jesus on the cross that would break your heart and bring you to Him. The wonder to me is that instead of one poor penitent thief, the whole mob didn't become a band of penitents and sob out their sorrow for the sins they had done.

I was preaching in Lawrence, Kansas, some time ago; and they told me about old Quantrell, the guerrilla who burned their houses and murdered their people. The Union army caught him and his gang down in Missouri and led them out to be shot.

Just as the soldiers were about to fire, the bushes parted, and a young man sprang out, ran up to the officer and, pointing to one of the condemned men in the line, said, "Let me take his place; I am just as guilty as he is, but you didn't catch me. He has a wife and four children. They have no one to take care of them but him. There's no one depending on me. Take me and let him go." The officer said, "If there is no objection, we will make the change." The change was made; the command to fire came, and the young man fell with the others.

Some years later a man passing through the cemetery down in Missouri saw another man bending down and parting the grass above a mound. He was planting a plain marble slab at the head of an uncared-for grave.

The man said, "I suppose you have some relative buried here."

"No," said the other.

"A friend then?"

"Yes, more than a friend." Then he told him the story.

"I saw him when he fell. I saw them take him up and bury him with the rest. I marked the spot; and when the soldiers had gone, I took his body and had it placed in this grave. I am a poor man; I have saved my wages for a long time to travel three hundred miles here so I could put this little stone at the head of his grave."

And the man looked down and saw on the stone this inscription:

SACRED TO THE MEMORY OF WILLIE LEAR.
HE TOOK MY PLACE.

And if you were to go to that graveyard today, you would find a handsome marble monument fifteen feet high over the grave. Though the man had become rich, he never forgot his saviour; and he put this heavy marble shaft at the head of his grave and on it carved just the same words:

SACRED TO THE MEMORY OF WILLIE LEAR.
HE TOOK MY PLACE.

Friend, instead of sitting out there and passing God up, you ought to be grateful to Jesus Christ for taking your place. You ought to say, and say it now, "If God will forgive my sins and all the dark past, I'll make this life a monument to the memory of His Christ and my Saviour. I'll make it sacred to the memory of Jesus Christ who took my place."

I hear someone say, "How can it be? Such good news is too good to believe." Well, that's because you don't know God. And here comes the other purpose of the Incarnation:

HE WAS MANIFESTED TO REVEAL THE FATHER

John 1:18 says that no man has ever seen God, but that Jesus Christ has revealed Him to us.

You say, "How did He do it?" Listen to Christ Himself. He says in John 14:9, "He that hath seen me hath seen the Father."

You've had an idea that God is vindictive and that He takes delight in letting a man go to Hell. But you don't know God if you think that.

The only perfect revelation God ever made of Himself, He made in Jesus Christ; and if you will look at Him through Jesus Christ, you will know what kind of a God He is. "He that hath seen me hath seen the Father."

Did you see Him moved with compassion for the restless multitude who were like sheep without a shepherd? That's God.

Did you see Him weeping in pity over Jerusalem? That's God.

Did you hear Him speak to blind Bartimaeus? When the disciples said, "Shut up, you beggar," Jesus said, "Bartimaeus, receive thy sight." That's God.

Did you hear Him speak to the poor woman with the scarlet stain of sin on her soul? When the crowd wanted to stone her, Jesus said, "Go in peace and sin no more." That's God.

Did you hear Him on the cross praying for the howling mob that nailed Him there? That's God.

Read the story of His wonderful life, full of tenderness, compassion and forbearance. And if you want a single word to characterize it, take four letters and write over it from beginning to end the word *Love*. That's God.

The old hymn says, "My God is reconciled," but I don't like it. When I took my concordance and looked up the word "reconcile," I found a good many places where it talked about our being reconciled to God; but I couldn't find any place where it said that God was reconciled to us. I know there is a sense in which God is said to be angry with the sinner on account of his sins, but that's in a judicial sense. Jesus revealed God as a Father; and as a Father, He does not need to be reconciled. He is waiting for you to come and be reconciled to Him. The only place in the Bible where God is represented as running is in the story of the Prodigal Son, where the Father ran out to meet His penitent, returning child.

I've always been glad that I could count among my friends Elijah P. Brown, the founder of the once famous "Ram's Horn." He was converted by coming to know that his father really loved him. He said something like this:

"I was a wayward boy who caused my father much anguish. We were never very close. It never entered my mind that I meant very much to him. So I took my destiny in my own hands and ran away.

"But I was taken sick, and having nowhere else to go I returned to my father's house. I was made welcome, but I repented in a few days that I had come. My father was very poor; he himself had been sick, and there was not bread enough for us all. Every piece I ate almost choked me for it seemed to have upon it the taste of blood.

"I told my father I would go away again. He begged me to stay; but when he saw I was determined, he took his hat and cane and walked a little piece with me. As we parted, he took me by the hand and, with a voice trembling with emotion, said, 'I never wanted to be rich before, but I do today. God knows it almost kills me to see you leave home because I am poor. Don't go, my son! Don't go. Come back. Help will surely come from somewhere. As long as we have a crust, a part of it is for you.'

"But when he saw he could not change my decision, he said, oh, so sadly, 'Goodbye; goodbye; God bless you,' then turned and started home.

"But he had taken only a step or two when he turned and called my name. As I looked I saw a tear leave his eye and wind down his cheek. It was the first tear I had *ever* seen my father shed for me. He put his hand in his pocket, took something out; then he pressed a fifty-cent piece in my hand and turned and walked away.

"I knew then what I had never known before, that my father loved me. I knew that fifty-cent piece was the last cent he had, and in the gift I saw my father's heart. I knew he would have given me a fortune just as gladly had it been his to give.

"As I realized this, I repented that I had ever caused him an anxious thought. I would have given anything to have blotted out the past, and I resolved I would be a better man and a better son to him.

"I went out into the cold and snow of that winter morning stronger and braver than I had ever been before because I knew my father loved me.

"All day long something seemed to be singing in my heart, 'Father loves me! Father loves me!' and I determined then that I would make life easier for him. And from that hour I have never consciously caused him another pang."

Said Mister Brown, "There was no change in my father. He had always loved me and I suppose had always been anxious that I should know it; but it seemed as though, until the moment came when he could make the sacrifice he did, there had been no way he could really reveal his heart to me."

Mr. Brown had been one of the most bitter infidels of this land, but he went to hear Mr. Moody preach his wonderful sermon on the Prodigal Son's father. He said, "If God is like that, I want to know Him."

That in brief is the story of how Elijah P. Brown found his way to Christ.

Say, if God is like that, can't you take Him and trust Him tonight? He is just like that. And just like that He is yearning for you.

This story is told by another man whose name was also Brown, an honored evangelist now in Glory. He had conducted a meeting in one of the towns of Wisconsin. He went away and a little later got a letter from an old man by the name of Stewart, telling him that his boy had left home saying he would come back but he did not know when. The letter said, "Mr. Brown, you travel a good deal; if you ever see my boy, tell him his father loves him and that his mother is dying to have him come home."

Two years later Mr. Brown went back to that town and the first man he saw as he stepped off the train was old Mr. Stewart. It was a cold, raw day; and Mr. Brown said, "Why, Mr. Stewart, what are you doing here?"

The old man said, "My boy."

"Why, hasn't he come yet?"

"No, but I'm sure he will, and I've met every train since he went away."

After eleven years Mr. Brown went again to this same town. As he stepped from the platform, the first person he saw was old James Stewart. His hair was now white like snow; his brow was wrinkled and his form bent. Mr. Brown said, "Good morning, Mr. Stewart." But the old man had forgotten him. He said, "Who are you?" Mr. Brown made himself known and asked him why he was there. The old man said, "I'm waiting for my boy."

"Why, hasn't he come yet?"

"No," said the old man, "we haven't heard anything, but I'm sure he's coming, and I thought he might be here this morning."

"Just then," said Mr. Brown, "I lifted up my eyes and saw a stalwart young man coming down the steps of the car. I said to myself, *If I were not sure the boy was dead I would say that was the son.*"

But other eyes had seen him, too, and the old man started, dropped his cane and ran as fast as his tottering limbs could let him. And in less time than I can take to tell it, the boy was in his father's arms.

The old white-haired man sobbed out, "O my son! Thank God, you have come! You have come!" Then turning to Mr. Brown he said, "Mr. Brown, I would have waited until I died."

Something like that is God's love for you. A yearning something like that is what God has in His heart for you tonight. He has been waiting for some of you now thirty, forty, fifty, sixty years, and you haven't come yet. But if Christ was made flesh and dwelt among us for the reasons we have seen tonight, and if God loves like a father and is a God like the God we have seen tonight, I think if I were you I'd come home tonight. I wouldn't keep Him waiting any longer.

W. B. RILEY
1861-1947

ABOUT THE MAN:

Dr. W. B. Riley was for 45 years pastor of First Baptist Church, Minneapolis, and pastor emeritus three years. His ministry there built this church to the largest membership in the Northern Baptist Convention.

But all over America Dr. Riley moved and swayed audiences. Thousands were won to Christ in great campaigns.

Riley's ministry was one of preaching the Gospel as well as fighting foes of the Gospel. He sometimes prefaced what he wrote with: *"As one who has given his life to the defense and propagation of fundamentalism."*

William Jennings Bryan once called him *"the greatest Christian statesman in the American pulpit."*

The teaching of evolution was a hot issue in his day, so his debates became another phase of his ministry. Bryan had died in 1925, so the mantle for fighting evolution passed to Riley.

One can well compare Dr. Riley with Charles Spurgeon in the largeness of his work: 1. Like that prince of preachers in London, the Minneapolis pastor-evangelist-crusader carried on for several decades an effective ministry; his church grew about as large as Spurgeon's. 2. Like Spurgeon, he turned out many books, including a 40-volume sermon-commentary. 3. Even as Spurgeon, he was a prophet to a whole nation of moral decline and infidelity in the church. 4. As Spurgeon withdrew from the Baptist Union, so Riley withdrew from the Northern Baptist Convention. 5. Like Spurgeon, he founded a growing training college and seminary. 6. Like Spurgeon, he was an editor, editing *The Christian Fundamentalist* and *The Northwestern Pilot.*

Truly, in the days of his strength, Dr. Riley was one of America's greatest preachers.

IX.

Christ's Deity and Man's Salvation

W. B. RILEY

"Many other signs therefore did Jesus in the presence of the disciples, which are not written in this book: but these are written, that ye may believe that Jesus is the Christ, the Son of God; and that believing ye may have life in his name." —John 20:30,31 (A.S.V.)

If one wished to select a single text that would answer the main point of our query, perhaps Acts 4:12 (American Standard Version) could not be surpassed, "In none other is there salvation: for neither is there any other name under heaven, that is given among men, wherein we must be saved."

It is not, however, our purpose to lay the whole emphasis upon the suggestion in "solitary," and hence we have preferred to present John 20:30,31 as more adequately compassing our theme.

When the Jew discusses the question, "Was Christ the Saviour?" no man doubts that he is sincere; when the Gentile evinces skepticism upon the same subject, we know that his query is not necessarily the result of prejudice, and yet it may easily be lacking the element of sincerity which characterizes the descendant of Jacob.

John Foster relates that two Unitarians called on an old member of the Society of Friends to find out his opinion of Christ. The Quaker replied to their questionings, as the apostle says,

"But we preach Christ crucified, unto the Jews a stumblingblock, and unto the Greeks foolishness; But unto them which are called, both Jews and Greeks, Christ the power of God, and the wisdom of God." —I Cor. 1:23,24.

There are three classes of persons presented in that reply: The Jews, who were prejudiced against Jesus because He came not as scribes and Pharisees had said; the Greeks, whose uninspired philosophies scarce made provision for the appearance of the Son of God; and the believers, from both Jews and Greeks, who saw in Him "the power of God, and the wisdom of God."

While purposing to treat this subject in such candor and fairness that even the demands of the critical mind may be met, we confess in advance our purpose to bring our auditors to join with this third class and consent that Jesus is the solitary Saviour.

To that end we propose three questions:

Is Jesus the Son of God?

There are points of evidence that may here be properly introduced. Permit the mention of three or four of these.

History should speak to this subject. If God was manifested in the person of Jesus Christ, it is quite incomprehensible that history should ignore or disregard that fact. The business of this branch of learning is to rehearse what has been. It is supposed also to lay the greatest importance upon the events of mightiest moment.

What one could match the incarnation of God? And history has spoken to this subject. No matter where one does his reading, whether in ancient, medieval or modern history, the Man of Nazareth meets him at every turn. The tale of His life, the record of His death, the report of His resurrection, the institution He founded, like the scarlet thread in the cable of the English navy, have become inextricably woven into every great historical event of the centuries.

The best history back of Christ is the Old Testament Scriptures. "They are they which testify of me." Skeptics, hard pressed for argument, have said, "Josephus, the historian, knows nothing of Jesus." But such a speech evinces ignorance and reveals a lack of logic. If Josephus had said not a word concerning Him, there would be poor comfort for the infidel in that circumstance, seeing that Josephus was a Jew of the strictest type, and the most bigoted spirit. But, unfortunately for the statement, the book of Josephus gives such prominence to Jesus that we are almost compelled to believe that the strongest of his statements is an interpolation. Read again Book 18, chapter 3, section 3, of the *Antiquities of the Jews.*

Now, there was about this time, Jesus, a wise Man, if it be lawful to call Him "a man," for He was a doer of wonderful works, a teacher of such men as received the truth with pleasure. He drew over to Him many of the Jews and many of the Greeks. He was Christ, and when Pilate, at the suggestion of the principal men amongst us, had condemned Him to the cross, those who loved Him at the first did not forsake Him, for He appeared to them alive again the third day, as the divine prophets had foretold. These and ten thousand other wonderful things concerning Him, and the tribe of Christians, so named for Him, are not extinct at this day.

If that is an interpolation, let us not forget that in *Antiquities of the Jews,* 18:5-2, he relates the story of the beheading of John; and in 20:9-1, tells the story of James the Just who, he says, "was the brother of Jesus, who claimed to be the Christ." No one disputes the validity of these latter chapters.

What is medieval history but a record of the misinterpretation of the message of Jesus? What modern history ignores Him? Could we write the history of England and leave out Christ? How account for the changes that made a continent of barbarians to be a church-going, Christ-believing nation? Could we write the history of America and leave out Christ? How account for the dreams and desires of Columbus? How explain the conduct of the Puritan Fathers? What disposition will you make of the uses to which the words "Christ" and "Church" are put, in the administration of the colonies and the establishment of the states and the attempt to evangelize the Indians?

Can you write the history of India and leave out Christ ? Who would attempt to do that and yet ignore Carey, Judson, and Boardman?

Can you write the history of China and leave out Christ? How will you explain the Boxer movement, not to speak of the long series of international conferences and complications involving the opening of China's doors to Christian missionaries?

Can you write the history of Africa and leave out Christ? Who would dare, making no mention of Livingstone and Moffat, not to speak of the modern movements inaugurated by Christian missionaries?

Can you write the history of the isles of the sea and leave out Christ? How will you explain why cannibalism ended and church spires sprang up on every hand?

The historian has not yet been born who has, or could ignore this name and yet command the respect of men. If He be not the Son of God, what is the secret of His success in forcing Himself into all human affairs? He was born in no palace; He was schooled in no great university; He was promoted to no position of honor; He commanded no mighty armies; He discovered no continents; He engaged in no scientific investigation; His career ended with a cross and not with a crown! Why has human history been compelled to accord Him such a place?

The Scriptures also testify to His deity. Passing over the Old Testament prophecies regarding Him about which men might argue, we come to indisputable things. The New Testament asserts, "And she shall bring forth a son, and thou shalt call his name JESUS: for he shall save his people from their sins" (Matt. 1:21).

If the Bible is to be believed in what it declares, God spake out of Heaven, saying, "This is my beloved Son, in whom I am well pleased." If He were not self-deceived, His sentence is, "I am in the Father, and the Father in me." If John were not deluded, his worthy testimony is this:

"In the beginning was the Word, and the Word was with God, and the Word was God. And the Word was made flesh, and dwelt among us, (and we beheld his glory, the glory as of the only begotten of the Father,) full of grace and truth." —John 1:1,14.

Paul certainly seemed to be a sane man, and you cannot explain him unless you believe also that he was an inspired man; and that apostle speaks of Jesus as being "the effulgence of his [Father's] glory, and the very image of his substance, and upholding all things by the word of his power" (A.S.V.).

But we will not go into the multiplication of texts to prove the deity of Jesus. No good student of the Scriptures denies their testimony, unless he has first derided their authority.

I have read somewhere of two gentlemen who were discussing the deity of Christ, and one of them said, "If He were God, it should have been more explicitly stated in the Bible."

To this the other replied, "How would you express it, to put it past dispute?"

"Why," said the first, "I would say that Jesus is the true God."

"You are very apt in the choice of words," answered his fellow, "for they are in accord with the inspired St. John, who says, 'This is the true God, and eternal life.' "

Christians also are credible witnesses to His deity. Experience has a testimony that cannot be gainsaid. Familiarity makes it possible for one to testify to facts. The world is full of people who claim to have an experience of the grace of Jesus, and a communion with Him which renders them competent to speak regarding His mission and character. Napoleon was profoundly impressed by the harmonious testimony of the multitude of believers. When John said,

"That which was from the beginning, that which we have heard, that which we have seen with our eyes, that which we beheld, and our hands handled, concerning the Word of life . . . that which we have seen and heard declare we unto you also, that ye also may have fellowship with us. . . ."—I John 1:1,3 (A.S.V.),

he introduced a form of argument, the strength of which has ever been confessed. Who shall dispute what they say who speak from experience and delightful fellowship? Who shall stand before the millions on millions that bear one testimony concerning what Jesus is to their souls?

Dr. O. P. Gifford, while yet pastor in Chicago, spoke one day concerning that wonderful Ferris wheel, the plan and construction of which was such a compliment to the ability of the young engineer. He told how, when the wheel was put into place, Mr. Ferris took his wife and a newspaper reporter and went down on a July day, when the wind was sweeping the earth with the strength of a hurricane, striking the wheel fairly on the face. Entering the car, Mr. Ferris closed the door behind him and gave the order to start the machinery; and suddenly the wheel began to move. The wind, like another Samson, seized it, pressed against it with mighty strength, strove to wrench it at every point, tore at the windows, shrieked like a maniac. But the great wheel moved on with scarcely a shiver until it had completed its revolution; and Mr. Ferris, his wife, and the reporter stepped out.

Mr. Ferris' faith in the wheel was a scientific faith. He knew its mechanical construction; he knew also its strength; like the apostle, he was persuaded that it was able to keep that which he had entrusted to it unto the end.

Mrs. Ferris' faith was purely personal. She knew little about the wheel; she believed in her husband's opinion and counsel, and like Ruth of old, said, "Where thou goest, I will go." Her confidence was not misplaced.

The newspaper reporter entered with fear and trembling, filled with doubts. But he had been commanded and dared not refuse. When the wheel had gone its round and he found himself again on the earth, he had the faith of experience and could testify also touching the ability of that wheel to keep what was committed to it.

The followers of Jesus join with the apostle and say, "We know whom we have believed." Their experience with Him has proven His power. Through strain and storm, through suffering and sorrow, through temptation and trial, they are kept. Who can gainsay the ground of their confidence in the deity of the Man of Nazareth?

If there were time we would "let His enemies bear witness also." Goethe, whose infidelity is well known, said, "The human mind, no matter how much it may advance in intellectual culture and in the extent and depth of the knowledge of nature, will never transcend the height and moral culture of Christianity as it shines and glows in the person of Jesus Christ."

Rousseau, another unbeliever, says,

> I confess that the purity of the Gospel has its influence on my heart. Is it possible that a Book at once so simple and sublime should be merely the work of man? Is it possible that the sacred personage whose history it contains should be Himself a mere man?
>
> What sweetness, what purity in His manners! What an affecting gracefulness in His delivery! What sublimity in His maxims! What profound wisdom in His discourses! What presence of mind in His answers!
>
> How great the command over His passions! Where is the man, where the philosopher who could so live and so die without weakness and without ostentation? If the life and death of Socrates were those of a sage, the life and death of Jesus were those of a God.

Strauss says, "Jesus represents within the sphere of religion the culmination point, beyond which posterity can never go, yea, which it cannot even equal. He remains the highest model of religion within the reach of our thoughts."

The words of Theodore Parker are interesting: "There is God in the heart of this youth—that mightiest heart that ever beat, stirred by the Spirit of God; how it wrought in His bosom!"

Renan concedes enough when he says, "The day on which Jesus uttered this saying, 'God is a Spirit: and they that worship him must worship him in spirit and in truth,' He was truly the Son of God."

Bob Ingersoll, blatant infidel as he was, still affirmed, "For the Man Jesus I have infinite respect."

Truly may one join with Moses in his wonderful psalm of Deuteronomy 32, where concerning the expectation of unbelievers as compared with that of believers, he said, "Their rock is not as our Rock, even our enemies themselves being judges."

But our theme involves more.

Is He the Solitary Saviour?

Is there no other person who can save? There was a day when the king put all the corn of Egypt into the hands of Joseph. Men must make their appeal to him or perish. Is it true of our Joseph that the stores of salvation are all in His hands? The Scriptures are strong: "And in none other is there salvation: for neither is there any other name under heaven, that is given among men, wherein we must be saved" (Acts 4:12, A.S.V.) Surely that phrase opposes the pretentions and promises of all others who essay to save.

Dr. Chapman tells us that a friend of his was about to climb the Matterhorn. He was besieged by men waiting at the base of the mountain ready to guide him up the difficult way. But when he asked them to show their papers, they all but one fell back. He came forward and presented his certificate which was signed by noted Americans and Englishmen, affirming that he had guided them up the Matterhorn in perfect safety.

If the professed saviours of the world are asked to show their certificates of appointment and their testimonials from the redeemed, they will be silenced. Jesus alone, by calling the roll of Heaven, including the great names of the Old and New Testament worthies (those of New Testament and modern times), can bring sufficient commendations and certificates to show that He is the all-sufficient Saviour.

There is no other way of salvation. Some willingly admit that Jesus is the only Son of God, but remind us that there are matters of merit which must be taken into account. They have done good works; shall they not therefore be saved? If a man does his best, will he miss Heaven and eternal bliss?

Let it be remembered that no man has done his best. The Scriptures and experience speak one thing, "There is none that doeth good, no, not one." And let it be further remembered, "By the deeds of the law there shall no flesh be justified in his sight."

If one reply, "But I am sorry for my sins, and have mourned them; will not that suffice to set me free?" we are compelled to answer that sorrow never reveals the attributes of a saviour; it quite as often dooms men as it helps them. It has drowned many a soul; but by itself it has never saved one.

Dr. Gordon says a very remarkable and yet scriptural thing when he remarks:

> Jesus let only His wounds be touched after His resurrection. Whereby I perceive that we can be united to Christ only by His sufferings. Many today are trying to be saved by imitating the earthly life of Christ; many others are trying to be saved by imitating the death of Christ. The world is pretty nearly divided between these two classes—those who are seeking salvation by copying Christ's life, and those who are seeking salvation by copying His death—the one looking for peace by self-morality and the other by self-mortification.

Both are doomed to disappointment. "Without shedding of blood is no remission." Even God, apart from Christ, cannot save, for, as Evangelist A. B. Earle said, "God the Father and God the Spirit cannot save because they have no blood." It is 'the blood of Jesus Christ His Son that cleanseth us from all sin.' Self-morality is sorry stuff; self-mortification cannot mean self-redemption.

One of our missionaries relates the terrible suffering of a heathen who had for many years lived with his body immersed in water, and at a later time had hung on hooks piercing through his flesh, trying to make peace with God through his own wounds. We recoil from even the report; but our civilized America is full of men and women who are attempting salvation by self-infliction. Vain endeavor! It is not ours to make peace with God through our sufferings, but to take the peace which Christ has made by His own sufferings. It is not ours to effect peace at all, but to receive the peace already perfected. True, "Godly sorrow worketh repentance," but not salvation. We do well to sing:

> **Weeping will not save me—**
> **Tho' my face were bathed in tears,**
> **That could not allay my fears,**
> **Could not wash the sins of years—**
> **Weeping will not save me.**
>
> **Faith in Christ will save me—**
> **Let me trust Thy weeping Son,**
> **Trust the work that He has done;**
> **To His arms, Lord, help me run—**
> **Faith in Christ will save me.**

To Thomas, Jesus said, "I am the way, the truth, and the life: no man cometh unto the Father, but by me."

What Then Is Essential?

That is the personal question; and we are never profited until we reach the personal question. "But these are written, that ye might believe that Jesus is the Christ, the Son of God."

To believe that Jesus is the Christ, the Son of God, is the first essential. Having seen that history accords Him that place; having remembered that the Scriptures affirm it; having listened to believers and even to the testimony of unbelievers, why should we imagine the voice heard from the Heavens, "This is my beloved Son," was other than the voice of God? The meaning of that language may not easily be misinterpreted. He meant by that speech to differentiate Him. "Unto which of the angels said he at any time, Thou art my Son, This day have I begotten thee?" (Heb. 1:5, A.S.V.).

No wonder the millions of Christians consent to this claim. Christ has made good!

Believe also that eternal life is with Him. "And this is the record, that God hath given to us eternal life, and this life is in his Son. He that hath the Son hath life; and he that hath not the Son of God hath not life" (I John 5:11). That proposition is plain; that declaration is decisive; that second step is absolutely essential.

But there remains another: *Believe that He gives you salvation now.* "That, believing, ye may have life in his name." "He that believeth on me hath everlasting life." The men who have tested this declaration of the Scriptures have found salvation demonstrated in their own hearts; the women who have brought to Him loyalty have come into the knowledge of life; the little children who have sought Him have been received and saved.

There were clean-cut distinctions in the language of a little maid Dr. George F. Pentecost met in Scotland, and the very way of life may be traced in her words. At Aberdeen, one night after nearly all the people had gone from the service, and Pentecost was about to leave the hall, this lassie timidly approached him. When he said, "What do you want?" she reached up on tiptoe as he bent down and whispered into his ear, "I want to get saved!"

"You want to get saved?"

"Aye, sir, I do," still whispering, but more intense in utterance.

"And why do you want to get saved?"

"Because I am a sinner."

"How do you know you are a sinner? Who told you so?"

"God says it in His Book, and I feel it right here," as she laid her hand on her little breast.

"Well," said Pentecost, "do you think I can save you?"

She passed from the whisper to clear, ringing tones, her eyes striking fire. "No, no, man, you cannot save me; no man can save a sinner!"

At his side, her hand in his, speaking as kindly as he knew how, he replied, "You are quite right; no man can save you. Tell me, why then do you come to me?"

Again her voice was dropped to a whisper as she said, "But Jesus can save me!"

"Yes," replied Pentecost, "but tell me how He can save you."

"Oh, sir, He died for me."

To test her knowledge again, he asked, "Then He is dead, is He? How can He save you if He is dead?"

The little thing, starting from her seat, her eyes suffused with tears, and yet flashing more fire than before, answered, "He is not dead! He is not dead! Man, Jesus is not dead. He is God's Son. Did you not tell us this night that God raised Him from the dead? Oh, man, I want to get saved. Do not fash me; but tell me all about it."

He did tell her, and she went away glad and thankful, for she knew that she had found Jesus, the world's solitary Saviour and the Guide of her own soul.

C. I. SCOFIELD
1843-1921

ABOUT THE MAN:

Born in Michigan, Cyrus Scofield became one of the foremost names among Bible students.

His mother died at his birth, but before she died, prayed this boy might become a minister.

His family moved to Tennessee, where he received his early education.

Although his parents were Christians and the Bible was read at home, Cyrus didn't consider it a book of investigative study but one to enjoy merely for its stories. So his religious experience prior to conversion was superficial.

The Civil War prevented him from entering the university, so he never received a formal collegiate education. At 17 he entered the Confederate Army. When the war was over, Scofield studied law in St. Louis and afterward moved to Kansas where he was admitted to the bar in 1869. He served in the Kansas State Legislature and at the age of 29 was appointed by President Grant as United States District Attorney for Kansas. Later he returned to St. Louis and re-entered law practice. During this time he drank heavily. However, this passion for drink was completely removed when he received Christ through the efforts of Thomas S. McPheeters, a YMCA worker.

Scofield immediately became active in Christian work. He was ordained in 1883 and became minister at First Congregational Church, Dallas.

As a result of diligent and systematic study of the Scriptures during his years of ministry, he produced the Scofield Reference Bible and the Scofield Bible Correspondence Course.

Scofield died on Sunday morning, July 24, 1921, at Douglaston, Long Island.

X.

The Deity of Jesus Christ

C. I. SCOFIELD, Editor, Scofield Reference Bible

"In the beginning was the Word, and the Word was with God, and the Word was God."—John 1:1.

I want to present to you, as best I may, the grounds upon which Christians receive Jesus Christ as God manifest in the flesh. Beyond all question, Christianity as a religion is committed to that proposition. Whatever it may call itself, anything less than that is not Christianity. Eliminate that and there is left a marvelous story, indeed, but like a box of wonderful gems to which the key is missing; there is left a wonderful ethic but without adequate authority; there is left the promise of a great spiritual kingdom, but the kingdom is without a king.

Christianity stands or falls by the proposition that Jesus of Nazareth was more than man; in other words, while being man, that He was God manifest in the flesh. That is a stupendous assertion, but God does not ask us to believe it without proof. What, then, are the reasons why we Christians receive Jesus Christ as God manifest in the flesh?

Now I shall feel more comfortable as I go on, if I say at the outset that the merits of my cause should not be judged by my ability in presenting it. Truth itself transcends the ability of any man to present it. All the more, then, if the reasons themselves shall seem to you to be convincing and the proofs shall seem to you to be adequate, will you as honest men be under compulsion to accept them. Give me, then, your attention to that cumulative body of truth which establishes beyond all question this proposition—that Jesus of Nazareth, the historic Christ, was God manifest in the flesh.

The Gospels Show Jesus As Absolutely Unique

First, the four Gospels present the record of a life and the impress of a character which are absolutely unique. The Jesus of the Gospels stands alone. He makes a class by Himself. There are points of resemblance between Cincinnatus and Washington; between Caesar and Napoleon; between Chaucer and Shakespeare; between Hesiod and Homer; between Dante and Milton; but Jesus is alone unique.

I will not stop to prove that, because no one denies it; but I ask you to take note of three respects in which the character presented in these four Gospels stands solitary among men.

First, in that it is absolutely without sin. Now neither in Scripture nor in history nor in fiction nor in our own observation, do we find another of which that can be said. History gives the record of no sinless men. Fiction has never yet presented a perfect character. The effort has been made a thousand times; but upon the most perfect character ever constructed by the genius of man is some fatal defect, some taint of imperfection.

Did it not lead too far from the subject, it would be interesting to take up some of the most perfect characters in the Bible, in history and in fiction, and show how true it is that, tested even by our own imperfect standards, there is, in the best of them, some obvious defect. They are too strong or too weak; they are too tender or too severe; they are all marked by excess in one direction and limitation in another. Not one but bears the mark of human frailty and imperfection.

But the four Gospels present a sinless life. It is not merely that the four evangelists assert that fact; they give us the life itself, so that we may see for ourselves that it was sinless.

Again, the Man of the Gospels is unique in that He is the only absolutely universal Man, the only catholic Man, the only Man with no race mark upon Him, and who, as He reaches the differing families of men, interposes no race barrier.

We know as a matter of history that He sprang out of Israel, that He was a Jew; and we are called to account for the fact that out of that most exclusive, most distinctive, most peculiar of all peoples, should have come the one universal Man, who has no mark of race upon Him.

You know how instinctively this has been brought out in art. As the Gospel spread through Europe, there sprang up great schools of Christian art. Men strove to put on canvas and to carve in stone their conception of the Christ. A very remarkable thing about it was that a Scandinavian always painted the Christ as blue of eye and fair of hair, just as an Italian always painted Him with dark locks and olive skin. It never seems to have occurred to them that He was not of their own race. One of the missionaries in Africa tells us that native converts in the heart of that country were greatly surprised when they were told that Christ was a white man. It never occurred to them that He was not black like themselves.

Now this universality would be singular enough if Christ came of Rome or of Greece, if He had been born in one of the world empires; but He came out of a little nation which has ever had the strongest marks of race distinction and race peculiarity. More than this, He grew to manhood in a remote village of Galilee, far from the slightest cosmopolitan influence.

Try to imagine a Scotchman two hundred years ago, who had grown to manhood in Inverness, having no marks of the Scot upon him. Shakespeare, who has been called the most impersonal of all men, was an Englishman to his fingertips; and Homer was a Greek through and through. No human being, save Christ, ever escaped a race mark.

The third respect in which the Man of the four Gospels is unique is that He was as perfect in the balance and proportion of His qualities as He was in His sinlessness. Not only was he a sinless Man, but He was a perfect Man, a rounded Man. Now all other wisdom has been marred by some folly; all other strength has gone over into excess or violence; all other sweetness has degenerated into weakness; but Jesus was wise without folly, strong without violence, sweet without weakness.

In these three respects, this Man of the Gospels stands alone among all men, the records of whose lives have come down to us or which have been invented by the genius of man.

Christ's Impact of Human History Is Without Parallel

Leaving the Gospels now, and coming on down the stream of time for the last 1900 or more years, we find the influence of Jesus in human history has been as unique as His sinlessness, His catholicity or His perfectness. In all history, no one else has influenced the course of human affairs or the trend of human lives just as the Man of the four Gospels has influenced them.

Napoleon, speaking of Alexander, Caesar and himself, said:

> We founded great empires, but we founded them on force. The principles upon which we founded our kingdoms were natural principles, but Jesus founded an empire which is indestructible, which

is growing day by day, which is ruled over by an invisible King, and which is founded upon love. I know man, and I tell you that Jesus was more than a man.

In history, then, we have the impress of Jesus Christ, and that impress is just as unique and peculiar as all else which concerns Him. These things are indisputable.

Now the startling fact concerning this entirely unique impress of Himself upon humanity is that Jesus said it would be so. He said, for instance, "I am the light of the world" (John 8:12). Think of the audacity of that statement. A young Jewish peasant, a carpenter by trade, without learning, without acknowledged rank, without wealth, announces to a little group of converted fishermen and harlots and tax gatherers, that He is the "light of the world."

When uttered, it was a mere assertion; but after 1900 years have passed, it is a statement which admits of disproof if it is not true or of verification if it is true. Think of the audacity of it! Not Homer, not Socrates, not Plato, not Moses—it is no one of these, but a peasant, who says, "I am the light of the world."

Well, after more than 1900 years, you may take the map of the world and shade that map according to the degree of enlightenment, moral and intellectual, which prevails today among the nations, and you will find that where your map comes nearest to perfect whiteness, there Christ is most known and most honored; and where your map shades off into absolute blackness, where the human mind today is in chains and darkness, where there is no picture, no statue, and no book, right there Christ is not known at all.

Dear friends, here are these undisputed phenomena. No one can or does dispute them, and they are to be accounted for. That explanation which *adequately* accounts for them *all* is the one upon which reason will set her seal. Is not that a reasonable statement? You may be interested to know that that formula belongs to the vocabulary of the exact sciences, not to theology. In the investigation of nature certain material phenomena are to be accounted for, and science says, "That explanation which adequately accounts for them all, is the true explanation," and reason says, "Amen!"

It can scarcely be necessary to refer to the various theories which have been propounded to account for the phenomena which we have been considering, but which have been abandoned as inadequate.

It was said, for instance, that Jesus was invented by the evangelists;

that the writers of Matthew, Mark, Luke and John invented the character which they present. It was pointed out long ago by the unbeliever Renan that "only a Jesus could invent a Jesus."

How does it happen that what the strenuous efforts of patriarch, prophet and priest failed to achieve, what the sublimest human genius failed to invent, these four writers accomplished with an ease, precision and naturalness to which every page of the artless narrative bears witness?

It puts a greater strain upon credulity to believe that four men could have created such a character as Jesus than to believe the simple, sublime and rational biblical explanation of Jesus.

How did it come that four different accounts, written by different men at different times, in a different style, and selecting for the illustration of this character different incidents very largely, should all succeed in producing identically the same impression? If you read Matthew, you get the impression of a sinless Being, perfectly wise and universal. If you read Mark, there comes to you the impression of the same sinlessness, the same universality, the same perfection of character. And if you read Luke and John, the impression is precisely the same.

It does violence to reason and probability to say that such men could invent such a character. But the theory has passed out of the minds of men as inadequate and irrational, and I refer to it merely to show how men have striven to avoid the only reasonable conclusion concerning this character.

Another theory which had possession of unbelieving minds for a time was the mythical theory of Strauss, the theory which said that the Jesus of the Gospels was a myth; that the Gospels, as we have them, were slowly built up through some four hundred years; that the first crude record was subjected to numberless prunings and increased by numberless inventions, until finally there came out the picture which we have of Jesus of Nazareth.

Well, even Strauss abandoned this theory before he died; and he did it for this reason: that the severest hostile criticism was compelled to concede the authenticity of at least four of the epistles of the Apostle Paul; that they were written within thirty or thirty-five years after the death of Christ; and because of these epistles of Paul there is the impress of the same character.

There are the same affirmations concerning His personality; the same doctrine concerning His work and the purpose that brought Him into the world, and Strauss admitted that thirty years was too brief a time for the development of a myth. So that theory was abandoned.

There has been discovered a work, known once to have existed, but believed to have perished, *The Diatesseron of Tatian,* the work of a man who was born in the year in which the Apostle John died; and this work proves that the four Gospels, as we have them, were then in existence. Exit, then, the mythical theory.

But the problem remains: we have to account for Jesus. How shall we do it? You know the biblical solution: "In the beginning was the Word, and the Word was with God, and the Word was God" (John 1:1), and "the Word was made flesh, and dwelt among us" (John 1:14).

That is the biblical solution. Now no one can question the adequacy of this solution; it perfectly accounts for all the phenomena. If this unique Being were indeed God, "manifest in the flesh," His sinlessness is accounted for; the absence of any race mark is accounted for; the rounded perfection of all the attributes of His character is accounted for. No one questions that; it is a complete solution of all the phenomena.

Christ's Becoming Man Was Necessary
to Reveal God

Now we are prepared to see how perfectly this solution harmonizes with adequate motives for an incarnation. First, if God was ever to be fully revealed to man, there lay upon Him the inevitability that He should do precisely that thing. All of nature, all of history, all of the Bible is in truth the unveiling, the self-disclosure of God.

If you look out upon the universe you see His handiwork. You remember how short and, it seems to me, unanswerable is the Apostle Paul's argument from the universe for the existence of God. "Every house is builded by some *man*; but he that built all things *is* God" (Heb. 3:4).

If we see a house, we do not think that it was built by anything less than a man. We look out upon this great universe and say, "Nothing less than God has been here." From the universe we get a revelation of God's power; we get a revelation of His wisdom. But how far off that God is from a mortal being on this earth, stumbling along a dark path which he never trod before, and will never tread again, to fall at last into an unexplained grave!

When God puts His self-revelation into words, there is of course an immeasurable advance, yet after all, a kind of incompleteness.

You know how we try sometimes to describe a thing in words. Then we do better than that; we make a picture of it. But when we are able to lead the person, to whom we are endeavoring to communicate the idea, to the very thing itself, then the description becomes intelligible, the picture full of meaning.

Suppose I were trying to describe to you the beauty of the sunset, and you had never seen a sunset. I might pile words upon words and fill them with color, yet I should give a very imperfect idea of a sunset. But if I could take you to some western slope, and let you stand there while the sun sank behind the cloud-palaces of the sky, fusing their dull greys into purple and scarlet and gold, and the glory and beauty of the sunset gave themselves to you, you would no longer need my words; you would know for yourself.

Now there is God, infinitely tender and beautiful and glorious, and here are we, finite and stupid and earthly—can you think of any way by which it would be possible for God really to make Himself known to us, except to enter into a human life and translate deity in its power and perfection, its light and its love, into the terms of human experience?

That this is the only perfect divine manifestation is felt dimly by all races; and there is no false religion (except Mohammedanism) which has not the thought of incarnation in it, the thought that the god they seek and whom they serve and worship has at some time incarnated himself in a human life. Incarnation inheres in the very necessity of the case; and when you think of God adopting this expedient and really clothing Himself with human flesh for the revelation of that which He is, through the stress and trial of a human life, you have a motive which is at once Godlike and adequate. If God had never been manifested in the flesh, if no prophet had ever predicted it, reason would compel us to anticipate the incarnation.

Now this very thing is declared to have been the purpose of the incarnation. John says, "No man hath seen God at any time; the only begotten Son, which is in the bosom of the Father, he hath declared him" (John 1:18).

If you think of Jesus Christ in this way, if you go back to the four Gospels and study them with the thought of Jesus Christ as God making Himself known to man, you find that the manifestation satisfies every demand of your heart and of your reason. The God revealed in Jesus Christ is the God who answers in every respect to human need. He is felt to be at once a God worthy of adoring worship. He is felt to be a God of power and a God of wisdom, and a God of matchless, inexpressible love.

No one has ever contemplated the character of Jesus Christ as the manifestation of God and has felt repelled from God by that manifestation. The power of God in nature may terrify, and the revelation of God through written words may perplex, but when we stand before God unveiled in Jesus Christ, we love and adore Him. It is impossible not to do so.

Again the prophets foretold the incarnation:

"And he said, Hear ye now, O house of David; Is it a small thing for you to weary men, but will ye weary my God also? Therefore the Lord himself shall give you a sign; Behold, a virgin shall conceive, and bear a son, and shall call his name Immanuel."—Isa. 7:13,14.

"For unto us a child is born, unto us a son is given: and the government shall be upon his shoulder: and his name shall be called Wonderful, Counsellor, The mighty God, The everlasting Father, The Prince of Peace."—Isa. 9:6.

Thus beyond all question, hundreds of years before Jesus was born in Bethlehem, a prediction was uttered that there should be born into the family of David One who in some mysterious way should also be God. We may or may not believe that the prophecy was fulfilled, but that it is there no one can dispute.

Now when we invoke prophetic testimony, my friends, we bring into court a witness never yet discredited. We have not only this prophecy that the Messiah should be in some mysterious way The Mighty God, The Everlasting Father, The Prince of Peace, but we have literally hundreds of other predictions, minute and specific, relating to nations, to countries and to individuals; and these predictions invariably have been literally and precisely fulfilled.

The prophets foretold the place of the Messiah's birth, and no one ever questioned that Jesus was born in Bethlehem. They foretold the family in which He should be born, the family of David; and no one ever disputed that He was born in the family of David. They foretold the tribe of which He should come, the tribe of Judah; and no one ever denied that Jesus came from the tribe of Judah.

If in the lifetime of Jesus Christ or in the years of the first proclamation of the Gospel, while the records were still in existence, the Jews had shown that Jesus was not born in Bethlehem, that He was not of the tribe of Judah, and not of the family of David, every disciple would instantly have forsaken Him. They were not able to do it; they never disputed it—never.

Of the many prophetic details concerning Jesus, I have called attention to three particulars which were literally fulfilled; and therefore reason compels us to give great weight to the prediction concerning His deity. If a witness has always testified truthfully, the presumption is that all of his testimony is true.

Jesus Plainly Claimed to Be God

A third incontestable proposition is that Jesus Himself claimed to be God manifest in the flesh. Read the following passages upon that point:

"Your father Abraham rejoiced to see my day: and he saw it, and was glad. Then said the Jews unto him, Thou art not yet fifty years old, and hast thou seen Abraham? Jesus said unto them, Verily, verily, I say unto you, Before Abraham was, I am. Then took they up stones to cast at him: but Jesus hid himself, and went out of the temple, going through the midst of them, and so passed by."—John 8:56-59.

There, then, was the distinct assertion upon the part of Jesus Himself that He existed before Abraham, and that He was the Jehovah of the Old Testament.

"While the Pharisees were gathered together, Jesus asked them, Saying, What think ye of Christ? whose son is he? They say unto him, The son of David. He saith unto them, How then doth David in spirit call him Lord?"—Matt. 22:41-43.

Another assertion of His deity:

"Jesus saith unto him, I am the way, the truth, and the life: no man cometh unto the Father, but by me. If ye had known me, ye should have known my Father also: and from henceforth ye know him, and have seen him. Philip saith unto him, Lord, shew us the Father, and it sufficeth us. Jesus saith unto him, Have I been so long time with you, and yet hast thou not known me, Philip? he that hath seen me hath seen the Father."—John 14:6-9.

You will remember that not once but many times this humblest of men, this meekest of men received the worship of His fellow men, an act of unspeakable blasphemy, a shocking violation of the First Commandment, if Jesus did not know Himself to be divine. We have a marked instance of that in chapter 20 of John:

"And after eight days again his disciples were within, and Thomas with them: then came Jesus, the doors being shut, and stood in the midst, and said, Peace be unto you. Then saith he to Thomas, Reach hither thy finger, and behold my hands; and reach hither thy hand, and thrust it into my side: and be not faithless, but believing. And Thomas answered and said unto him, My Lord and my God."—Vss. 26-28.

Here let me anticipate an objection. You are saying that this is what Jesus says of Himself. Very true; but it shuts a candid investigator up to one of two alternatives. Either Jesus was the Son of God or He, the only sinless Being of whom any record has come down to man, was a conscious impostor, a blasphemous wretch or a deluded enthusiast, one or the other. It does not matter which of these latter alternatives you take—the position is abhorrent to reason. That a sinless Being would consciously, deliberately commit the most flagrant of all sins in the violation of the First Commandment, "Thou shalt have none other gods before me" (Deut. 5:7), could be explained only on the ground of insanity.

But the whole record of Jesus' life impresses a candid observer with His sanity, His strength of mind, His perfect wisdom and self-poise; and the effect of faith in Him as divine has ever been to purify the character and lift it up and sanctify it. On the other hand, were Jesus a weak religious enthusiast, you have to account for the undeniable fact that a self-deceived fanatic was the author of the only perfectly pure religion which, when applied to sinful lives, has demonstrated its power to transform them into holiness.

By either alternative, we are shut up to a greater inconsistency and to a greater demand upon our credulity than to receive as true the simple and sublime statement of the Word of God; that for the purpose of making Himself known to a race which had gone astray from Him, He in His infinite love and pity clothed Himself with flesh and lived among men that they might know Him, come to Him, trust Him and love Him.

Lost, Sinful Man Must Have Such a Divine Saviour

Remember, too, that other all-compelling motive to incarnation which grows out of our guilt. The most evidently Godlike thing in all Scripture is the record of the self-sacrifice of Jehovah for the sins of His creatures. Only a sinless One could make that sacrifice; only deity could gather all sins into one expiatory act; only in the flesh could deity become a sacrifice.

Well, you have here a great mystery; and if the doctrine is true, that needs must be.

"In the beginning was the Word, and the Word was with God, and the Word was God." —John 1:1.

There is one mystery—God. How much do we know about God after all? How much are we, under human limitations, capable of knowing about God? "The Word was made flesh, and dwelt among us" (John 1:14)—another mystery. We know a little more about man than we do about God, but men are great mysteries. Two mysteries—the mystery of God and the mystery of man, and these brought together in the Incarnation. Indeed it would be a difficult religion to believe if there were no mystery in it. That there are mysteries in Christianity is the very mark of God upon it.

We have, then, the fact of the deity of Jesus Christ and it accounts perfectly for all the phenomena of His life and His character and of the influence of that life and character upon personal experience and human history. No other theory will account for all those phenomena. Furthermore, it agrees with the predictions of the prophets and the testimony of Christ Himself.

Are we not, by these very processes of reasoning, shut up to the necessity of believing that this explanation is the only one credible to sound, human reason? Philosophy and Scripture agree in the consent that this explanation is adequate; it accounts for all the facts and accounts for them perfectly.

There remains the testimony, upon which I will not dwell, of personal experience. Let it suffice to say, that for 1900 years, faith in Jesus Christ as a divine Saviour and Lord has laid hold upon the most degraded human lives and lifted them up into purity. Faith in the deity of Jesus Christ has transformed barbarous into civilized nations. It has established a new standard of right and wrong. Even those who do not accept the personal authority of the Divine Jesus know that that human personality is the fountainhead of every blessing of light, liberty and law under which they live.

As we stand before that gentle and loving and mighty Jesus, shall not our hearts confirm with trust and love the verdict of our reason, which compels us to proclaim the deity of Jesus Christ to be the essence of Christianity?

"In the beginning was the Word, and the Word was with God, and the Word was God." —John 1:1.

HARRY RIMMER
1890-1952

ABOUT THE MAN:

Dr. Harry Rimmer wore many hats in his lifetime—lecturer, scientist, archaeologist, author, pastor, crusader, debater, fundamentalist, soul winner—and one of America's most thrilling speakers.

As president of the Science Research Bureau, he delved into all the so-called evidences for evolution and with scientific evidence proved it a foolish and untenable theory.

After his lecture about the creation, the Flood, Joshua's long day, the miracles, the Bible account seemed the most reasonable and scientific thing in the world, while the guesses of the evolutionary theory proved to be scientifically ridiculous. A Christian who heard him did not long feel like a shipwrecked mariner clinging with despair to the broken pieces of his ship of faith in a stormy sea. Instead, he felt like he was on an unsinkable ocean liner driving steadily on a proper course to a well-known haven under the safe hands of a master Mariner! He made you want to stand up and cheer for the Bible. No man in America could more strengthen your faith in the Bible than this man.

Dr. Rimmer was a working scientist, for years spending six months in excavation and examination of fossils and in other scientific research, then six months on the platform.

He was long pastor of the First Presbyterian Church of Duluth, Minnesota.

He was author of many books; among them: *Dead Men Tell Tales, Harmony of Science and Scripture,* and *Modern Science and the Genesis Record,* all highly recommended to young people.

In March of 1953 he slipped across that "Valley of Deep Shadow" to occupy his bit of property—for after taps comes reveille for the Christian!

XI.

The Voice of the Centurion

HARRY RIMMER

Text: Matt. 27:50-54

We have often heard the superficial critic question the evidence of the crucifixion of Jesus Christ, on the ground that the testimony was all given by men who loved Him and had a sentimental interest in establishing the spiritual value of His sacrifice.

The Centurion's Background

In the voices that come to us from the place called Calvary, there is, however, one voice that is as divorced from sentiment as a human voice can be. This is the cry of the Roman centurion. After the Roman custom of commissioning men for foreign service, this man was a veteran of the fiercest wars. He was a man of blood and violence who had often rallied his armed band for intrepid deeds of conquest and slaughter. There was nothing "sentimental" or soft in the nature of the man who had risen to command a band in a Roman legion in a land as tumultuous and embroiled as was Palestine.

Steeped in the legends of his own people, the centurion was unconcerned with the gods of Palestine. It mattered not to him whether they named their God Jehovah, Adonai, or Mars. To the Roman psychology, the gods of Palestine were defeated with the people who worshiped them. He reasoned, as did all Romans, that if those gods were unable to keep the land from the grasp of Roman hands, then the Roman gods were superior to the gods of the conquered land. So if he ever thought about the Jewish faith, it was with scorn and rejection.

The Centurion Observes the Crucifixion

On that day a Man was delivered to him for crucifixion. To him it was just a familiar chore. There was nothing unusual or startling about this task; it was all in the day's work. Whenever the volatile people of Jerusalem rose in their might and clamored in public riot and disorder, the Roman legionnaires leaped to their arms and took their places in the ranks.

So throughout all the shouting and the excitement of that morning, this centurion had probably been busy watching the turbulent mob. In that case he would have known nothing of the trial and the reasons for the condemnation. Until the Prisoner was handed over to him for execution, the centurion was utterly unconcerned with the merits of the case. He may have supervised the scourging, and certainly it was his voice of authority that drafted Simon and compelled him to the high and noble act that became the fondest memory of the Cyrenean's later years.

This centurion was a witness of strange events. He was used to the railing and the blasphemy that came from the lips of the crucified. He had heard the suffering victims curse Rome and shout anathemas upon the executioners. His ears were calloused to the condemnations that came with the agonized breath of those who twisted in the misery of crucifixion. But never had he heard such words as fell from the mouth of this One who prayed in gentle tones for those who slew Him!

Subconsciously keyed to withstand the first words of bitterness and anger he expected would be uttered by the chief Victim of that day, his entire mentality was startled when those suffering lips opened to say, "Father, forgive them; they know not what they do."

While his troubled heart pondered the almost superhuman courage and gentleness displayed in those words, the light of the sun began to dim, as the face of the earth turned gray and then black under the supernatural darkness. For three hours the sun hid its face from a planet that could tolerate such an awful deed. The tragedy being the darkest in all history, the sky itself joined in with a physical reaction and added blackness to the scene.

We have often heard skeptics dismiss this evidence with the contemptuous phrase, "Probably an eclipse." This explanation is sheer folly. The ancients were very familiar with the phenomena of eclipses. The Chaldeans had kept records of their occurrence as far back as 2200 B. C. The ancients had worked out a systematic table of the cycles and tandems of eclipses, and in that somewhat more enlightened day of Roman culture they would probably have kept records that would have told them that this one was due. We must not forget, also, that an eclipse only obscures the light, and that for swiftly passing minutes.

This darkness *was total, and it lasted for three hours.* The date of the crucifixion is fairly well established, and there is no astronomical record that an eclipse was due at the time when this darkness fell upon the earth. The simple explanation, and the only one that can be received as a fact, is that creation thus mourned the suffering of its Creator-God. So to the bewildered mind of this enlightened Roman, that unnatural darkness brought a tremendous appeal.

Then, also, there hung in the Temple the famous veil that was the pride and boast of all Israel. The Romans were inveterate sightseers; and whenever they entered a new land, they hunted works of art that might be wrested from the conquered and carried home to grace their own palaces and pavilions.

Unquestionably, this man knew of that woven veil in the Temple. It was made of finely twined linen, blue, purple, and scarlet. It was embroidered with the figures of cherubim, and it was the pride of that ancient city.

Now, suddenly, a whisper begins to spread through the mob, and their voices are hushed in wonder. The watchful captain, to whom there was committed not only the crucifixion of the famous Prisoner but the peace of the city as well, noted the fear of the people. When he inquired for the reason, he was told by awe-stricken voices that the veil of the Temple had been rent in twain. Upon the natural question as to the identity of the one who had done this deed of vandalism, the shivering priests replied that no human hand was involved; the veil was rent from the top down! No man could have reached the top of that veil; no human arm had power to tear it!

While the centurion pondered this thought in his mind, the quivering earth began to twist beneath his feet.

The rending rocks lent their doleful diapason to the mournful song of murder and death, as the earth shuddered at the sickening sight of God being slain by sinful hands.

To cap the climax, the dead came forth!

Matthew has told us that at this supernatural demonstration of God's power as the earth was rent, 'the bodies of many saints that slept arose, and were seen in Jerusalem,' after the resurrection of Jesus.

This, of course, was but the fulfillment of another Old Testament type, that of the "firstfruits." When the grain had been planted and God in

His beneficence had brought a rich harvest, a handful of the increase was offered to God as a significant confession that the whole belonged to Him. One was planted; many were reaped! So the Lord Jesus was able to ascend into the presence of God with a handful brought from the dead, as type of the coming harvest.

The Centurion's Emotional and Verbal Response to Calvary

The mighty impact of these amazing events could not fail to have a tremendous influence upon the superstitious mind of this powerful Roman.

He feared!

This veteran of Rome recognized the supernatural element in all these events and cried out in startled, spontaneous tones, "Truly this was the Son of God!"

This was not the natural cry of a pantheist. There was no more complete pantheon in all antiquity than that of Rome. To her own vast number of deities, she added the acceptable gods of all the peoples whom she conquered. The proper phrase from a pantheist would have been, "Truly this was a son of a god." This cry, however, was particular and specific. The centurion designated the dying Man as "*the* Son of God."

The voice of the centurion echoes today in the heart of every child of God who has ever studied with unprejudiced interest the record of this mighty Person!

The Modern Objection to the Centurion's Testimony

The modern objection to the testimony of that Roman is advanced by those who were not there. We could pass over all of the vapid vaporings of modernism by the simple refutation that people born eighteen hundred years after an event are not creditable authorities concerning that event. However, we would prefer to deal kindly but logically with the recent critics who would refute the centurion's testimony with this false assertion, "All men are sons of God."

This is not quite accurate. All men are sons of Adam. The New Testament tells us that Jesus "came unto his own, and his own received him not. But as many as received him, to them gave he power to *become* the sons of God." Nowhere in all Scripture, in philosophy or in science, is there a single line which says that you or any other man needs power to become a child of Adam. By the very fact of our birth, we inherit our nature by descent from Adam.

If all men are children of God, then what means that strange denunciation from the lips of Jesus, who confuted the critics of His day by saying, 'Ye are the children of your father, the devil, and the works of your father ye will do'? The simple summary of this entire doctrine, as it is set forth in the New Testament, may be reduced to this one phrase: We become the children of God *by faith in Jesus Christ.*

There is no such thing as an unregenerate Christian. Christianity begins for us when Jesus Christ is formed in our hearts through faith by the operation of the Holy Spirit. Thus we are born again.

The Unique Meaning of "Son" as Applied to Jesus

Of Jesus Christ, in another sense, the word "Son" is used. The Hebrew epistle states: 'Of no angel at any time saith he, Thou art my Son, this day have I begotten thee'—and if angels cannot claim this Sonship, how much less can men! We repeat that all human beings may become the children of God by regeneration, and that only by faith in Jesus. Whence, then, did Jesus get this power?

If we are children of God in the same sense that Jesus was, and we become such through Him, the Gospel becomes both futile and chaotic. If Jesus Christ became the Son of God by regeneration, then He also had a sinful and fallen nature, and we who follow after Him are still lost in the consequence of our own sin.

But of Jesus it is stated in John's famous passage that "God so loved the world that he gave his only begotten Son." The word in the Greek is *monogenes.* "Only begotten" is a very poor translation of that word. The word *monogenetos,* which is common in the Septuagint version, is used in the New Testament, as in Luke 7:12 and 8:42, and occurs only in connection with the Person of Christ, in such passages as John 1:14 and 1:18.

In all these the emphasis is upon the fact that as the "only" Son of God, He has no equal, and is able fully to reveal the Father. In the rich sources, however, that have come to us from archaeological investigations into the common meaning of the language of the New Testament, as it was upon the lips of the people in the early centuries, we find that the word John used, namely, *monogenes,* means "unique," or literally "only one of its kind." Since we have covered this discussion more extensively in another work, we merely call attention to the fact that those who were familiar with the Greek language when the New Testament was written, understood what John meant. To them it was clear that John was saying, "For God so loved the world, that he gave the only-one-of-its-kind Son, that whosoever believeth in him should not perish, but have everlasting life."

So there now comes to us and to this generation a voice from the first century that helps to bear out the testimony of the centurion and establish the fact to which he gave utterance.

No more important voice came from Calvary than the voice of this amazed Roman, whose spontaneous testimony was, "Truly this was the Son of God."

WITNESSES TO THE TRUTH OF THE CENTURION'S CRY

A mighty company of independent witnesses could be gathered to establish the truth of the cry of this centurion.

The Testimony of God the Father

It was expressly stated by God in the third chapter of Matthew, where in the record of the baptism of Jesus, we have the testimony of the Heavenly Father. It is there recounted that when Jesus was baptized, He went up straightway out of the water. The heavens were opened unto Him; and the Spirit of God descended like a dove and lighted upon Him. Then came an audible voice from Heaven saying, "This is my beloved Son, in whom I am well pleased."

The centurion, of course, was not present at that remarkable episode of the baptism of Jesus, to which the Saviour had submitted for the purpose of completely fulfilling all the forms and ceremonies of the law. So the centurion's cry is an additional proof of a fact that was pre-established by the voice of God Almighty.

Again, God spoke with almost this same utterance on the Mount of Transfiguration. Once more, men in the flesh were awed almost beyond their power to bear, when the bright cloud overshadowed them. Out of that cloud there came the Heavenly Voice which said, "This is my beloved Son, in whom I am well pleased; hear ye him." Although faint with fright at the time the phenomenon occurred, these men attested the credibility of the event in later times.

The first record of this Heavenly Voice was written by Matthew, who happily was a tax-collector. Humanly speaking, one of the shrewdest things that Jesus ever did for the sake of future generations was to call Matthew to be an historian of these events.

Matthew, after the fashion of that day, worked on what might be termed a commission, or a "cost-plus" basis. He was skilled in detecting every shrewd device for deceit that the ingenuity of man could concoct. No greater testimony to the honesty of the intent of Jesus could ever be erected than the fact that He took the skeptical, suspicious, highly trained Matthew to be a witness of all the miracles and phenomena of His amazing ministry. If Matthew attests a fact, it must be so.

We have also the corroborating testimony of Peter, who in his second Epistle states, "This voice which came from heaven we heard, when we were with him in the holy mount." Again we note the records of Mark and Luke, who testify to this same fact. So the law of witnesses was here abundantly satisfied. This law stated "that in the mouth of two or three witnesses every word may be established," and here we have four.

When Heaven opened and the voice of the God who was the Father of Jesus Christ spoke to establish the Sonship of Jesus, the message came in almost the same words that the centurion used.

Certainly the kinship with God accorded to Jesus by the centurion was often and specifically claimed by the Lord Himself. The whole Gospel as nearly as it may be summarized in a few words, is found in John 3:16-18. Three times in those three verses Jesus made the claim that He was the unique, the only-one-of-its-kind, Son of God. In verse 16 we read, "He gave his only begotten Son." Again, in verse 17, it is written "that God sent not his Son into the world to condemn the world." Verse 18 expresses it in these words, "He that believeth not is condemned already, because he hath not believed in the name of the only begotten Son of God."

The Testimony of Christ Himself

Even more specific was the claim of Jesus to this high and holy relationship in the episode that followed the healing of the blind man in the Temple. When this man, who had felt the power of Christ, was cast out of the Temple for praising the Lord Jesus who had restored him, the Saviour met him outside. To the one who had been healed the Lord Jesus said, "Dost thou believe on the Son of God?"

The blind man replied, "Who is he, Lord, that I might believe on him?"

In simple words Jesus said to him in substance, "He is speaking to you now." Whereupon the healed, believing man fell at His feet and, confessing his faith, worshiped the One who had proved His deity by the use of miraculous power.

Perhaps the most striking of all the episodes wherein Jesus Christ claimed the thing the centurion confessed was when He stood on trial before Caiaphas. When Caiaphas framed his shrewd question, "Tell us plainly, Art thou the Son of the Blessed?" Jesus knew that death would be the penalty for an affirmative reply. To the Jew, this was blasphemy. Caiaphas knew that if he could wring a reiteration of this oft-repeated claim from the lips of the famous Prisoner, the sentence of death was inevitable. So when the Lord Jesus drew Himself up in calm assurance and said, 'Thou sayest; I am,' it was the simple, dignified, but amazing acceptance of death for testifying to that which He could not deny, namely, the Sonship which the centurion later confessed.

The Testimony of the Apostle Paul

The voice of the centurion is also supported by the united witness which is maintained by all New Testament writers. The writers of the four Gospels are not the only ones who have a strong testimony concerning the relationship that Jesus had to the Heavenly Father. The claim that Jesus made, that He was one in essence and in substance with God, is often made by Paul, who said such things as these:

"Concerning **his Son**, Jesus Christ our Lord."

"Declared to be **the Son of God** with power."

"For God is my witness, whom I serve with my spirit in the gospel of **his Son**."

"We were reconciled by the death of **his Son**."

"God sending **his own Son** in the likeness of sinful flesh."

"He that spared not **his own Son**, but delivered him up for us all."

"Even the **Father of our Lord Jesus** Christ."

"God is faithful, by whom ye were called into the fellowship of **his Son** Jesus Christ our Lord."

"For the **Son of God**, Jesus Christ who as preached among you."

"Blessed be God, even the **Father of our Lord** Jesus Christ."

"I live by the faith of the **Son of God**, who loved me."

"God sent forth **his Son**, made of a woman."

"For this cause I bow my knees **unto the Father** of our Lord Jesus Christ."

"We give thanks to God, **the Father** of our Lord Jesus Christ."
"God, who at sundry times . . . spake . . . unto the fathers by the prophets, Hath in these last days spoken unto us by **his Son.**"
"Unto **the Son** he saith, Thy throne, O God, is for ever and ever."
"Seeing then that we have a great high priest . . . **Jesus the Son of** God."

The Testimony of Christ's Resurrection

The theme of the centurion's cry which was also expressly **stated** by God, specifically **claimed** by Jesus, and **maintained** by all New Testament writers, was further demonstrated by the resurrection of Jesus from the dead. If the centurion was right, and it was the Son of God who died on the cross that day, it is folly to presume that He could ever have remained dead.

We go back in memory to the events of His ministry, and we hear the crowd requesting a sign of His deity. Once more we hear the Saviour say, 'There shall no sign be given you, save the sign of the prophet Jonah. As Jonah was three days and three nights in the belly of the sea-monster, so must the Son of Man be three days and three nights in the heart of the earth.' Specifically, when the mob said to Jesus, "Prove your deity," He retorted, "I will, by rising from the dead."

That this proof was acceptable is evidenced by the strange conduct of Thomas. He has often been called, "Doubting Thomas," and the name is applied somewhat in derision. We think that the condemnation of this man is scarcely just. Thomas was evidently a man of "scientific" leaning. He wanted proof for everything that he was asked to believe. The evidence of the resurrection would never have been complete without the specific, skeptical, physical demands advanced by this man Thomas.

In no uncertain terms he said, "You can't fool me. I will never believe that the dead body we took down from Calvary and laid in the tomb has come to life again, unless I see the physical marks of the crucifixion in a living fleshly form." When, therefore, Jesus appeared to Him after His resurrection, He offered Thomas the physical evidence of the nail holes in His hands and feet and the gap of the spear in His riven side. Thomas received with a triumphant shout this proof of the resurrection by saying, "My Lord and my God!"

This indeed was the thought that the centurion had voiced, "This was the Son of God."

So closely is the fact of the resurrection allied with the proof of the deity of Jesus, that faith in this fact logically becomes a premise of salvation. We are told in the Romans Epistle that two things are essential to those who would become the children of God by virtue of regeneration. The quotation, familiar to all, is found in this verse: "That if thou shalt confess with thy mouth the Lord Jesus, and shalt believe in thine heart that God hath raised him from the dead, thou shalt be saved."

If Jesus Christ was the Son of God, He could not stay dead. If He did rise from the dead, He then attested His every claim to absolute deity and thus established His power to save the lost!

The voice of the centurion is the voice of the united company of the truly believing in the church of Jesus Christ today. No man or woman of real understanding could survey the events of Calvary and come to any other conclusion than that which throbs in the voice of the centurion, **"Truly this was the Son of God!"**

(From *Winona Echoes*, 1936.)

BILLY SUNDAY
1862-1935

ABOUT THE MAN:

William Ashley (Billy) Sunday was converted from pro baseball to Christ at twenty-three but carried his athletic ability into the pulpit.

Born in Ames, Iowa, he lost his father to the Civil War and lived with his grandparents until age nine when he was taken to live in an orphanage. A life of hard work paid off in athletic prowess that brought him a contract with the Chicago White Stockings in 1883. His early success in baseball was diluted by strong drink; however, in 1886 he was converted at the Pacific Garden Mission in Chicago and became actively involved in Christian work.

Sunday held some three hundred crusades in thirty-nine years. It is estimated that a hundred million heard him speak in great tabernacles, and more than a quarter million people made a profession of faith in Christ as Saviour under his preaching. His long-time associate, Dr. Homer Rodeheaver, called him "the greatest gospel preacher since the Apostle Paul."

Billy Sunday was one of the most unusual evangelists of his day. He walked, ran, or jumped across the platform as he preached, sometimes breaking chairs. His controversial style brought criticism but won the admiration of millions. He attacked public evils, particularly the liquor industry, and was considered the most influential person in bringing about the prohibition legislation after World War I.

Many long remembered his famous quote: "I'm against sin. I'll kick it as long as I've got a foot, and I'll fight it as long as I've got a fist. I'll butt it as long as I've got a head. I'll bite it as long as I've got a tooth. And when I'm old and fistless and footless and toothless, I'll gum it till I go home to Glory and it goes home to perdition!"

Those who heard him never forgot him or his blazing, barehanded evangelism.

The evangelist died November 6, 1935, at age 72. His funeral was held in Moody Church, Chicago, the sermon by H. A. Ironside.

XII.

The Faultless Christ

BILLY SUNDAY

(As preached at Richmond, Indiana, 1922.)

"I find no fault in him."—John 19:4.

Some things must be faultless in order to be valuable.

The value of a diamond depends on its quality, not its quantity. When I was in New York I went down to Tiffany's. Picking up the famous Tiffany diamond, I asked, "How much is that worth?"

"One hundred thousand dollars."

I picked up a rope of pearls. "How much is this worth?"

"Two hundred thousand dollars."

I picked up a string of black pearls found over in southern California. "How much is that worth?"

"Eighty-five thousand dollars."

I picked up a little two-carat pigeon-blood ruby. "How much is that worth?"

"Five thousand dollars."

One of the most valuable stones in the world, as well as the rarest, is the pigeon-blood ruby. Only ten percent of the diamonds on the market are what they call first class or first water. The others are either a little off in color, size, or shape, or have a flaw that reduces their value.

We have a pure food law which says that nothing adulterated shall be in composition of food, because that would jeopardize our health.

To be valuable, a horse must be without a flaw. If he kicks or runs away, has the heaves, is blind, or epizootic, those are flaws, making him less valuable.

To be a masterpiece, a picture must be flawless. With a flaw, its value is reduced.

A man may be known by five things:

First, his character—what he is.

Second, his conversation—what he says.

Third, his conduct—what he does.

Fourth, his contributions—what he gives.

Fifth, his creed—what he believes.

Love is the greatest thing in the world. Character is the grandest. It will remain when all things else are taken away. You can't lose character. It will stay when money is gone, when your friends forsake you. You can burn up money, your house, your clothes; but you can't burn up your character. It won't blow away. It can't be lost.

You can't buy character. A reputation may be lost in one act of your life which has taken a lifetime to build up.

Character needs no epitaph on its tombstone. You may bury a man, but his character will beat the hearse back from the cemetery. He will walk the streets long after his name has been obliterated by time from the tombstone. Men who lived in this city years and years ago—you have forgotten their names, but they are still living, either reproduced in a benediction or a curse.

Character has to be flawless; and I bring before you Jesus Christ.

Can You Find Flaw in His Claim?

He claimed to be the Son of God. Can you prove that that claim was false? I challenge you to find any flaw in that claim. Didn't He talk like the Son of God should have talked? Didn't He talk like you would have had you been the Son of God? Did He say anything that you wouldn't have said had you been the Son of God?

Did any of His recorded words show that He had no right to say what He said, or do what He did? Can you find any utterances that are out of place in the Son of God? Doesn't your own heart say that every word Jesus Christ said was true?

He declared God to be what every true heart wants God to be. He declared that God loves men and was willing to forgive men who had gone astray if they would repent. Can you find any fault with that? Isn't that what you feel that God must be in order to be God?

No matter what you have done, God says, "All I am waiting for you to do is to express your sorrow for that sin; then forgiveness, full, free, perfect and eternal is yours."

Every word shows that God is good, merciful, patient, forbearing.

There is not a word said about God's anxiety to punish. He wants to make us all good. Can you find any fault with that?

Do you object to the physician who wants to make you well? Do you object to anybody wanting to do something that will make you tell the truth? Do you object to anybody wanting you to be sober?

Why does a man refuse to be a Christian, refuse to receive Christ? God has no pleasure in the death of the wicked. God knows that if a man dies a sinner, he will go directly to Hell. God has no pleasure in the death of the wicked, because He knows the wicked man isn't ready to die. Not at all! God sent Jesus into the world, not to condemn the world, for the world was condemned before Jesus Christ came, but to open up a plan of redemption to save the world.

I didn't come here to preach anything to condemn you; you were already condemned before you ever heard of me. If you came in here tonight to be saved, I am not coming here to condemn you but to preach to you, to tell you what to do to be saved.

You came in here condemned; you may go out without condemnation. Jesus didn't come to condemn the world; He came to save, to give a man a chance to be redeemed. If God loves the world and if this world has gone into sin, God must do something to win it back to prove that He does love it.

If you will take the New Testament and study what Jesus said about the Father, you will say every word of that is true.

He said the time would come when God would wipe out this world and separate the good from the bad, like the shepherd separates the sheep from the goats. Well, we do that same thing. We separate the sick from the well, the coal from the slag, the wheat from the chaff, the criminals from those who will keep the law.

We all know God could not be God and pen the good and bad up in the same place. Heaven wouldn't remain Heaven. This earth would be Heaven if there were no sin here, and this earth would be Hell if there were no Christianity here.

This old earth is neither Heaven nor Hell because it has some good and some bad in it. If it were all good, it would be Heaven; if it were all bad, it would be Hell. So the only thing that makes it decent to live in is due to the salvation through Jesus Christ. If Jesus Christ had said that God wouldn't or couldn't put the good and bad in different places, that would have been enough to convince me that He was a fraud and not the Son of God.

Can you find any fault with His condition?

Can You Find Anything Which Jesus Did That Dishonored God?

Can you find anything Jesus did or said that was dishonoring to God? Can you put your finger on anything that was out of place? I challenge you to do it. What did Jesus Christ ever do that wasn't for the benefit of human beings?

What has Jesus Christ ever asked you to do that wasn't for your good? What did you ever refuse to do that God wanted you to do that you weren't a fool for refusing? God doesn't want you to do anything that isn't for your betterment. So if you want the best there is, God has it waiting for you.

And did Jesus Christ ever injure anybody in thought or deed? No! Did Jesus ever lie? No! Did He ever misrepresent? No! Did He ever say, "That's all wool," when it was half cotton? No! Did He ever say it was imported when it was made in Chicago? No! Did He ever raise a finger against anything that was good? No!

If Jesus Christ lived in this city, do you think He would stay here for five weeks and not poke His head around this tabernacle? No! Did Jesus ever turn His back on anybody in trouble? No! Did He ever refuse to help anybody who asked Him? No! Wherever He went lives were made happier, men and women were made purer.

Can you find any fault with that in the transforming power of God?

Over in the trenches of France was a French soldier named Maurice. The Y.M.C.A. was distributing little Testaments of John printed in French. Somebody had thrown away a copy and Maurice found it one day in the mud under his feet in the trenches. He picked it up and read it.

In the back was a place where he could sign his name to indicate he was accepting Jesus Christ as his Saviour. He read this Gospel of John and signed his name there.

Maurice had a cousin in the trenches named Jacques, an infidel. On his day off he came to visit Maurice. When he came in, he said, "Maurice, what's the matter with you? Your face shines so."

"I found Jesus Christ and here's where I found Him," was his reply. He handed Jacques this little Testament. "Here's where I found Him."

Jacques read it and was also converted. He said, "I could answer to my own satisfaction all arguments about God, all arguments about Christ, all arguments about Heaven, all arguments about Hell; but I couldn't answer the argument of the bright, cheerful look on Maurice's face."

Christ Proved God's Love

Wherever the Gospel of Christ goes, it makes lives brighter and shines up this old world. He said that God loved everybody, and He went about trying to show that to be true.

He cured the sick. He opened the eyes of the blind. He unstopped the ears of the deaf. He raised the dead. He cleansed the leper. He helped everybody who asked Him, and He helped a good many who didn't ask Him. The only one who ever went away with a sorrowful heart was the rich young ruler who would not repent. And if you go away with a sorrowful heart, it is your own fault.

If you will let Him help you, you will be joyful. This young fellow thought he had so much that he could get along well without Jesus.

Jesus never attended a funeral, never followed anybody to the grave. He came that they might have life and that they might have it more abundantly.

The sober man has life more abundantly than the drunkard. The honest man has life more abundantly than the thief. The virtuous one has life more abundantly than the one living in vice. The believer in Christ has life more abundantly than the infidel who doesn't believe in Christ.

Once when Moody was asked to preach a funeral sermon, he tried to find in the Bible what Jesus said and did at a funeral for his standard to go by. But to his surprise and delight he found that Jesus Christ broke up every funeral procession that He ever met by raising the dead. He turned the house of sorrow into joy, tears into laughter. Can you find any fault with that?

"I find no fault in him." Don't you wish He had come to your house before the hearse had called? Don't you wish He had come and raised the dead and put your loved one back in your arms?

"I find no fault in him." Do you consider yourself honorable and decent to favor what Christ is against? Do you think you ought to be respected by decent people when you are in favor of everything that Jesus Christ is against? You forfeit the right there, whether you be a millionaire or a hobo.

Jesus Against All Wrong

Has anybody cheated or defrauded you? Jesus Christ is against it.

Has anybody lied about you? Jesus Christ is against it.

Are you in favor of honesty? So is Jesus. Are you in favor of purity? So is Jesus. Do you believe that every man ought to have a fair equivalent in return for the brain or muscle that he gives in working? So does Jesus.

Do you believe that every employer ought to pay honest wages to every employee? So does Jesus. Do you believe that every working man ought to give honest, square work for the wages he is paid? So does Jesus.

Do you believe that capital ought to give labor a square deal? So does Jesus. Do you believe that labor ought to give capital a square deal? So does Jesus.

Do you believe there ought to be thirty-six inches in every yard? So does Jesus. Do you believe there ought to be four pecks in every bushel? So does Jesus. Do you believe there ought to be twelve inches in every foot? So does Jesus. Do you believe there ought to be two thousand pounds in every ton? So does Jesus. A hundred cents in every dollar? So does Jesus.

Jesus is against all crookedness. Are you? Jesus is against all dishonesty. Are you? Jesus is against everything where men feed and fatten and gormandize upon the misfortunes and sins of others.

Jesus Christ never dealt in generalities. He never went around Robin Hood's barn to get at a point; invariably He cut across lots; and when He got there, nobody had any doubt who He meant or what He meant.

If Jesus Christ should become pastor of one of the leading churches in this city and talk as straight to them as He did to the treacherous Jerusalem set in the Temple, I wonder how long He would hold His job? Some of these elders would be pulling their long whiskers. Then the prudential committee would get on its high horse, and the vestrymen would hit the ceiling. Then the stewards who are always making a mess out of the stew, and the church dignitaries who are digging for the Devil, would kick.

See His rebuke to the Jerusalem crowd and see if He was always the weak, two-by-four, three-carat, sissified Jesus a lot of people are always trying to picture Him to be.

I am disgusted with those who try to picture Jesus Christ as though He were a doughfaced nonentity. He was the bravest preacher who ever breathed. Why, that invective in Matthew 23 stings in words like a whiplash or a cat-o'-nine-tails; and as a piece of concentrated damnation, it is without a peer in literature! Why, the hot metaphors, whatever they are, race upon the heels of one another, surging out of an ocean of wrath, speeded by a master's command as they were hurled into the sins and passions of the day!

He shot His preaching into the biggest guns of the synagogues. He said:

"Woe unto you! You devour widows' houses and for a pretence, you make longwinded prayers and you will have the greater damnation.

"Woe unto you! You do everything to make a proselyte, and when you have made him, he is twofold more the child of Hell than one of you.

"Woe unto you! You shut up the kingdom of Heaven against men and you won't go in yourself and you are keeping everybody else out. You are a dog in the manger. You neither eat the hay nor let the horse have it.

"Woe unto you! You have done the small things, but you neglect the weightier matters of the law, such as mercy, equity, truth, love thy neighbor as thyself.

"Woe unto you! Oh, you are like the outside of a cup. You look nice and clean on the outside, but you are full of rottenness.

"Woe unto you! you whited sepulchres. You are like a grave. You look fine on the outside, but on the inside you are full of rottenness and dead men's bones.

"Woe unto you! you fools and blind.

"Woe unto you! You strain at a gnat and swallow a camel.

"Woe unto you! you generation of vipers. Woe unto you! how can you escape the damnation of Hell. You ought to be in jail, the whole dirty bunch of you."

Can you find any fault with that? That is when Jesus handed them the hot end of the poker. Jesus stood before the church, all the cultured highbrows of the day, and said those things. That's Jesus talking!

Now He never has a harsh word for a penitent sinner nor a good one for a Pharisee. And when a man claims to be a Christian, he ought to do what Jesus would do.

If a man puts out a sign announcing himself a carpenter or plumber, I expect him to carry on the business that he announces by the sign. I don't go to a barber shop to get an automobile, nor to a butcher shop to buy a suit of clothes, nor to a jewelry store to get potatoes and celery.

Something is expected of a Christian that isn't expected of a godless man. I expect something more of an elder than I do of a brewer. For a man to be a member of a church and have nothing in his life or conduct which resembles Jesus Christ is as much out of place as a Y.M.C.A. over a brewery or over a house of ill fame. You are expected to carry on the things that you announce under the sign.

That is the reason I go to a barber shop to get a haircut, and to a jewelry store to get my watch fixed. When a man hangs out a sign and says he is a Christian, I have a right to expect something.

No Fault With His Courage, His Faith

There is something about His courage that wins our applause. It compels our admiration, commendation, emulation and several other "-ations" that I can't think of now.

Did Jesus ever show the white feather? No! No! When the mob charged upon Him with clubs and stones and the disciples forsook Him and fled, He stood His ground as immovable as Gibraltar. They spat upon Him, stoned Him, damned Him, scourged Him.

He bore Himself like a king when He stood before old Pilate. Not once did He turn pale. Not once did He show concern or fear. Not once, my friends, can you find any fault with Him.

The first recorded word of Jesus was when he was twelve years old. "Wist ye not that I must be about my Father's business?" His last recorded words were on the cross, "It is finished."

When at thirty-three He hung on the cross, and in the twenty-one years crowded in between the first recorded words and the last recorded words, nothing found place in His life that wasn't for the glory of God and the good of humanity.

"I find no fault in him," said his bitter enemy, Pilate. If there had been, you may be sure, old Pilate would have dug it out, for he was looking for a chance to put something over on Him if he could. No, "I find no fault in him."

He had faith in His Father. Faith says, "God did it. Christ says it; I believe it; that settles it."

He had faith in His Father. A man's faith links him to God. I am chained to God not by money, culture or such things, but by faith.

Take what faith you have and start out. If you know enough now to start and if you use it, you will get more.

Mind you, there isn't one man in business today who didn't start poor. Did J. P. Morgan start rich? No! Did Rockefeller? No! Did Judge Gary? No! Did Vanderbilt? No! George Perkins? No! Peter Armour of Chicago?

No! Marshall Field? No! Field used to be a traveling man who sold goods for $100.00 a month.

Andrew Carnegie started for $1.00 a week as a stockboy in a mill; Charley Schwab crawled out of the dirt, soot and coal of Homestead and Bradford. None started rich.

Take what you have, use it and you will get more. Start with your faith, use it and it will grow.

Farm your faith like a seed. Put it into the ground and you will get more. Drop a kernel of corn into the ground and it will produce a hill of corn. A hill on an average will produce two ears. An ear of corn will produce 800 kernels. Twice eight is 16, so I get 1,600 times more than I put into the ground.

Farm your faith. Start with what you have and God will give you more all the way through. Without faith there wouldn't be a factory, nor a railroad, nor any trucking. We can't do business without it.

Almost all the business in this country is done on credit—credit cards, drafts, mail orders and other credit devices.

The Milwaukee railroad made an extension from South Dakota to Puget Sound, costing hundreds of millions of dollars. They hadn't sold a ticket, hadn't contracted for a pound of freight. They had only faith, faith to believe that people would travel and that freight would be shipped over the road.

Without faith there would have been no electricity. Thomas Edison thought he could find a better way to illuminate the home than with a tallow candle.

Without faith there wouldn't have been the automobile. Henry Ford started out in the Y.M.C.A. in Detroit in 1908 in the little department there where they had sort of a forge. He went in there and went to work. He had an idea. He thought he could put together an automobile, and he did. He had to get money. One after another refused him. Finally he found a man who backed him with $10,000.00. The fellow had faith.

Everything you see today in business started with faith. Begin with what faith you have and see how it will grow in this old world.

There is not one who didn't first believe before he ever invented. Fulton had visions of his steamboat before she ever puffed up the Hudson. Elias Howe had visions of a sewing machine before it took tangible form. Whitney had visions of his cotton gin before he ever invented it.

Men got to South America, to South Africa, to the Klondike, to Australia, because they were told they could; and they believed they could find gold. Faith gives us energy and backbone. Faith is the grandest word in the lexicon of any man or woman.

Had Abraham not had faith in God, there would have been no Jewish nation. God would have started the nation with somebody else. But Abraham, father of the nation, believed; and so we have the Jewish nation today.

Faith is the hand by which my soul touches God. I can't touch God with my hand. I can touch you. You are flesh, bones, and so am I. God is a Spirit. I can't touch God with my hand. I can touch Him with my faith. Faith is a sort of wireless telegraphy which communicates with the sky. Faith is to the soul what the law of gravitation is to the world.

I hold this book in my hand; when I take my hand away, it falls. What made it fall? Gravitation yanks everything toward the center of the earth. Faith is to my soul what the law of gravitation is to the world. The law of gravity pulls everything down toward the center of the earth. So faith changes the center toward which spiritual gravity pulls. Instead of swearing, we pray. Instead of being impure, we are pure. Instead of being drunk, we are sober. Instead of lying and cheating, we are honest. Instead of going to the saloon, we go to church. Instead of going to Hell, man can go to Heaven. Faith changes the center. So when the power of Christ comes in, these other things go out.

Now you do these things, and now you go here. The power that pulls you there is faith in Jesus Christ. So gravity pulls everything to the center of this old earth.

The Faultlessness of Jesus Christ

Can you find any fault with what He said about Himself? Can you put your finger on any spot that He didn't make good? He said, "I am the light of the world." You take out of this world all that Jesus Christ has done for it, and it wouldn't be worth a rummage sale. If you take out of this world all that Jesus has for it, you are taking down every church; you close up every Sunday school; you disband every charitable organization. Everything that is done for the benefit of humanity comes through the principles of Jesus Christ.

Go to the library and select every book which contains a verse of poetry or prose reference to Jesus Christ and take them and turn them into ashes; what is left?

Then go to the galleries of art and slash and cut and daub the achievements of man—Dore, Millet, Murillo, Michelangelo, Raphael, da Vinci, Rubens, Munkacsy's "Christ Before Pilate"; what do you have left?

Then go to the hospitals and throw the sick into the streets. Tear down the buildings, close up the asylums for the poor, the maimed, the blind, the halt, the old men and the old women, boys and girls.

Go to the conservatories of music, tear out all the songs, "Jesus, Keep Me Near the Cross," "Jesus, Lover of My Soul," "Pass Me Not, O Gentle Saviour," until the world stands voiceless, songless, and dumb; what do you have left?

Then go to the cemeteries; go from tombstone to tombstone; chisel out every verse that tells of the world to be. Sir Walter Scott had Old Mortality chasing around with chisel and mallet to make more distinct the partly obliterated epitaphs on the tombstone. Cut off every verse that your mother pillowed her head on when she swept out into Glory to meet Jesus Christ. Take out of this world all that Jesus Christ has ever done for it; what have you got left?

"I find no fault in him." A holy Christ for my Saviour, a holy Bible for my staff, a holy church for my field. "I find no fault in him." Hasn't He made good, my friends?

He said, "Believe on the Lord Jesus Christ, and thou shalt be saved" (Acts 16:31). You show me somebody who is saved who didn't believe in Jesus Christ, or one who ever will be saved when he didn't believe in Him.

We are always helped or hindered by our belief. Wrong belief makes everybody wrong. Right belief makes everything right. Belief should result in action which harmonizes with your belief.

If you believe wrong, you will act wrong. Your actions should be in harmony with your belief, and your belief may be father to your act. If you believe right, you will usually act right. Therefore, belief should result in actions in harmony with your belief.

"Oh," you say, "It doesn't make any difference what a man believes as long as he is sincere."

You are a fool! A man may sincerely believe he can handle nitroglycerine and it not hurt him; but if he monkeys with it, they will look for him with a spyglass, and take him up with a whisk broom and dustpan.

They say Sydney Harbor in Australia is one of the most beautiful harbors in the world. They have what is called North Head and South Head. In between those two heads is the entrance to the harbor; then the harbor runs off and dips down to the coastline and shuts up abruptly.

There is a lighthouse down there. One night when the steamer *Duncan Dunbar* was coming to make the harbor at Sydney it mistook the South Head for the North Head and steered in between these two, running over the rocks. It went down. Everybody was lost but three.

The captain was sincere, but he was wrong. His sincerity didn't save the lives of the fifty people on the steamer *Duncan Dunbar*.

A man who believes that God is his Father ought to live like his Father.

No Fault With His Atonement

He tasted death for every man. He did for every man what man couldn't do for himself.

Many years ago up in St. Paul, a man was tending bar. One day in came an old sidekick of his, the champion middleweight prizefighter of the Northwest. The bartender said, "Have a drink."

The man said, "No, I don't want it."

He said, "You don't want it?"

"No, I don't want it."

"Then what do you want to drink?"

"I don't want anything."

"Oh," said the bartender, "you mean you want to drink, but you won't."

"No, I don't want anything, nor do I want to drink."

"Are you taking the Keeley Cure?"

"No, I have something better than that."

"What is it?"

"It is a blood cure."

"What do you mean?"

"I have found Jesus Christ, and He saved me and has kept me sober for seven months."

"Is that so?" said the astonished bartender.

"Yes. Come up and I will tell you about it."

They went to the meetings. The bartender heard the story and gave his heart to Jesus Christ and resigned from tending a bar.

He started out, my friends, but the cops would get their eyes on him; then he would have to move on, for he had left a record behind him where he had done time.

He went straight and lived for God for years. Then he went to Chicago to one of our great lawyers, Luther Lann Mills, and said, "Will you give me a letter to Carter Harrison" (then the mayor of Chicago)?

The lawyer gave him the letter. He went to the mayor and said, "You have my measurements here in the police department. I am going square and I'd like to have all the records you have." So all the records against him were torn out of the police records.

Then he went to my friend, Billy Pinkerton, and said, "Billy, you have my records here and I'd like to have them. The police department of Chicago has torn out all their records. I have a letter to Carter Harrison." Then they wiped out every scratch of the pen they had against him in the detective bureau.

Then his picture was down at the Joliet penitentiary. So he wrote to get it. "You have my records and I'd like to have my picture and Bertillion records from there. I have found Jesus Christ and I am going straight." The warden wrote back, "You made the record; we didn't. You may have gotten your records from the police in Chicago, but you can't get them away from the State of Illinois."

He didn't know what to do, so he went to telling his story to everybody. He went to Battle Creek, Michigan, to take a rest at the sanitarium. Three governors were there—Altgeld of Illinois; Culbertson of Texas; Johnson of Mississippi.

He went to Mr. Altgeld of Illinois, and asked him to help him get the record away from Joliet. The governor said, "That's an unusual request. I don't know whether it can be done, but I will be glad to help anybody who wants to do right. But I will make no promise. Give me your address."

About a month later, he received a big fat envelope. Up in the corner it read: "Executive Mansion, Springfield, Illinois." He broke it open and it said, "It gives me great pleasure to comply with your request. I am enclosing all the records that were in Joliet against you. There is now not the scratch of a pen in any institution against you. I wish you well, and may God's blessing be upon you. And may you be a blessing to the world."

Go down to Hadley Mission and take my friend John Callahan by the hand. He is one of the cleanest-cut, most upright men who walks in shoeleather. I have known John for twenty years and he is as clean as a hound's tooth. He is 124 karats fine and worth one hundred cents to the dollar. I will back John to the limit.

Can you find any fault with that? That is what this Jesus does that I am talking about.

No Fault With His Promises

Can you find any fault with His promises? He said,

"Come unto me, all ye that labour and are heavy laden, and I will give you rest."

 Has He made good?

"And this is the will of him that sent me, that every one which seeth the Son, and believeth on him, may have everlasting life."

"Whosoever therefore shall confess me before men, him will I confess also before my Father which is in heaven."

"In my Father's house are many mansions; if it were not so, I would have told you. I go to prepare a place for you."

Robert Bruce said when he was king of Scotland, the English refused to acknowledge the claim. They came up against Sterling castle. Then Bruce and his followers fled.

Then the English opened their kennels and turned the bloodhounds loose and chased Bruce and his brave followers over the hills and through valleys. When Bruce and his followers came to the river, they plunged into the water, backtracked them, then climbed up the banks. The bloodhounds, with the tongues lolling from their mouths, came to the river; but the scent was lost, and they stood barking on the banks of the stream.

Oh, all the bloodhounds of Hell can bay on your track; but if you have plunged beneath that stream drawn from Immanuel's veins, you need not fear.

No Fault With His Teaching

"I find no fault in him." Can you find any fault with what His teaching has done for the world? Wherever His teaching has been accepted and believed, it has made the desert blossom as the rose. Homes have been made happy. Drunkards have been made sober. Tears have been dried on the cheeks. Mothers have been able to sleep.

Old libertines have been made pure. Blasphemers have been made to pray. Girls who sold their womanhood now go home with tears of repentance coursing down their cheeks. Men have been made true to their wives, and employers true to those who toil.

Before Jesus Christ came there wasn't a hospital on earth. There wasn't an asylum on earth. There wasn't a home for the aged or the infirm, or for the boys and girls. His teachings have caused mankind to care enough to build them, until today they are as thick as the sands on the seashore. That's what Jesus Christ did and is doing for the world.

"I find no fault in him." Before Jesus came, woman was a slave. She was looked upon as something having no soul. Today the respect and honor that is paid to womanhood is due to the restraining influence of Jesus Christ. You are an ungrateful wretch if you refuse to arise and put the crown upon the brow of Him who has brought such wonderful blessings to womanhood; and He has come to help all who need it.

A father and son were in the same company. At the close of the Battle of Franklin, when the roll was called, the son was missing. The father went out, stumbling over the dead and dying, calling, "John Harkman! John Harkman!"

Away in the distance he heard a faint voice. At last he stood beside his son. He dragged him back to the hospital, where he was nursed back to health and strength.

Jesus Christ's mission on earth was to bind up the broken heart and help those who needed help.

No Fault With His Peace

"I find no fault in him." Do you find any fault with His peace? "My peace," He said, "I leave with you."

Some men, when they die, leave their land to their children. Other men, when they die, leave a bad character to their children. And others, when they die, bequeath weak, anemic bodies to their children. Still others, when they die, bequeath idiotic minds to their children. Others bequeath to them tainted blood. But Jesus said, "My peace I leave with you."

I will give you something better than that. Some people couldn't wear any longer faces than they do, if they were dead sure God was dead. When they smile, they do it in a way that makes you think it hurts; and you are glad when they quit.

Some people who look like that are praying for the Lord to use them. You ought to pray God to help you stop looking sour, for He can't use a map like yours.

If Paul and Silas had gone to jail looking as sour as some folks do who come to the tabernacle, that Philippian jailer wouldn't have been converted yet. It is a great mistake to think that God wants you to look solemn when you put on your Sunday clothes and start for church.

This Faultless Christ Died for You

Years ago a great plague swept Paris, causing people to die by the thousands. It baffled the skill of the physicians of the day. Finally they held a consultation and agreed the only way to find out what it was, was for someone to make a diagnosis of one who had died. But who would do it? It meant sure death to that one who did.

The doctors sat in silence for half an hour, then a famous French surgeon arose and said, "Gentlemen, I will make the examination."

He wrote out his Will. He stepped into a room with the corpse of one who had died from the dreadful malady. He made his diagnosis, the result of which he wrote on paper and cast that into a jar of vinegar where all could read it.

In six hours the doctor was a corpse. But his diagnosis stopped the dreadful malady and saved the lives of perhaps thousands. A monument arose to perpetuate the sacrifice of the doctor for the people of Paris.

God tells me if I will accept Jesus Christ as my Saviour, I am saved. God tells me I am going to Heaven. I believe it. I don't bother about it but trust Him. His words are true.

I went to visit the Waltham watchworks. Down in the basement was what they call the master clock. It is surrounded by several thicknesses of wall and kept at a normal temperature the year 'round.

They have in there a thermostat automatically lighted by electricity. When the temperature reaches a certain degree, the light will go on; and when it gets to another certain degree, it will go out.

Now that clock is resting upon a foundation that goes down below the river. They have attached to it a little machine with a cylinder. On that is a piece of paper, and fastened on that is a fountain pen. As the clock ticks, that fountain pen makes a little mark on this cylinder.

Out yonder stands an observatory—one of the finest in the United States—resting upon a foundation that goes 50 feet below the bed of the river. Expert men, astronomers with a huge telescope, sit and watch the stars. As the stars go by, they push a button which records it with a fountain pen on another cylinder down in the basement near this great master clock.

Every twenty-four hours they compare these two cylinders. If the one made by the tick of the clock doesn't harmonize with the cylinder made by the astronomers, then the clock is wrong. The stars—never.

Let me tell you something! Do you regulate your life by the Bible? You are wrong! God—never. Adjust yourself and see what He will do.

If Jesus Christ were only a man, I would still cleave to Him and to Him only! But if Jesus Christ is God, and the only God, I will follow Him through Heaven, Hell, earth, sea and air! I find no fault in Jesus. My greatest joy will be to hear my Saviour say, "I find no fault with thee."

A steamer tied up at her wharf in Detroit. She had just come down from Toronto. After she had discharged her cargo, a drunken sailor was seen staggering up Woodward Avenue. He staggered on and on, up to the old White opera house. He said to the lady in the ticket office, as he reeled back and forth, "How do you do, lady? Is Jesus Christ here?"

She said, "No, sir, but we have His picture."

(In Philadelphia, one of John Wanamaker's homes had burned. He couldn't get out the master picture in its frame— "Christ Before Pilate" — so he cut it out of the frame and brought it out of the burning house to his store. He paid $75,000.00 for the original of Munkacsy's "Christ Before Pilate.")

The sailor said, "Jesus ain't here?"

"No, but His picture is."

"Maybe that's what Ma meant. When I left Toronto she made me promise I'd come down here and see Him. She said He was in here. How much is it?"

"A quarter," she said. So he reached down and dug up a quarter.

She asked, "Do you want a catalog?"

"What is that?"

She told him and he said, "Yes, I might as well get it. How much?"

"Ten cents." So he pulled out a dime and went in.

The ticket lady followed him to see what effect a painting of such grandeur would have upon a man of such evident illiteracy and sin.

He walked in and sat down with his hat on. He looked up to the picture and said, "Who is that fellow sitting up there in that chair with his hair cut short?"

She said, "That is Pilate, the Roman governor."

"Who are those fellows around there in those blue, red, yellow and green clothes?"

"Those are the Pharisees, there to accuse Jesus."

"Who is that fellow there with that spear in his hand and that thing on his head?"

"That is a Roman centurion, a soldier. He is keeping the mob back. They are trying to get at Jesus to kill Him."

"Who is that gang out there holding up their hands?"

"That is the mob. They are crying, 'Crucify Him! Crucify Him!' "

"Who is that fellow standing out there in the middle, with long hair and the white dress on and His hands tied?"

"That is Jesus."

"What has He done?"

"Nothing."

"Are they trying to put something over on Him?"

"Yes." And then she left him.

She went back in about ten minutes. Listen! His hat and catalog were on the floor. He had grabbed the back of the seat in front of him and buried his face in his hands. He was sobbing. Big tears were dropping on the floor.

She put her hand on his head and said, "What do you think about it?"

He looked up, wiped his eyes and nose with his sleeve and said, "Lady, I never—I never—thought anything about Him. I have damned Him all my life. I have been drunk so much of the time. But I know He is all right because Ma loves Him and He made her what she is. She prays to Him every day. She taught me, when I was a little boy, to say, 'Now I lay me down to sleep,' and I know He is all right. Lady, I am going to become a Christian and follow Him, too."

"I find no fault in him."

JOHN R. RICE
1895-1980

ABOUT THE MAN:

Preacher . . . evangelist . . . revivalist . . . editor . . . counselor to thousands . . . friend to millions—that was Dr. John R. Rice, whose accomplishments were nothing short of miraculous. Known as "America's Dean of Evangelists," Dr. Rice made a mighty impact upon the nation's religious life for some sixty years, in great citywide campaigns and in Sword of the Lord Conferences.

At age nine, after hearing a sermon on "The Prodigal Son," John went forward to claim Christ as Saviour. In 1916, with only $9.35 in his pocket, he rode off on his cowpony toward Decatur Baptist College. He was now on the road to becoming a world-renowned evangelist, although he was then totally unaware of God's will for his life.

There was many a twist and turn before Rice rode through the open door into full-time preaching—the army, marriage, graduate work, more seminary, assistant pastor, pastor—then FINALLY, where God planned to use him most—in full-time evangelism.

Dr. Rice and his ministry were always colorful (born in Cooke county, in Texas, December 11, 1895, and often called "Will Rogers of the Pulpit" because of their likeness and mannerisms)—and controversial. CONTROVERSIAL—and correctly so—because of his intense stand against modernism and infidelity and his fight for the Fundamentals.

Dr. Rice lived and died a man of convictions—intense convictions. But, like many other strong fighters for the Faith, Rice was also marked with a sincere spirit of compassion. Those who knew him best knew a man who loved them. In preaching, in prayer, and in personal life, Rice wept over sinners and with saints. But there is more . . . .

Less than seventy-one hours before the dawning of 1981, one of the most prolific pens in all Christendom was stilled. Dr. John R. Rice left behind a legacy in writing of more than 200 titles, with a combined circulation of over 61 million copies. And through October 1981, a total of 24,058 precious souls reported trusting Christ through his ministries, not counting those saved in his crusades nor in foreign countries where his literature has been translated.

And who but God knows the influence of THE SWORD OF THE LORD magazine which he started and edited for forty-six years!

And while "Twentieth Century's Mightiest Pen" —and man—has been stilled, thank God, the fruit remains! Though dead, he continues to speak.

XIII.

The Virgin-Born Saviour

JOHN R. RICE

"Therefore the Lord himself shall give you a sign; Behold, a virgin shall conceive, and bear a son, and shall call his name Immanuel." — Isa. 7:14.

"Now the birth of Jesus Christ was on this wise: When as his mother Mary was espoused to Joseph, before they came together, she was found with child of the Holy Ghost." —Matt. 1:18.

"Then said Mary unto the angel, How shall this be, seeing I know not a man? And the angel answered and said unto her, The Holy Ghost shall come upon thee, and the power of the Highest shall overshadow thee: therefore also that holy thing which shall be born of thee shall be called the Son of God." —Luke 1:34,35.

The Scriptures teach that the Lord Jesus was born with a human mother but without a human father. Mary was a virgin when Christ was conceived; she was still a virgin when He was born. The Holy Spirit came upon her, and she conceived the holy child Jesus. This is a blessed and vital teaching of the Bible.

Jesus was born of a woman so that He might be "the Son of man." If Christ were not virgin-born, then He is not God. If Christ were not virgin-born, then He could not be our Saviour. All Christianity stands or falls with the doctrine of the virgin birth.

If Jesus had a human father, then the book of Isaiah, the Gospel of Matthew, the Gospel of Luke and the Gospel of John are all false, for these clearly teach that the Saviour was begotten of God, not of a human father. There is no way to believe in the inspiration of the Bible if one denies its claim of this.

If Jesus were born of a human father and the Bible teaching that He was born of a virgin is untrue, then no sensible man would believe in His pre-existence with the Father as taught in the first chapter of John.

If He be not deity in human form, begotten of God, miraculously born, a supernatural being, no sensible person could believe that He is the Creator of the world, as claimed in Hebrews 1:2 and Colossians 1:16.

If Jesus be not a supernatural being, God in human flesh, therefore born of a virgin without a human father, then no sensible person could believe that He will be the final Judge of all the earth.

If Jesus had a human father and mother just as other men, then His death on the cross could not atone for the sins of mankind.

All Christianity, I say, stands or falls with the Bible doctrine of the virgin birth of Christ. The doctrine of the virgin birth and the doctrine of the deity of Christ are one and the same. The doctrine of the virgin birth and the doctrine of the blood atonement are so interrelated that they cannot be separated. They are Siamese-twin doctrines. Neither can stand without the other. The virgin birth of Christ and His Saviourhood are one and the same doctrine.

Then anybody who denies the virgin birth is an infidel. He has already rejected Christianity, already denied the inspiration of the Bible and the blood atonement of Christ. The man who denies the virgin birth may be counted a minister of the Gospel; but actually he is a brother of Bob Ingersoll, Tom Paine, and of every infidel, Christ-denier and Bible-hater.

If anyone says that the deity of Christ is not essential, then he does not even know what essential Christianity is. To deny the virgin birth is to deny Christ Himself!

I. THE VIRGIN BIRTH IS PLAINLY STATED
IN SCRIPTURE

That the mother of Jesus was a virgin when he was conceived, not having known any man carnally, and a virgin still when the Saviour was born, is as specifically and positively stated as any doctrine in the Bible. Please consider the following Scripture statements about the virgin birth.

1. *Isaiah prophesied the Saviour's virgin birth some 740 years before it happened!*

Isaiah 7:14 says, "Therefore the Lord himself shall give you a sign; Behold, a virgin shall conceive, and bear a son, and shall call his name Immanuel." The sign is given, as the preceding verse shows, to the whole house of David. A young woman was to conceive and bear a Son while she was yet a virgin; and He should be called Immanuel, meaning "God with us." This virgin-born Child was to be God incarnate, God dwelling for a little while with men!

2. *Matthew, the first Gospel, plainly teaches the virgin birth of Christ.*
Read the following beautiful account of how God explained to Joseph how his sweetheart Mary was to become the mother of our Lord.

"Now the birth of Jesus Christ was on this wise: When as his mother Mary was espoused to Joseph, before they came together, she was found with child of the Holy Ghost. Then Joseph her husband, being a just man, and not willing to make her a publick example, was minded to put her away privily. But while he thought on these things, behold, the angel of the Lord appeared unto him in a dream, saying, Joseph, thou son of David, fear not to take unto thee Mary thy wife: for that which is conceived in her is of the Holy Ghost. And she shall bring forth a son, and thou shalt call his name JESUS: for he shall save his people from their sins. Now all this was done, that it might be fulfilled which was spoken of the Lord by the prophet, saying, Behold, a virgin shall be with child, and shall bring forth a son, and they shall call his name Emmanuel, which being interpreted is, God with us. Then Joseph being raised from sleep did as the angel of the Lord had bidden him, and took unto him his wife: And knew her not till she had brought forth her firstborn son: and he called his name JESUS."—Matt. 1:18-25.

The traditional date of the writing of Matthew's Gospel is A. D. 37, probably four years after the crucifixion. Even modernists agree that the Gospel according to Matthew was the first one written. And this Gospel gives the longest and most detailed account of the virgin birth. It quotes Isaiah 7:14 and announces that that Scripture was fulfilled!

The simple explanation is that the Child in the womb of Mary was conceived by the Holy Ghost. God was literally the Father of our Lord Jesus Christ and so Jesus was "God with us"—Immanuel. The same Scripture announces that "thou shalt call his name JESUS: for he shall save his people from their sins."

A Christ not born of a virgin, a Christ with a human father and a natural conception and birth, could never be a saviour.

3. *The Gospel of Luke, written by "the beloved physician," Luke, also states the fact of the virgin birth.*
Read the following in Luke 1:26-38.

"And in the sixth month the angel Gabriel was sent from God unto

a city of Galilee, named Nazareth, To a virgin espoused to a man whose name was Joseph, of the house of David; and the virgin's name was Mary. And the angel came in unto her, and said, Hail, thou that art highly favoured, the Lord is with thee: blessed art thou among women. And when she saw him, she was troubled at his saying, and cast in her mind what manner of salutation this should be. And the angel said unto her, Fear not, Mary: for thou hast found favour with God. And, behold, thou shalt conceive in thy womb, and bring forth a son, and shalt call his name JESUS. He shall be great, and shall be called the Son of the Highest: and the Lord God shall give unto him the throne of his father David: And he shall reign over the house of Jacob for ever; and of his kingdom there shall be no end. Then said Mary unto the angel, How shall this be, seeing I know not a man? And the angel answered and said unto her, The Holy Ghost shall come upon thee, and the power of the Highest shall overshadow thee: therefore also that holy thing which shall be born of thee shall be called the Son of God. And, behold, thy cousin Elisabeth, she hath also conceived a son in her old age: and this is the sixth month with her, who was called barren. For with God nothing shall be impossible. And Mary said, Behold the handmaid of the Lord; be it unto me according to thy word. And the angel departed from her."

Here again we are told that Mary was a virgin, that she was engaged to Joseph. The problem of how she should bear a child without a human father troubled Mary, so the angel explained, "The Holy Ghost shall come upon thee, and the power of the Highest shall overshadow thee: therefore also that holy thing which shall be born of thee shall be called the Son of God." The virgin birth was essential were Christ to actually be the Son of God, that is, physically begotten of God.

Obviously the doctrine of the virgin birth is as clearly stated as any doctrine in the Bible.

II. VIRGIN BIRTH ALSO TAUGHT ELSEWHERE IN THE BIBLE

Isaiah, Matthew and Luke all expressly state that Christ was born of a virgin. But a number of other Scriptures, without using the term "virgin," teach that Joseph was not the father of Jesus and that therefore He was conceived of the Holy Ghost.

1. *The prophet Jeremiah foretold that Joseph could not be the father of Jesus.*

Here is a most interesting study. Jeremiah 22:30 says of Coniah (also called Jeconiah, Jechonias and Jehoiachin), "Thus saith the Lord, Write ye this man childless, a man that shall not prosper in his days: for no man of his seed shall prosper, sitting upon the throne of David, and ruling any more in Judah."

Only five verses below this statement that Coniah, or Jeconiah, should be counted childless, that none of his seed should prosper reigning upon the throne of David, the Lord tells us, "Behold, the days come, saith the Lord, that I will raise unto David a righteous Branch, and a King shall reign and prosper, and shall execute judgment and justice in the earth" (23:5). And in the following verse we are told that His name should be called "THE LORD OUR RIGHTEOUSNESS."

Although Coniah's seed should not reign and prosper on David's throne, the coming Messiah would come and reign on David's throne. So the coming Saviour could not be descended from Jeconias.

But what does this have to do with the virgin birth of Christ? Simply that Coniah, or Jechonias, was a direct descendant of King Solomon and King David and reigned in Judah until he was carried away captive to Babylon.

Now look at the genealogy of Joseph in Matthew 1:12, "And after they were brought to Babylon, Jechonias begat Salathiel . . . ." Then verse 16 continues the same genealogy: "And Jacob begat Joseph the husband of Mary, of whom was born Jesus, who is called Christ." Joseph was descended from Coniah (Jechonias); and if Joseph were the father of Jesus, then the Scripture says no one of this line should prosper, sitting upon the throne of David and ruling any more in Judah.

But in Luke 1:32,33 the Angel Gabriel told Mary about the Saviour, that great Son she should bear: "He shall be great, and shall be called the Son of the Highest: and the Lord God shall give unto him the throne of his father David: And he shall reign over the house of Jacob for ever; and of his kingdom there shall be no end."

During His earthly ministry, of course, Jesus did not reign in Judah nor over Jerusalem. But Jesus is coming again, and God will give Him the throne of His father David, and He will rule over the house of Jacob.

Revelation 5:10 says, "And hast made us unto our God kings and priests: and we shall reign on the earth." Revelation 20:6 says that those in the first resurrection "shall be priests of God and of Christ, and shall reign with him a thousand years." Christ is to reign on David's throne.

Was it clearly intended by the Holy Spirit who dictated the Scriptures that Jeremiah 22:30 should be used as proof that Jesus was not the son of Joseph? Obviously so. For after Jeremiah 22:30 says that no man of the seed of Coniah "shall prosper, sitting upon the throne of David, and ruling any more in Judah," the fifth and sixth verses thereafter say:

"Behold, the days come, saith the Lord, that I will raise unto David a righteous Branch, and a King shall reign and prosper, and shall execute judgment and justice in the earth. In his days Judah shall be saved, and Israel shall dwell safely: and this is his name whereby he shall be called, THE LORD OUR RIGHTEOUSNESS."

No seed of Coniah should reign and prosper in Judah; but Christ, "THE LORD OUR RIGHTEOUSNESS," *shall* reign and prosper on David's throne ruling over Judah and the whole earth! So Coniah, the ancestor of Joseph, could not be the ancestor of Jesus. Jesus was not born of Joseph!

2. *The genealogy of Jesus, through Mary, does not give Coniah (Jechonias) at all, proving that Jesus was descended from David through another line, not Joseph's line.*

We have mentioned the genealogy of "Joseph the husband of Mary," in Matthew 1:1-16. But the genealogy of Mary is in Luke 3:23-38. At first glance one might think that this was the genealogy of Joseph and wonder why the two were different. Matthew 1:16 says, "And Jacob begat Joseph the husband of Mary." But in Luke 3:23 we are told, "And Jesus himself began to be about thirty years of age, being (as was supposed) the son of Joseph, which was *the son* of Heli."

Actually the words "the son," used the second time in this verse, are in italics, meaning they were not in the Greek. There is no doubt that Joseph was son-in-law of Heli. The Gospel of Matthew speaks of Jesus as the King of the Jews, and so gives the genealogy of Joseph, His foster father, as an official record showing that, humanly speaking, He would be entitled to the throne of Israel. The Gospel of Matthew was more clearly directed to the Jews.

But the Gospel according to Luke pictures Jesus as the Son of man and gives His genealogy, not just to Abraham, the father of Jews, as does the genealogy in Matthew, but traces it all the way back to Adam! So the genealogy in Luke naturally gives the actual human parentage of Jesus, that is, His mother Mary and her ancestry.

The Scofield Reference Bible has this note on Luke 3:23:

In Matthew, where unquestionably we have the genealogy of

Joseph, we are told (1:16) that Joseph was the son of Jacob. In what sense, then, could he be called in Luke "the son of Heli"? He could not be by natural generation the son of both Jacob and Heli. But in Luke it is not said that Heli *begat* Joseph, so that the natural explanation is that Joseph was the son-in-law of Heli, who was, like himself, a descendant of David. That he should in that case be called "son of Heli" ("son" is not in the Greek, but rightly supplied by the translators) would be in accord with Jewish usage (cf. I Sam. 24:16). The conclusion is therefore inevitable that in Luke we have Mary's genealogy; and Joseph was "son of Heli" because espoused to Heli's daughter. The genealogy in Luke is Mary's, whose father, Heli, was descended from David.

Now note this interesting thing. The genealogy of Mary, and therefore the literal human genealogy of Christ, is not traced through Coniah (Jechonias), not even through King Solomon, but is traced through Nathan, another son of David (Luke 3:31)!

Jesus was actually, literally descended, through Mary, from King David. But He was not descended from Jechonias. God gave that additional proof in the Old Testament, before the Saviour was born, that Joseph could not be His father.

3. *The Scripture repeatedly speaks of Jesus as the only One who was begotten of God, "the only begotten Son of God."*

This clearly refers to the fact that Jesus was born of a virgin, with God as His Father. The Scripture tells us that "Jacob begat Joseph the husband of Mary" (Matt. 1:16), but many Scriptures tell us that God begot Jesus Christ. Psalm 2:7 prophesies the coming of the Saviour and says, "The Lord hath said unto me, Thou art my Son; this day have I begotten thee." All Bible students agree that that refers to Jesus Christ.

Now Jesus was in the very beginning with God. John 1:1-3 says, "In the beginning was the Word, and the Word was with God, and the Word was God. The same was in the beginning with God. All things were made by him; and without him was not any thing made that was made." If Jesus was in the beginning with the Father, then surely it could not be said that He ever had a beginning, in His pre-existent state with the Father.

So when we speak of Jesus as "the only begotten Son" of God, we refer to His human beginning.

On the mother's side we say that a child is conceived. On the father's side we say that the child is begotten. So when the Holy Spirit overshadowed Mary, God begot Jesus Christ; therefore He is called the only begotten Son of God. No one else was ever physically begotten by God, as Jesus was, so He is "the only begotten Son."

The first chapter of John has much to say about Jesus as the pre-existent Word of God, as the Creator of all things. "And the Word was made flesh, and dwelt among us, (and we beheld his glory, the glory as of the only begotten of the Father,) full of grace and truth" (vs. 14).

When the Word was made flesh, that is, when Christ was made flesh, then He was begotten of the Father; and what the beloved John is here saying by divine inspiration is that they, the disciples, beheld the glory of Christ, and could tell by His glory that He was deity, that He was physically begotten of God! John means that anyone who saw the glorified Saviour on the Mount of Transfiguration, and again after His resurrection, as well as all the days of His ministry, would have to agree that Jesus had no human father, but was begotten of God, conceived and born to a virgin.

It is true that once or twice the Bible speaks of Christians as begotten of God, but that is a figurative use of the term. Five times in the New Testament Jesus is called the *only* begotten Son of God: in John 1:14,18; 3:16,18; and I John 4:9.

So the Gospel of John and the first epistle of John unite with the books of Isaiah, Matthew and Luke in declaring the virgin birth of our Saviour!

4. *Another reference to the virgin birth of Christ is given in Jeremiah 31:22.*

There in a prophecy of the coming Saviour the prophet says, "How long wilt thou go about, O thou backsliding daughter? for the Lord hath created a new thing in the earth, A woman shall compass a man."

Certainly it would not be a new thing for a woman to conceive and bear a man-child. That is not what God means. He says, "The Lord hath created a new thing in the earth"—an entirely new thing: a woman without any human intervention, without knowing any man carnally, would "compass a man," that is, conceive, carry and deliver a man-child! That virgin birth of Christ would be a unique event, a wholly new thing. Certainly this must be a reference to the virgin birth of the coming Saviour.

III. THE VIRGIN BIRTH IMPLIED THROUGHOUT THE BIBLE

I have shown that the virgin birth is expressly stated in Isaiah, Matthew and Luke, and that it is taught elsewhere very clearly. But that is not all. The birth of Jesus without a human father and His deity as a result are implied throughout the Bible. I have mentioned three of the Gospels: Matthew and Luke expressly say that Jesus was born of a virgin, and John, that Jesus was the only person ever begotten of God, was God's only begotten Son.

And the Gospel of Mark leaves no room for doubt on this question. While it does not expressly state that Jesus was born of a virgin, it emphatically teaches that Jesus was the pre-existent Son of God, which necessarily means that He was not the son of Joseph.

Mark 1:1 says, "The beginning of the gospel of Jesus Christ, the Son of God." The first word that Mark has to say about the Saviour is that He is the Son of God! And the first chapter proceeds only to the eleventh verse before it reports God saying from Heaven, "Thou art my beloved Son, in whom I am well pleased."

All through the Gospel of Mark Jesus is spoken of as the miracle-working God in human form. That necessarily means that He was born of a virgin. Although Mark does not tell the story of the angel's coming to Mary and of the Saviour's miraculous conception and birth, that truth is implied throughout the Gospel.

So it is all through the Bible. In Isaiah 9:6 it is prophesied, "For unto us a child is born, unto us a son is given: and the government shall be upon his shoulder: and his name shall be called Wonderful, Counsellor, The mighty God, The everlasting Father, The Prince of Peace." Though this verse does not specially tell of the virgin birth of Christ, it calls Him, "The mighty God, The everlasting Father." That forever set Him apart from every man-child ever born of natural generation, and necessarily compels a belief in the deity of Christ.

Isaiah 53 tells of the atonement—how Christ bore our griefs and carried our sorrows, how He was wounded for our transgressions and bruised for our iniquities, how the chastisement of our peace was upon Him and how with His stripes we are healed.

If one Man can stand before God for the whole race of men; if one Man's suffering can pay the debt of all the sinners in the universe, then He is no ordinary man. He could be only a God-Man, God in human form, begotten of God in a virgin's womb. That is why all those who deny the virgin birth of Christ likewise deny His deity and deny His atoning death, His substitutionary sacrifice for our sins.

Throughout the Bible we are taught that Christ is the Creator who made all things and upholds all things now.

We are taught that He is to judge the world, and that the Father has committed all judgment to the Son (John 5:22; Acts 17:31).

We are told that the same Jesus who was crucified arose from the dead.

We are told that He ascended to Heaven, and then two angels promised that the same Jesus should return again (Acts 1:9-11).

Jesus Himself said, "If I go and prepare a place for you, I will come again, and receive you unto myself" (John 14:3). "In him dwelleth all the fulness of the Godhead bodily" (Col. 2:9).

The virgin birth is implied in every chapter in the Bible; so to deny the virgin birth of Christ is to deny that the Bible means what it says, to deny that it is the Word of God. To deny the virgin birth is to deny historic Christianity and turn one's back on the God of the Bible.

IV. OBJECTIONS TO THE VIRGIN BIRTH ANSWERED

Unbelievers, haters of the Bible and rejectors of Christ object to the Bible doctrine of the virgin birth. But their objections are not sensible, as investigation will prove.

1. *They say, "It is only mentioned in two or three places in the Bible."*

That is not true. We have shown that the virgin birth is clearly taught in Isaiah, Jeremiah, Matthew, Luke, John and the first epistle of John, and implied throughout the Scriptures everywhere. If it were only stated one time in the Bible, that would be enough for any Christian. But the virgin birth is as clearly taught as any Bible doctrine, and as often repeated.

2. *"Jesus Himself did not claim to be born of a virgin," says the modernist and infidel.*

That is not true. Those who deny the virgin birth are not scholarly, and they do not know what the Bible really teaches. Jesus clearly said, "For the bread of God is he which cometh down from heaven, and giveth life unto the world" (John 6:33); then He said, "I am that bread of life" (John 6:48). Jesus said that He came down from Heaven.

That could not be said of any other man in the world. That involved His pre-existence with God the Father and His deity, and necessarily presumes that God begot Him at His conception. Jesus plainly called Himself the "only begotten Son" of God (John 3:16). He was the only Man ever begotten physically by God.

Jesus told Nicodemus that He (Jesus) was "He that came down from heaven, even the Son of man which is in heaven" (John 3:13). To the Pharisees, Jesus said, "Ye are from beneath; I am from above: ye are of this world; I am not of this world. I said therefore unto you, that ye shall die in your sins: for if ye believe not that I am he, ye shall die in your sins" (John 8:23,24). Jesus said He came from above, that He was not of this world as other men were, and that therefore He was God and that anyone who would not believe Him to be what He claimed to be—God in human form—should die in his sins! The virgin birth, the deity of Christ, and salvation by faith in Him, are all taught in these words of Jesus Christ. Certainly He claimed to be the virgin-born Son of God!

And all the enemies of Christ in His own lifetime knew that was what He claimed. John 5:18 says, "Therefore the Jews sought the more to kill him, because he not only had broken the sabbath, but said also that God was his Father, making himself equal with God." Jesus certainly claimed deity, insisted that He was begotten of God, that is, virgin-born, and came down from Heaven, as no other man did.

2. *"But scientists cannot believe in the virgin birth of Christ because there are no scientific records of any other case of one being born without a human father," says some scoffer.*

Indeed! But we are not claiming that men are born every few days without a human father! We are not claiming that anybody else was ever born of a virgin. In fact, we are claiming just the opposite, that Jesus is the only person so conceived—with a virgin mother and without a human father. We are not talking about an ordinary man, but a God-Man, God incarnate in human flesh!

If you should tell me that any scientist or statesman, any genius or philanthropist of this day were born of a virgin, I would not believe you. If you should tell me that any of them rose from the dead, I would laugh at you. The late President Roosevelt, for example, was a man who attained high honor; nevertheless he was only a man, born as other men, died like other men. Nothing about Roosevelt indicated that he was God, that he created the world, that he one day will be judge of all the universe.

The virgin birth would not fit Franklin D. Roosevelt nor any other man who ever lived. It does fit Jesus Christ, who is God in human form.

A few years ago scientists announced that by the use of an electric impulse, the ova of a female rabbit had been stimulated into growth and development and that this mother rabbit had borne a baby rabbit without intercourse with a male rabbit. In other words, scientists were able to induce the virgin birth of a rabbit.

They have not been able to produce the same effect on a human ova.

But what scientists did by an electrical impulse in the womb of a rabbit, could not the Almighty God do in the conception of His Son Jesus Christ in the womb of a virgin? The virgin birth fits the nature and life of Jesus, and it is easy for anybody to believe who accepts Him as the Son of God who came into the world to save sinners.

4. *"But that would be a miracle, and I cannot believe in miracles,"* *says an unbeliever.*

A miracle? Certainly! But sensible scientists have long ago decided that only miracles could account for many things.

Where did matter come from? It was created by a miracle, of course. How were the planetary systems arranged and balanced and set in motion? Unquestionably by some miracle of God. How did life originate and begin? No scientist in the world now believes that life can come from dead matter of itself. Scientists believe that the earth was once a fiery mass where life could not exist. They know that now life is on this planet. Where did it come from? Without any other explanation possible, life came as a miracle of God's creation. One who cannot believe in miracles is an ignoramus and an unthinking enemy of fact.

A miracle, the conception of Christ and His virgin birth? Certainly! Christ Himself is the God of miracles. He worked many miracles Himself. He died for our sins, died as no one else died, then miraculously rose from the dead. Miraculously He appeared to the disciples, then ascended visibly to Heaven. He is coming again.

The Bible is a miracle. Creation was a miracle. Every time a soul is regenerated and made into a new creature, that is a miracle. Certainly the virgin birth of Christ is a miracle.

I heard Dr. L. R. Scarborough, once president of the Southwestern Baptist Theological Seminary at Fort Worth, tell in our class in evangelism how one of his sons, only six or eight years old at the time, came from Sunday school one day and announced, "Dad, I don't believe that stuff they told us today about a whale swallowing Jonah."

"But, son, if God could make a whale and could make a man, why couldn't He make the whale swallow the man and keep the man alive three days in the whale?"

"Oh, well," said the boy, "if you are going to put God in it, I can believe it, too!"

So, like that lad, if you put God in it, I can believe in the virgin birth. And all who put God in it have to believe in the virgin birth. If Jesus was God come in human form, the only begotten Son of God, then that means He was born of a virgin. Certainly that is a miracle. But the Bible is a miracle book, and Christianity is a miracle religion, and no one can be a Christian who does not believe in these essential miracles.

5. *"But intelligent people do not believe in the virgin birth,"* some *ungodly teacher tells the innocent young people in his class.*

He could not face an intelligent and informed Christian leader on such a question; but he sets out to break down the faith of boys and girls with immature minds, parroting infidelity because he is against God and the Bible and has not made any honest investigation.

But what is true? Do intelligent and educated people believe in the virgin birth?

The answer is that every great creed in Christendom has stood for the virgin birth, from the Apostles' Creed on down to the Westminster Confession or the New Hampshire Statement of Faith. All the apostles believed in the virgin birth. So did all the great church fathers, all the reformers, including Martin Luther, John Calvin, and John Wesley. All the great teachers and preachers of Christianity—Spurgeon, Moody, Finney, Torrey—all the great Bible-believing theologians, evangelists, pastors and students have agreed on the virgin birth of Christ.

The only ones who deny the virgin birth are infidels who do not believe the Bible, do not believe in the deity of Christ, and do not trust Him as their own personal Saviour. Of course modernists, infidels, those who join Bob Ingersoll, Voltaire, Tom Paine, and Hitler, deny the virgin birth. But no true Christian denies it.

Great scientists like Sir Isaac Newton, Sir James Simpson, Lord Kelvin, Louis Pasteur and statemen like Gladstone, Lloyd George, Winston Churchill, George Washington, Abraham Lincoln, Woodrow Wilson, Herbert Hoover and William Jennings Bryan believed in the deity of Jesus Christ and in His virgin birth. Everywhere that good men, profoundly intelligent men, love the Lord Jesus and believe the Word of God, they believe in the virgin birth as taught so plainly in Scripture.

Then let every Christian be happy in his faith. You have the best wisdom, the best character, the greatest fellowship of the ages on your side. And if all the world beside still denied the virgin birth of Christ, any Christian who has been born again, who knows Christ as a personal Saviour, would know that He is all He claimed to be—the virgin-born Son of God.

Let us teach the virgin birth to our children. It is a beautiful, holy mystery that they can believe and grasp. Let all of God's people give to the dear lord Jesus the reverence and worship which belong to Him as the Creator of the world, God come in human form, born of a virgin, living a perfect, sinless life, dying for our sins on the cross, buried and rising again from the dead and ascending into the heavens, and one day to return again to receive us to Himself!

CHARLES H. SPURGEON
1835-1892

ABOUT THE MAN:

Many times it has been said that this was the greatest preacher this side of the Apostle Paul. He began preaching at the age of 16. At 25 he built London's famous Metropolitan Tabernacle, seating around 5,000. It was never large enough. Even when traveling he preached to 10,000 eager listeners a week. Crowds thronged to hear him as they came to hear John the Baptist by the River Jordan. The fire of God was on him as on the Prophet Elijah facing assembled Israel at Mount Carmel.

Royalty sat in his Tabernacle, as did washerwomen. Mr. Gladstone had him to dinner; and cabbies refused his fare, considering it an honor to drive for this "Prince of Preachers." To a housewife kneading bread, he would say, "Have you ever tried the Bread of Life?" Many a carpenter was asked, "Have you ever tried to build a house on sand?"

He preached in all the principal cities of England, Scotland and Ireland. And although invited to the United States on several occasions, he was never able to visit this country.

HOW GREAT WAS HIS HEART: for preachers, so the Pastors' College was founded; for orphans, so the orphans' houses came to be; for people around the world, so his literature poured forth in an almost unmeasurable volume. He was a national voice; so every national issue affecting morals, religion or the poor had his interpretation, his counsel.

Oh, but his passion for souls! You can see it in every sermon.

Spurgeon published thousands of poems, tracts, sermons and songs.

HIS MESSAGE TO LOST SINNERS WILL LIVE AS LONG AS THE GOSPEL IS PREACHED.

XIV.

"His Name—Wonderful!"

CHARLES H. SPURGEON

"For unto us a child is born, unto us a son is given: and the govern-ment shall be upon his shoulder: and his name shall be called Wonder-ful."—Isaiah 9:6.

The person spoken of in our text is undoubtedly the Lord Jesus Christ. He is a child born, with reference to His human nature; He is born of the virgin, a child. But He is a Son given, with reference to His divine nature, being given as well as born. Of course, the Godhead could not be born of woman. That was from everlasting, and is to everlasting. As a child, He was born; as a Son, He was given. "The government shall be upon his shoulder: and his name shall be called Wonderful."

Beloved, there are a thousand things in this world that are called by names that do not belong to them; but in entering upon my text, I must announce at the very opening that Christ is called Wonderful because He is so. God the Father never gave His Son a name which He did not deserve. There is no panegyric here, no flattery. It is just the simple name that He deserves; they that know Him best will say that the word doth not overstrain His merits, but rather falleth infinitely short of His glorious deserving.

His name is called Wonderful. And mark, it does not merely say that God has given Him the name of Wonderful—though that is implied; but "his name shall be *called*" so. It *shall* be; it is at this time called Wonderful by all His believing people, and it shall be. As long as the moon endureth, there shall be found men, and angels, and glorified spirits, who shall always call Him by His right name. "His name shall be called Wonderful."

I find that this name may bear two or three interpretations. The word is sometimes in Scripture translated "marvelous." Jesus Christ may be called marvelous; and a learned German interpreter says that without doubt the meaning of miraculous is also wrapped up in it. Christ is the marvel of marvels, the miracle of miracles. "His name shall be called *Miraculous,*" for He is more than a man; He is God's highest miracle. "Great is the mystery of godliness: God was manifest in the flesh."

It may also mean separated or distinguished. And Jesus Christ may well be called this, for as Saul was distinguished from all men, being head and shoulders taller than they, so is Christ distinguished above all men; He is anointed with the oil of gladness above His fellows; and in His character and in His acts, He is infinitely separated from all comparison with any of the sons of men. "Thou art fairer than the children of men; grace is poured into thy lips." He is "the chief among ten thousand and altogether lovely." "His name shall be called the *Separated One,*" the distinguished One, the noble One, set apart from the common race of mankind.

We shall, however, this morning, keep to the old version and simply read it thus, "His name shall be called Wonderful." And first I shall notice that Jesus Christ deserveth to be called Wonderful for *what He was in the past;* second, that He is called Wonderful by all His people for *what He is in the present;* and in the third place, that He *shall* be called Wonderful *for what He shall be in the future.*

I. CHRIST'S WONDERFUL PAST

First, Christ shall be called Wonderful for WHAT HE WAS IN THE PAST. Gather up your thoughts, my brethren, for a moment, and center them all on Christ, and you will soon see how wonderful He is.

1. His Eternal Existence

Consider His eternal existence, "begotten of His Father from before all worlds," being of the same substance with His Father: begotten, not made, co-equal, co-eternal, in every attribute "very God of very God." For a moment remember that He who became an infant of a span long, was no less than the King of ages, the everlasting Father, who was from eternity and is to be to all eternity. The divine nature of Christ is indeed wonderful.

Just think for a moment how much interest clusters round the life of an old man. Those of us who are but as children in years look up to him with wonder and astonishment as he tells us the varied stories of the experience through which he has passed. But what is the life of an aged man? How brief it appears when compared with the life of the tree that shelters him. It existed long before that old man's father crept, a helpless infant, into the world. How many storms have swept over its brow, how many kings have come and gone, how many empires have risen and fallen since that old oak was slumbering in its acorn cradle!

But what is the life of the tree compared with the soil on which it grows? What a wonderful story that soil might tell! What changes it has passed through in all the eras of time that have elapsed since "in the beginning, God created the heaven and the earth." There is a wonderful story connected with every atom of black mold which furnishes the nourishment of the oak.

But what is the history of that soil compared with the marvelous history of the rock on which it rests—the cliff on which it lifts its head? Oh, what stories might it tell, what records lie hidden in its bowels! Perhaps it could tell the story of the time when "the earth was without form, and void; and darkness was upon the face of the deep." Perhaps it might speak and tell us of those days when the morning and the evening were the first day, and the morning and the evening were the second day, and could explain to us the mysteries of how God made the marvelous piece of miracle—the world.

But what is the history of the cliff compared with that of the sea that rolls at its base—that deep blue ocean over which a thousand navies have swept, without leaving a furrow upon its brow?

But what is the history of the sea compared with the history of the heavens that are stretched like a curtain over that vast basin? What a history is that of the hosts of Heaven—of the everlasting marches of the sun, moon, and stars! Who can tell their generation, or who can write their biography?

But what is the history of the heavens compared with the history of the angels? They could tell you of the day when they saw this world wrapped in swaddling bands of mist—when, like a newborn infant, the last of God's offspring, it came forth from Him, and the morning stars sang together, and the sons of God shouted for joy.

But what is the history of the angels that excel in strength compared with the history of the Lord Jesus Christ? The angel is but of yesterday, and he knoweth nothing; Christ, the eternal One, chargeth even His angels with folly, and looks upon them as His ministering spirits that come and go at His good pleasure.

O Christians, gather with reverence and mysterious awe around the throne of Him who is your great Redeemer; for "his name is called Wonderful," since He has existed before all things, and "by him all things were made; and without him was not any thing made that was made."

2. Christ's Wonderful Incarnation

Consider again the incarnation of Christ, and you will rightly say that His name deserveth to be called "Wonderful."

Oh, what is that I see? Oh, world of wonders, what is that I see? The Eternal of ages, whose hair is white like wool, as white as snow, becomes an infant. Can it be? Ye angels, are ye not astonished? He becomes an infant, hangs at a virgin's breast, draws His nourishment from the breast of woman. Oh, wonder of wonders! Manger of Bethlehem, thou hast miracles poured into thee! This is a sight that surpasses all others. Talk ye of the sun, moon, and stars; consider ye the heavens, the work of God's fingers, the moon and the stars that He hath ordained; but all the wonders of the universe shrink into nothing when we come to the mystery of the incarnation of the Lord Jesus Christ.

It was a marvelous thing when Joshua bade the sun to stand still, but more marvelous when God seemed to stand still, and no longer to move forward, but rather, like the sun upon the dial of Ahaz, did go back ten degrees and veil His splendor in a cloud.

There have been sights matchless and wonderful, at which we might look for years, and yet turn away and say, "I cannot understand this; here is a deep into which I dare not dive; my thoughts are drowned; this is a steep without a summit, I cannot climb it; it is high, I cannot attain it!" But all these things are as nothing compared with the incarnation of the Son of God.

I believe that the very angels have never wondered but once, and that has been incessantly ever since they first beheld it. They never cease to tell the astonishing story, and to tell it with increasing astonishment, too, that Jesus Christ, the Son of God, was born of the virgin Mary, and became a Man. Is He not rightly called Wonderful? Infinite, and an infant—eternal, and yet born hanging on a woman's breast—supporting the universe, and yet needing to be carried in a mother's arms—King of angels, and yet the reputed son of Joseph—heir of all things, and yet the carpenter's despised Son. Wonderful art Thou, O Jesus, and that shall be Thy name forever.

3. His Amazing Humiliation

But trace the Saviour's course, and all the way He is wonderful. Is it not marvelous that He submitted to the taunts and jeers of His enemies—that for a long life He should allow the bulls of Bashan to gird Him round, and the dogs to encompass Him? Is it not surprising that He should have bridled His anger, when blasphemy was uttered against His sacred person? Had you or I been possessed of His matchless might, we should have dashed our enemies down the brow of the hill, if they had sought to cast us there; we should never have submitted to shame and spitting; no, we would have looked upon them, and with one fierce look of wrath, have dashed their spirits into eternal torment. But He bears it all—keeps in His noble spirit—the Lion of the tribe of Judah, but bearing still the lamblike character of

The humble man before His foes,
A weary man, and full of woes.

I do believe that Jesus of Nazareth was the King of Heaven; and yet He was a poor, despised, persecuted, slandered Man; but while I believe it I never can understand it. I bless Him for it; I love Him for it; I desire to praise His name while immortality endures for His infinite condescension in thus suffering for me; but to understand it, I can never pretend. His name must all His life long be called Wonderful.

4. Wonderful, Shameful Death of Jesus

But see Him die. Come, O my brothers, ye children of God, and gather round the cross. See your Master. There He hangs. Can you understand this riddle: God was manifest in the flesh and crucified of men? My Master, I cannot understand how Thou couldst stoop Thine awful head to such a death as this—how Thou couldst take from Thy brow the coronet of stars which from old eternity had shone resplendent there; but how Thou shouldst permit the thorn-crown to gird Thy temples astonishes me far more. That Thou shouldst cast away the mantle of Thy glory, the azure of Thine everlasting empire, I cannot comprehend; but how Thou shouldst have become vailed in the ignominious purple for awhile, and then be bowed to by impious men who mocked Thee as a pretended king, and how Thou shouldst be stripped naked to Thy shame, without a single covering, this is still more incomprehensible.

Truly Thy name is Wonderful. Oh, Thy love to me is wonderful, passing the love of woman. Was ever grief like Thine? Was ever love like Thine, that could open the floodgates of such grief. Thy grief is like a river, but was there ever spring that poured out such a torrent? Was ever love so mighty as to become the fount from which such an ocean of grief could come rolling down?

Here is matchless love—matchless love to make Him suffer, matchless power to enable Him to endure all the weight of His Father's wrath. Here is matchless justice, that He Himself should acquiesce in His Father's will, and not allow men to be saved without His own sufferings. And here is matchless mercy to the chief of sinners, that Christ should suffer even for them. "His name shall be called Wonderful."

But He died! He died! See Salem's daughters weep around. Joseph of Arimathea takes up the lifeless body after it has been taken down from the cross. They bear it away to the sepulcher. It is put in a garden. Do you call Him Wonderful now?

> Is this the Saviour long foretold
> To usher in the age of gold?

5. The Lord Jesus Wonderful in Resurrection

And is He dead? Lift His hands! They drop motionless by His side. His foot exhibits still the nailprint; but there is no mark of life. "Aha," cries the Jew, "is this the Messiah? He is dead; He shall see corruption in a little space of time. Oh! watchman, keep good ward lest His disciples steal His body. His body can never come forth, unless they do steal it; for He is dead. Is this the Wonderful, the Counselor?"

But God did not leave His soul in Hades, nor did He suffer His body—"his holy one"—to see corruption. Yes, He is wonderful, even in His death. That clay cold corpse is wonderful. Perhaps this is the greatest wonder of all, that He who is "death of death and Hell's destruction" should for awhile endure the bonds of death.

But here is the wonder. He could not be holden of those bonds. Those chains which have held ten thousand of the sons and daughters of Adam, and which have never been broken yet by any man of human mold, save by a miracle, were but to Him as green withes. Death bound our Samson fast and said, "I have Him now; I have taken away the locks of His strength; His glory is departed, and now He is mine." But the bands that kept the human race in chains were nothing to the Saviour;

the third day He burst them; and He rose again from the dead, from henceforth to die no more.

Oh! Thou risen Saviour—Thou who couldst not see corruption— Thou art wonderful in Thy resurrection. And Thou art wonderful, too, in Thine ascension, as I see Thee leading captivity captive and giving gifts unto men. "His name shall be called Wonderful."

6. Surpassingly Wonderful

Pause here one moment, and let us think—Christ is surpassingly wonderful. The little story I have told you just now—not little in itself, but little as I have told it—has in it something surpassingly wonderful. All the wonders that you ever saw are nothing compared with this.

As we have passed through various countries we have seen a wonder, and some elder traveler than ourselves has said, "Yes, this is wonderful to you, but I could show you something that utterly eclipses that." Though we have seen some splendid landscapes with glorious hills, and we have climbed up where the eagle seemed to knit the mountain and the sky together in his flight, and we have stood and looked down, and said, "How wonderful!" saith he, "I have seen fairer lands than these, and wider and richer prospects far."

But when we speak of Christ, none can say they ever saw a greater wonder than He is. You have come now to the very summit of everything that may be wondered at. There are no mysteries equal to this surprise; there is no astonishment and admiration that we feel when we behold Christ in the glories of the past. He surpasses everything.

7. Forever to Be Wondered At

And yet again, wonder is a short-lived emotion; you know, it is pro-verbial that a wonder grows gray-headed in nine days. The longest period that a wonder is known to live is about that time. It is such a short-lived thing.

But Christ is, and ever shall be, wonderful. You may think of Him through threescore years and ten, but you shall wonder at Him more at the end than at the beginning.

Abraham might wonder at Him when he saw His day in the distant future; but I do not think that even Abraham himself could wonder at Christ so much as the very least in the kingdom of Heaven of today wonders at Him, seeing that we know more than Abraham, and therefore wonder more.

Think again for one moment, and you will say of Christ that He deserves to be called Wonderful, not only because He is always wonderful, and because He is surpassingly wonderful, but also because He is altogether wonderful.

There have been some great feats of skill in the arts and sciences; for instance, if we take a common wonder of the day, the telegraph— how much there is about that which is wonderful! But there are a great many things in the telegraph that we can understand. Though there are many mysteries in it, still there are parts of it that are like keys to the mysteries, so that if we cannot solve the riddle wholly, yet it is disrobed of some of the low garments of its mystery.

But now if you look at Christ any how, any where, any way, He is all mystery; He is altogether wonderful, always to be looked at and always to be admired.

8. Jesus Christ Is Universally Wondered At

And again, He is universally wondered at. They tell us that the religion of Christ is very good for old women.

I was once complimented by a person who told me he believed my preaching would be extremely suitable for Blacks. He did not intend it as a compliment, but I replied, "Well, sir, if it was suitable for Blacks, I should think it would be very suitable for Whites; for there is only a little difference of skin; and I do not preach to people's skins, but to their hearts."

Now of Christ we can say that He is universally a wonder; the strongest intellects have wondered at Him. Our Lockes and our Newtons have felt themselves to be as little children when they have come to the foot of the cross. The wonder has not been confined to ladies, to children, to old women and dying men; the highest intellects and the loftiest minds have all wondered at Christ.

I am sure it is a difficult task to make some people wonder. Hard thinkers and close mathematicians are not easily brought to wonder, but such men have covered their faces with their hands and cast themselves in the dust and confessed that they have been lost in wonder and amazement. Well then may Christ be called Wonderful.

"His name shall be called Wonderful."

II. HE IS WONDERFUL FOR WHAT HE IS
IN THE PRESENT

And here I will not diverge, but will just appeal to you personally.

Is He wonderful to *you!* Let me tell the story of my own wonderment at Christ, and in telling it, I shall be telling the experience of all God's children.

1. Jesus Christ Wonderful in Saving Sinners

There was a time when I wondered not at Christ. I heard of His beauties, but I had never seen them; I heard of His power, but it was nought to me; it was but news of something done in a far country—I had no connection with it, and therefore I observed it not.

But once upon a time there came one to my house of a black and terrible aspect. He smote the door; I tried to bolt it, to hold it fast. He smote again and again, till at last he entered; and with a rough voice he summoned me before him; and he said, "I have a message from God for thee; thou art condemned on account of thy sins." I looked at him with astonishment; I asked him his name. He said, "My name is the Law"; and I fell at his feet as one that was dead. "I was alive without the law once; but when the commandment came, sin revived, and I died." As I lay there, he smote me. He smote me till every rib seemed as if it must break, and the bowels be poured forth. My heart was melted like wax within me; I seemed to be stretched upon a rack—to be pinched with hot irons—to be beaten with whips of burning wire. A misery extreme dwelt and reigned in my heart.

I dared not lift up mine eyes, but I thought within myself, *There may be hope; there may be mercy for me. Perhaps the God whom I have offended may accept my tears and my promises of amendment, and I may live.*

But when that thought crossed me, heavier were the blows and more poignant my sufferings than before, till hope entirely failed me; and I had nought wherein to trust. Darkness black and dense gathered around me; I heard a voice as it were, of rushing to and fro, and of wailing and gnashing of teeth. I said within my soul, *I am cast out from His sight; I am utterly abhorred of God; He hath trampled me in the mire of the streets in His anger.*

And there came One by of sorrowful but of loving aspect, and He stooped over me and He said, "Awake thou that sleepest, and arise from the dead, and Christ shall give thee light." I arose in astonishment, and He took me, and He led me to a place where stood a cross, and He seemed to vanish from my sight. But He appeared again hanging there. I looked upon Him as He bled upon that tree. His eyes darted a glance of love unutterable into my spirit; and in a moment, looking at Him, the bruises that my soul had suffered were healed; the gaping wounds were cured; the broken bones rejoiced; the rags that had covered me were all removed; my spirit was white as the spotless snows of the far off North; I had melody within my spirit, for I was saved, washed, cleansed, forgiven, through Him who did hang upon the tree.

Oh, how I wondered that I should be pardoned! It was not the pardon that I wondered at so much as the wonder was that it should come to me. I wondered that He should be able to pardon such sins as mine, such crimes, so numerous and so black, and that after such an accusing conscience He should have power to still every wave within my spirit and make my soul like the surface of a river, undisturbed, quiet, and at ease.

His name then to my spirit was Wonderful. But, brethren and sisters, if you have felt this, you can say you thought Him wonderful then—if you are feeling it, a sense of adoring wonder enraptures your heart even now.

2. Wonderful to His Own in Trouble

And has He not been wonderful to you since that auspicious hour when first you heard Mercy's voice spoken to you? How often have you been in sadness, sickness, and sorrow! But your pain has been light, for Jesus Christ has been with you on your sickbeds; your care has been no care at all, for you have been able to cast your burden upon Him. The trial which threatened to crush you rather lifted you up to Heaven; and you have said, "How wonderful that Jesus Christ's name should give me such comfort, such joy, such peace, such confidence."

Various things bring to my recollection a period now removed by the space of nearly two years. Never shall we forget, beloved, the judgments of the Lord, when by terrible things in righteousness He answered our prayer that He would give us success in this house. We cannot forget how the people were scattered—how some of the sheep were slain, and the shepherd himself was smitten.

I may not have told in your hearing the story of my own woe. Perhaps never soul went so near the burning furnace of insanity and yet came away unharmed. I have walked by that fire until these locks seemed to be crisp with the heat thereof. My brain was racked. I dared not look up to God; and prayer, that was once my solace, was the cause of my affright and terror, if I attempted it.

I shall never forget the time when I first became restored to myself. It was in the garden of a friend. I was walking solitary and alone, musing upon my misery, much cheered as that was by the kindness of my loving friend, yet far too heavy for my soul to bear, when on a sudden the name of Jesus flashed through my mind. The person of Christ seemed visible to me. I stood still. The burning lava on my soul was cooled. My agonies were hushed. I bowed myself there, and the garden that had seemed a Gethsemane became to me a Paradise. And then it seemed so strange to me that nought should have brought me back but that name of Jesus. I thought indeed at that time that I should love Him better all the days of my life.

But there were two things I wondered at. I wondered that He should be so good to me, and I wondered more that I should have been so ungrateful to Him. But His name has been from that time "Wonderful" to me, and I must record what He has done for my soul.

3. Wonderful in Fellowship Is Jesus

And now, brothers and sisters, you shall all find every day of your life, whatever your trials and troubles, that He shall always be made the more wonderful by them. He sends your troubles to be like a black foil, to make the diamond of His name shine the brighter. You would never know the wonders of God if it were not that you find them out in the furnace. "They that go down to the sea in ships, that do business in great waters; These see the works of the Lord, and his wonders in the deep." And we shall never see the wonders of God except in that deep; we must go into the deeps before we know how wonderful are His power and His might to save.

I must not leave this point without one more remark. There have been times when you and I have said of Christ, "His name is wonderful indeed, for we have been by it transported entirely above the world, and carried upward to the very gates of Heaven itself." I pity you, beloved, if you do not understand the rhapsody I am about to use.

There are moments when the Christian feels the charms of earth all broken, and his wings are loosed, and he begins to fly. Up he soars, till he forgets earth's sorrows and leaves them far behind. Up he goes, till he forgets earth's joys, and leaves them like the mountain tops far below, as when the eagle flies to meet the sun. Up, up, up he goes, with his Saviour full before him almost in vision beatific. His heart is full of Christ; his soul beholds his Saviour, and the cloud that darkened his view of the Saviour's face seems to be dispersed.

At such a time the Christian can sympathize with Paul who said, "Whether in the body or out of the body, I can not tell: God knoweth!" but I am, as it were, "caught up to the third heaven."

And how is this rapture produced? By the music of flute, harp, sackbut, psaltery, and all kinds of instruments? No. How then? By riches? By fame? By wealth? Ah, no. By a strong mind? By a lively disposition? No. By the name of Jesus. That one name is all-sufficient to lead the Christian into heights of transport that verge upon the region where the angels fly in cloudless day.

III. JESUS WONDERFUL IN THE FUTURE

I have no more time to stay upon this point, although the text is infinite, and one might preach upon it forever. I have only to notice that His name shall be called Wonderful in the future.

1. Wonderful in Judgment

The day is come, the day of wrath, the day of fire. The ages are ended; the last century, like the last pillar of a dilapidated temple, has crumbled to its fall. The clock of time is verging to its last hour. It is on the stroke. The time is come when the things that are made must disappear.

Lo, I see earth's bowels moving. A thousand hillocks give up the slumbering dead. The battlefields are clothed no more with the rich harvests that have been manured with blood; but a new harvest has sprung up. The fields are thick with men. The sea itself becomes a prolific mother; and though she hath swallowed men alive, she gives them up again; and they stand before God, an exceeding great army.

Sinners, ye have risen from your tombs; the pillars of Heaven are reeling; the sky is moving to and fro; the sun, the eye of this great world, is rolling like a maniac's, and glaring with dismay. The moon that long has cheered the night now makes the darkness terrible, for she is turned into a clot of blood. Portents, signs and wonders past imagination, make the heavens shake and make men's hearts quail within them.

Suddenly upon a cloud there comes one like unto the Son of Man. Sinners, picture your astonishment and your wonder when you see Him. Where art thou, Voltaire? Thou saidst, "I will crush the wretch." Come and crush Him now! "Nay," saith Voltaire, "He is not the man I thought

He was." Oh, how will he wonder when he finds out what Christ is! Now, Judas, come and give Him a traitor's kiss! "Ah! nay," says he, "I knew not what I kissed. I thought I kissed only the son of Mary, but lo, He is the everlasting God!"

Now, ye kings and princes that stood up and took counsel together against the Lord and against His anointed, saying, "Let us break his bands asunder, and cast his cords from us," come now; take counsel once more; rebel against Him now!

Oh, can ye picture the astonishment, the wonder, the dismay, when careless, godless infidels and Socinians find out what Christ is? "Oh," they will say, "this is wonderful! I thought not He was such as this"; while Christ shall say to them, "Thou thoughtest that I was altogether such as yourselves; but I am no such thing; I am come in all My Father's glory to judge the quick and dead."

Pharaoh led his hosts into the midst of the Red Sea. The path was dry and shingly, and on either shore stood, like a wall of alabaster, the clear white water, stiff as with the breath of frost consolidated into marble. There it stood. Can you guess the astonishment and dismay of the hosts of Pharaoh when they saw those walls of water about to close upon them? "Behold, ye despisers, and wonder, and perish!" Such will be your astonishment when Christ, whom ye have despised today— Christ, whom ye would not have to be your Saviour—Christ, whose Bible ye left unread—Christ, whose Gospel ye rejected, shall come in the glory of His Father and all His holy angels with Him. Ay, then indeed will ye "behold . . . and wonder, and perish," and shall say, "His name is Wonderful."

2. Wonderful, Eternal Peace and Salvation for the Redeemed, Forgiven Ones

But perhaps the most wonderful part of the day of judgment is this: Do you see all the horrors yonder—the black darkness, the horrid night, the clashing comets, the pale stars, sickly and wan, falling like figs from the fig tree? Do you hear the cry, "Rocks, hide us; mountains, on us fall"? "Every battle of the warrior is with confused noise." But there never was a battle like this. This is with fire and smoke indeed. But do ye see yonder? All is peaceful, all serene and quiet. The myriads of the redeemed—are they shrieking, crying, wailing? No. See them! They are gathering—gathering round the throne. That very throne that seems to scatter, as with a hundred hands, death and destruction on the wicked, becomes the sun of light and happiness to all believers.

Do you see them coming, robed in white, with their bright wings, while gathering round Him they veil their faces? Do you hear them cry, "Holy, holy, holy, Lord God of hosts, for Thou wast slain, and Thou hast risen from the dead; worthy art Thou to live and reign, when death itself is dead"? Do ye hear them? It is all song, and no shriek. Do ye see them? It is all joy, and no terror.

His name to them is Wonderful; but it is the wonder of admiration, the wonder of ecstasy, the wonder of affection, and not the wonder of horror and dismay.

Saints of the Lord, ye *shall* know the wonders of His name when ye shall be like Him in the day of His appearing. Oh, my enraptured spirit, thou shalt bear thy part in thy Redeemer's triumph, unworthy though thou art, the chief of sinners, and less than the least of saints. Thine eye shall see Him and not another; "I know that my redeemer liveth, and that he shall stand at the latter day upon the earth: And though after my skin worms destroy this body, yet in my flesh shall I see God."

Oh, make yourselves ready, ye virgins! Behold the Bridegroom cometh. Arise and trim your lamps, and go ye out to meet Him. He comes— He comes—He comes! And when He comes, you shall well say of Him, as you meet Him with joy, "Thy name is called Wonderful. All hail! all hail! all hail!"

R. G. LEE
1886-1978

ABOUT THE MAN:

R. G. Lee was born November 11, 1886, and died July 20, 1978.

The midwife attending his birth held baby Lee in her black arms while dancing a jig around the room, saying, "Praise Gawd! Glory be! The good Lawd done sont a preacher to dis here house. Yas, sah! Yes, ma'am! Dat's what He's done gone and done."

"God-sent preacher" well describes Dr. Lee. Few in number are the Baptists who have never heard his most famous sermon, "Payday Someday!" If you haven't heard it, or read it, surely you have heard some preacher make a favorable reference to it.

From his humble birth to sharecropper parents, Dr. Lee rose to pastor one of the largest churches in his denomination and head the mammoth Southern Baptist Convention as its president, serving three terms in that office. Dr. John R. Rice said:

"If you have not had the privilege of hearing Dr. Lee in person, I am sorry for you. The scholarly thoroughness, the wizardry of words, the lilt of poetic thought, the exalted idealism, the tender pathos, the practical application, the stern devotion to divine truth, the holy urgency in the preaching of a man called and anointed of God to preach and who must therefore preach, are never to be forgotten. The stately progression of his sermon to its logical end satisfies. The facile language, the alliterative statement, the powerful conviction mark Dr. Lee's sermons. The scholarly gleaning of incident and illustration from the treasures of scholarly memory and library make a rich feast for the hearer. The banquet table is spread with bread from many a grain field, honey distilled from the nectar of far-off exotic blossoms, sweetmeats from many a bake shop, strong meat from divers markets, and the whole board is garnished by posies from a thousand gardens.

"Often have I been blessed in hearing Dr. Lee preach, have delighted in his southern voice, and have been carried along with joy by his anointed eloquence."

XV.

The Only Begotten of the Father

R. G. LEE

"The only begotten Son of God."—John 3:18.

"God sent his only begotten Son into the world, that we might live through him."—I John 4:9.

Jesus has many names—all of them great names, names transcendently meaningful. And not the least, but among the greatest, of the names He has is "The Only Begotten Son."

"Father" is an official title designating activities. So also is "Son" an official title designating activities. "Father," meaning source, refers to the infinite, eternal and invisible Source of all. "Son" means that which, carrying forward omnipotently and omnisciently and omnipresently, expresses the Father.

All that the Father ever **has** done, **is** doing, and **will** do is through the sinless Son—the objectification of Deity, the executive of Deity. The Father's holiness, the Father's love, the Father's shepherd heart, the Father's redeeming compassion were mightily and beautifully manifest in Christ's earthly life. Everything that Jesus—the living, dying, rising-again Word of God—did in the days of His flesh spoke of the heart of Him with whom He was coexistent, coequal, coeternal, coessential. Jesus was the Light—God seen; the Word—God heard; the Life—God felt.

Consider the Only Begotten of the Father in the glory of His

I. PREINCARNATION

He had glory with God before the world was, and was loved by the Father before the foundation of the world (John 17:5,24). His life on earth was a momentous episode between two eternities—the one reaching back before all worlds, the other forward forever. Before "by faith Abraham . . . went out, not knowing whither he went," Jesus' will was the law of angels and archangels in the midst of the glories of Heaven. And He Himself said: "Before Abraham was, I am" (John 8:58).

Before the infant earth lay, wrapped in swaddling clothes of light, in the arms of the great Jehovah, Jesus was the central Sun which guided the hosts of Heaven.

Before, on earth, any flowers ever bloomed, before any fountains gushed forth liquid blessings, before any stars ever shone in the sky like glowing embers on hearthstones of blue, the Heaven of heavens was "filled with the odors of His life-giving essence."

Before the sun shone forth from His tabernacle in the heavens, before any fires burned in dark corners and continents of chaos, before the phosphorescent foam of surging seas gleamed in the light of the full moon, pinned like a huge cameo on the breast of the sky, "all the hosts of heaven were upborne on the swelling tide of His unfolding perfections."

Before the first ray of light sped forth like some flaming archangel with garments afire across the uncharted dark, Jesus "emitted and absorbed all the glory of the eternal past" and this is He who had preeminence in creative power, having no associate in creating the universe—which is a vast autograph album, made up of motes and mountains and molecules, atoms, and seas with islands studded, with Christ's signature written everywhere, in every corner of every continent. That creation in concept is the product of His wisdom we learn when we read:

"All things were made by him; and without him was not any thing made that was made."—John 1:3.

That creation in its wondrous perfection is the product of the power of Him "who spake, and it was done; he commanded, and it stood fast," we acknowledge when we read:

"For by him were all things created, that are in heaven, and that are in earth, visible and invisible, whether they be thrones, or dominions, or principalities, or powers: all things were created by him, and for him: And he is before all things, and by him all things consist."—Col. 1:16,17.

That Jesus, "whom [God] hath appointed heir of all things, by whom also he made the worlds," is at the center and the circumference, as the One who hath all power in Heaven and earth, we assert when we read:

"Who being the brightness of his glory, and the express image of his person, and upholding all things by the word of his power." —Heb. 1:3.

And with the four and twenty elders, who "fall down before him . . . and worship him that liveth for ever and ever," we would say:

"Thou art worthy, O Lord, to receive glory and honour and power: for thou hast created all things, and for thy pleasure they are and were created." —Rev. 4:11.

Consider, too, the Only Begotten of the Father as the subject, the fulfillment of—

II. PROPHECY

To the two on the road to Emmaus, who were "slow of heart to believe all that the prophets have spoken," Jesus, "beginning at Moses and all the prophets . . . expounded unto them in all the scriptures the things concerning himself" (Luke 24:27).

To those who looked upon Him through Jewish eyes of malicious enmity, Jesus said:

"Search the scriptures; for in them ye think ye have eternal life: and they are they which testify of me . . . there is one that accuseth you, even Moses, in whom ye trust. For had ye believed Moses, ye would have believed me: for he wrote of me." —John 5:39,45,46.

And Abraham, talking to the rich man in Hell, said: "They have Moses and the prophets; let them hear them" (Luke 16:29).

Foolish are we if we forget that the Old Testament and the New Testament alike tell of Jesus. Of the whole inerrant Word of God truly it can be said that Christ, the Glory of God, "[doth] lighten it, and the Lamb is the light thereof."

Verily the Old Testament conceals Christ and the New Testament reveals Christ. Just as the Old Testament infolds Christ, the New Testament unfolds Christ. The Old Testament promises Christ; the New Testament presents Christ. The Old Testament pictures Christ; the New Testament produces Christ. The Old Testament prophesies Christ; the New Testament proclaims Christ. The Old Testament localizes Christ; the New Testament universalizes Christ. The Old Testament symbolizes Christ; the New Testament sacrifices Christ. The Old Testament is law which Christ fulfilled; the New Testament is love, which Christ exhibited.

The name of Jesus, the Supreme Personality, the center of a world's desire, is on *every page*—in expression or symbol or prophecy or psalm or proverb. Through the Bible, the name of Jesus runs like a line of glimmering light. The thought of Jesus, literature's loftiest ideal and philosophy's highest personality and criticism's supremest problem and theology's fundamental doctrine and spirituality's cardinal necessity, threads the great Book as a crystal river winds its way through a continent.

All the Bible's analogies, all the Bible's types, all the Bible's pictures, all the Bible's truths, are so related to Christ that Christ alone explains them. And the explanation is filled with such perfection of harmony in every detail—the relationship between them and our Lord Jesus is so strikingly self-evident—that any discussion of it would be useless.

No one ought to have to argue to get folk to see that the diversified and systematic sacrifices of the Jews, the significant shadows of redemptive entity still ahead, the adumbrations of a substance yet to come, were elemental, preparatory, rudimental, introductory—and pointed to Christ, the propellent Center to which the faith of mankind, before and since, gravitated.

The promises to fallen man in Eden and the ceremonies of Judaism mean Christ. The music of Israel's sweetest harps and the light that burns in prophecy mean Christ. Jesus is the vital substance that gives meaning to the Bible's genealogies, meaning to its histories, meaning to its chronologies. Take Jesus out of the Bible and it would be like taking calcium out of lime, carbon out of diamonds, truth out of history, invention out of fiction, matter out of physics, mind out of metaphysics, numbers out of mathematics. For the Jesus of prophecy is the secret of its unity, its strength, its beauty. And all the prophecies read, since Jesus came, more like history than prophecy—more like a description of events already done than a declaration of events yet to be.

Now think of the Only Begotten of the Father—

III. PRESENTED

Isaiah, the evangelist of the Old Testament, in whose preaching was the growl of the Assyrian wolf, wrote:

"Therefore the Lord himself shall give you a sign; Behold, a virgin shall conceive, and bear a son, and shall call his name Immanuel."— Isa. 7:14.

Thus did the prophet tell how He would be presented to the world as the unspeakable Gift of God's love. The Incarnate Son of God entered into a body of flesh that He might render to God adequate penance and sorrow for the sins of men, that He might adequately compensate God's government by an equivalent to man's offense and offer mercy abundantly in consistence with divine integrity.

Born in a barn amid cattle was He—and at a time when religion and idolatry were not only lovers but affectionate bedfellows. He who is called the Desire of all nations was born when "the scepter was frozen with the tyranny of impeached civilizations." Born in a little town which has been called "a weed patch by Roman highways" while Athens, the intellectual center of the world, was drunk with the wine of skepticism, His birth was not marked by clocks and calendars.

Jesus, in whom was life, and that life the light of men, was of the Virgin born when old Persia had on her brow a funeral wreath—born when old sleepy Egypt was on the way to becoming a shabby sexton of splendid tombs. This compassionate Christ who, grown to Manhood, wept over Jerusalem, was born when the Coliseum, stained with human blood, "typed the cruelty of the heart of the Roman Empire"—an empire believing itself to be invulnerably bulwarked in every part.

This virgin-born Christ, His entrance into the realm of human flesh by a virgin's womb being the seal of the Father's approval affixed to the claims Jesus made as the Only Begotten of the Father, was presented as God's will, God's thought, God's purpose swathed in mortality—His every nerve divine handwriting, His every bone divine Scripture, His every muscle a pulley divinely swung, His every breath divine whisper, His every heartbeat divine pulsation, His every cry divine wooing.

In view of the truth that Jesus was Head of the human race and responsible for its creation, is it not most difficult to understand how any person can deny His miraculous conception? Was it not a necessity and His own desire to be conceived, to be born, to pass through the stages of human growth? Was not the virgin birth the most natural and most sacred way to enter the world? Know men not that the natural procreative force of mankind produces new persons, but not so in the case of Jesus?

Know ye not, ye scholars, ye doubting physicians, that no new person came into existence with His conception and birth? Know ye not, ye readers of the Scriptures, that He was already existing as the Son of God when He entered into the experience of mankind? Know ye not that this Christ who was ages older than His mother, was, in His Incarnation, embodied in human flesh, demonstrated in human life, exemplified in human action, crystallized in human form? Know ye not, ye who have heard much preaching, that the Only Begotten of the Father, given in grace for our redemption, linked His deity with our humanity (apart from sin) and was thus God and Man in one adorable Person?

Now give thought, please, to the Only Begotten of the Father in—

IV. PAIN

"A man of sorrows, and acquainted with grief," He said on one occasion, "My soul is exceeding sorrowful, even unto death" (Matt. 26:38)—a sorrow far beyond Paul's "great heaviness and continual sorrow" of heart. Behold, and see if there be any pain like unto His pain—pain wherewith the Lord afflicted Him in the day of His fierce anger, when sin was ordered to execution in the Person of the Only Begotten of the Father.

Paul was His because He was "not of the world," yet was "sent into the world"—the world uncongenial and hostile—sent from an assembly seraphic to an assembly diabolic, from the songs of angels to the hoots of mobs, from the hallelujahs around God's throne to the Hell-brewed hissing of satanic assault in the wilderness, from the throngs that acclaimed Him worthy of praise and honor and worship to the groups which found Him deserving of death.

Pain was His because of the misunderstandings all along the way—misunderstandings which sharpened the thorns of His only earthly crown as those nearest and dearest misconstrued Him.

In pain was He—pain of soul—because men were unresponsive to the magnanimity of His nature—because men were blind to the beauty of His character—because they were deaf to the significance of His teaching—because they were ungrateful in the presence of His ministries of mercy—because He saw behind the loveliest scenes of village and city and countryside the hearts of people smitten with sin, burdened with care, wrung with anguish.

In pain often was He—because of men's lack of faith. Pained with the abuses of men. Pained by the agony of Gethsemane. Pained by the fists of men that beat Him. Pained by the fingers that pulled out His beard. Pained by the scourge that seamed His quivering flesh to the bone. Pained by the thorns that punctured His brow. Pained by the palms that slapped Him. Pained by the nails that pinioned Him to the cross. Pained by the pangs of thirst. Pained by the sorrows of His soul. Pained by the tortures of Calvary.

Traveling the painful road from Edom, with dyed garments from Bozrah, glorious in His apparel, traveling in the greatness of His strength, He retrod the way of man's retreat, opened the way to the tree of life, liquidated the bond of inexorable law, sheathed the sword of justice behind the blood-drenched Mercy Seat. Pained when He made His sinless soul an offering for our sins. Pained when He was "made a curse for us." Pained when He who knew no sin was made sin in our behalf that we might become the righteousness of God in Him.

> **"O the cruel pain He bore,**
> **When the crown of thorns He wore."**

In pain was He because of the hostile forces that allied themselves against Him—hostile forces of hate deployed from the Sanhedrin, detailed from the standing army, the vagabonds of the streets joining men from Caesarean palaces in venting their spite against Him.

Was not Bethlehem, place of His birth, against Him? And Nazareth— place of His toil? And Capernaum—place of His miraculous healing? And Jerusalem—with evil girt with diadem inside her walls? And Galilee where His ministries were as rains in drought-smitten lands? Yes, all these. And, besides, the courts. Moreover, the army. And Rome, too, and the world also. And all Hell.

"Though he were a Son, yet learned he obedience by the things which he suffered." —Heb. 5:8.

In life, His enemies, setting their pickets to watch Him, hounded His every step. They saw into which house He went—and when He came out. They watched what He ate—and how much. They saw what He drank—and how much. They knew with whom He stayed—and how long. They heard what He said—and lied about the intent thereof.

At last the most dreadfully painful suffering of all came—at Calvary, where all the furies of Hell and all the hatreds of earth joined their wicked hearts and murderous hands in unholy alliance to do Him to death. There by His pain of body and pain of soul culminating in awful death, He purchased our redemption—purchased us who believe off the slave market so that we can never be put up for sale again.

Coming from a throne to a footstool, from the top of glory to the bottom of humiliation, He let wicked men thrust the lances of pain through His vitals for us—for us, Hell-deserving sinners all. As someone has said, though I may somewhat take from or somewhat add to his words:

He came and wrapped Himself in all the agonies which we deserve for our misdoings. He stood at the point where all earthly and infernal hostilities charged on Him at once, with keen sabers—our SUBSTITUTE. When did ever attorney endure so much for a pauper client? When did ever physician suffer so much for patient in the lazaretto? When did mother ever suffer so much to bring a child into the world? When did any suffering ever equal the pain of soul and the pain of body which Christ suffered for us—for you—for me? The thunderbolts struck Him from above, hurricane after hurricane of pain, cyclone after cyclone of pain, when, all the worlds witnessing, He paid the price, the bitter price, the transcendent price, the awful price, the glorious price, the infinite price, the eternal price that sets us free.

Knowing that He died a spiritual death as well as a physical death, founding our joy in the deep bitterness of His own soul, we say—

> **See, from His head, His hands, His feet,**
> **Sorrow and love flow mingled down:**
> **Did e'er such love and sorrow meet,**
> **Or thorns compose so rich a crown?**

And we, saved from wrath through Him, recall that in love—

> **Out from the realm of the glory light**
> **Into the far-away land of night,**
> **Out from the bliss of worshipful song**
> **Into the pain of hatred and wrong,**
> **Out from the holy rapture above**
> **Into the grief of rejected love,**
> **Out from the life at the Father's side**
> **Into the death of the crucified,**
> **Out of high honor and into shame**
> **The Master willingly, gladly came.**

And now give thought to the Only Begotten of the Father as the One—

V. PLACED

"He was buried." The body of Him who, before He was made flesh, placed the pillars of the earth in their sockets, was placed in the grave. The body of Him who, before He "was made of a woman," placed the whirling worlds in their places, was placed in the tomb where, for the first time in thirty-three years, the cruel world left Him alone.

And, let us ask, who were present at the placement in the tomb of the body marred and scarred with the stigmata of the cross? Joseph of Arimathea, a rich man, who owned the tomb. He it was who asked

Governor Pilate for the body. He it was who took the body, not a bone of it broken, and washed the dirt and spit and blood and dust therefrom. Then in the presence of Nicodemus (the same who came to Jesus by night), in the presence of women, the body was wrapped in clean linen and perfumes, and placed in the tomb which the Roman government sealed—afraid that the disciples would come and steal the body and play resurrection.

A regiment of soldiers from the Tower of Antonia was detailed to guard that mausoleum. At the door of that tomb a fight took place which decided the question for all graveyards and cemeteries. Sword of lightning against sword of steel. Angel of God against military. God against Rome.

But He was not placed there **permanently.** "Up from the grave He arose." He shattered His tomb so that it can never be rebuilt. All the trowels and masonry of earth cannot mend it. Forever and forever it is a broken tomb. The King of Terror must go down before the King of Grace. For Jesus, "the Ancient of days," 'cut off in the midst of His days,' resumed His power, recovered His challenged rights, regained His waning influence, reasserted His sacred grandeur, sent down the ages the blest assurance that He who was born in denial of the laws of life was raised from the dead in defiance of the laws of death.

Think now of the Only Begotten of the Father as the One—

VI. PREACHED

"Preached unto the Gentiles." Yes. And "believed on in the world."

Preached—by men with hearts on fire and tongues aflame.

Preached—by apostles daring dungeons and defying the oppressors of the truth.

Preached—by men who preferred the duty they owed to God to any danger that might come from men.

Preached—with rattle of chain and creak of torture rack.

Preached—with fervor by loving hearts, though the fires of the stake threatened.

Preached—with love, though scourging whips were ready for the using.

Preached—with faithfulness, though rotten eggs and dead cats, on occasions, were thrown.

Preached—though the preachers were hissed at, laughed at, maltreated at whipping posts, and made to rot in sunless dungeons, dark and dank and deadly.

Preached—from behind prison bars.

Preached—from the midst of martyrs' flames.

Preached—from the blood-stained sands of murderous arenas.

Preached—before slaves.

Preached—before kings and rulers.

Preached—"from Greenland's icy mountains to India's coral strand."

Preached—where the Eskimos feed on putrid blubber amid the ice floes of the North.

Preached—where Chinamen feed on rats in Hong Kong.

Preached—where cannibals drink human blood out of human skulls.

Preached—where African Hottentots wear no clothes and know no shame.

Preached—where Indian worshipers of turtles burn wives on their husbands' funeral pyre.

Preached—where savages utter their wild war whoops.

Preached—where Chinese opium sots make of themselves beasts of the lowest type.

Preached—where Korean demon-worshipers make the night hideous with their cries.

Preached—where Confucian scholars grope in the dark.

Preached—where Mohammedan fanatics call from their towers to prayer.

Preached—where assemble the poor to whom a crust is a feast.

Preached—where meet the rich, oft poor in spiritual wealth.

Preached—where the streets of Sodom are filled with riotous throngs.

Preached—where many are content with the religion of the organ and the aisle.

Preached in the first century—Judaism declined.

Preached in the third, fourth and fifth centuries—and pagan philosophy was conquered.

Preached in the seventeenth century—and French skepticism was conquered.

Preached in the eighteenth century—and English deism met defeat.

Preached in this century—and the tides of materialism—materialism which would reduce the supernatural to ignorance—will not rise so high.

Preached in Virginia—and John Albert Broadus, yielding his will to Christ at sixteen, stays on double duty as preacher and educator all his days, and sings with his last whispered breath, "Jesus, Lover of my soul."

Preached in Puerto Rico—and, as we are told, a policeman, Delfino

Muler, is saved, and then becomes an evangelist with his tongue catching fire from a heart that burned fervently.

Preached in British America—and Benjamin Cameron, the Indian, who in his savage days had shot and had eaten his own wife, as Villiers tells us, is born again—and goes forth to greet every stranger with the questions: "Are you a Christian? Do you love my Saviour? Will you give me your hand if you do?"

Preached in New Guinea—and Ruatoka, himself born a heathen, by faith sees Christ's wounded hands and feet, repents and believes and is saved. Then he writes to the London Missionary Society, even as we read in "Hurry Call," regarding the cannibals who had murdered Chalmen: "I ask of you a great privilege—permit me to go to the place where he was killed, and tell his murderers about the love of God in Christ."

Preached in the Philippines where many, knowing not the liberating truth of Christ, are in bondage to relics and friars—and Si Loy becomes a Baptist deacon who cries out, when mobbed and beaten, "I cannot strike back; for there is a great love in my heart."

Preached in Japan where there are agile seekers for the world's trade and military powers that seek world domination—and some have solemnly sworn to devote their entire time and talents to Christ's cause.

Preached in China where millions were slaves of a long and drowsy past—and many turn their eyes from the tombs of their ancestors and their gods to the cross and to the Christ of that cross.

Preached in Africa where Livingstone held out emaciated hands toward Christ, where Burns and Camphor made themselves meet for the fellowship of martyrs—and over that African highway, marked by the tombstones of martyr missionaries, Ethiopia stumbles with outstretched hands toward God.

Preached in India with its millions of gods and dire poverty—and Krishua Pal, a carpenter, became Carey's first Hindu convert who—later—wrote a hymn in which are the words:

**"O thou, my soul, forget no more
The Friend who all thy sorrows bore."**

Preached in Mexico where multitudes of dark-faced people, held back by centuries of illiteracy, and clouded by agelong superstitions, came to know the sweetness of the words of the Christ: "He that followeth me shall not walk in darkness, but shall have the light of life."

Preached in lanes, in alleys, in countrysides, in mines, in villages, in cities—and many have come out of their bondage, their sorrow, their night, into Christ's freedom, Christ's gladness, Christ's light— "out of the depths of ruin untold, into the peace of Thy sheltering fold."

But why say more? All the words of all languages, most skillfully combined and most eloquently spoken, can express only a meager measure of the wonder contained in the words, "Preached unto the Gentiles."

But now, in conclusion, let us give thought to the Only Begotten of the Father as—

VII. PREEMINENT

"And he is the head of the body, the church: who is the beginning, the firstborn from the dead; that in all things he might have the preeminence."—Col. 1:18.

"He that cometh from above is above all: he that is of the earth is earthly, and speaketh of the earth: he that cometh from heaven is above all."—John 3:31.

"Christ came, who is over all, God blessed for ever. Amen" (Rom. 9:5). Preeminent in preincarnate glory—this Christ. Preeminent in creative power—this Christ. Preeminent in redemption—showing how His infinite holiness could be reconciled to embrace the unclean—this Christ! Preeminent as the Revealer of God—this Christ—expressing the soul of God with entire precision and finality. "He that hath seen me hath seen the Father; and how sayest thou then, Shew us the Father?" (John 14:9). "God was in Christ." "God manifest in the flesh" was Jesus. And let us never forget that without Christ, the Revealer of God, as Saviour and Lord, man is a failure, the world is a carcass, and eternity is a vast horror.

Phenomenally preeminent this Christ is in all things—by the purpose and will and power of God. You can match every good man the world has ever known with one or more equally as great or good.

Homer of the Greeks was great, reaching from pole to pole with the wings of his poetic fancy. But you can match him with Virgil who wielded a pen that ploughed its way as far as Homer's wings of fancy could fly.

Demosthenes, the silver-tongued orator of Greece, finds his equal in Cicero, the Roman.

Edmund Burke whose impeachment speech withered all the flowers of hope in Warren Hasting's garden is equaled or surpassed by Henry Grady who, at the New England banquet, reminded people of an animated aurora with all the variations of a luminous sunset, and by William Jennings Bryan whose words were flights of golden arrows.

Dante, whose ears heard Hell's infernal drums roll the eternal bass in Hell's uproar, beating time to the ceaseless groans of the lost, in the hot breath of Hell's inferno, runs not one step ahead of Milton, the blind Baptist bard, whose ears were attuned to the hallelujah choruses of Heaven.

Shakespeare, from whose pen words dropped like golden pollen from the stems of shaken lilies, has his place disputed by Bacon, one of the greatest intellects of centuries.

Tennyson, with his "Crossing the Bar," has a high pedestal. But along beside him is Longfellow with his "Psalm of Life."

Scotland lifts up her voice in praise to Walter Scott, whose pen was a Niagara of power. But in the same breath they praise with as great joy and honor Robert Burns whose pen seemed to be a golden cage from which choruses of nightingales and sobbing angels were imprisoned and let loose.

Among preachers, Wesley whose prescription for good health was a little more work, stands in equal splendor with Whitefield and Jonathan Edwards who threw revival fires that burned out the dross of nations. Spurgeon was great. And Carroll, the theological juggernaut. But so also was Henry Ward Beecher who let all the bells in his belfry ring for God. So was Broadus whom God kept on double duty as teacher and preacher for half a century. Alexander conquers the world. But so does Caesar. Napoleon was a great general. But he is defeated at Waterloo by Wellington.

You may put side by side—Plato and Socrates, Peter and Paul, Savonarola and Chrysostom, Luther and Wycliffe, Cromwell and Pitt, Lincoln and Lee, Beethoven and Mendelssohn, Angelo and Millet, Molly Pitcher and Grace Darling, Florence Nightingale and Ann Hasseltine, Rogers and Cobb, John Gough and Sam Jones, Lindberg and Wiley Post, Frances Willard and Henrietta Hall Shook. There is no name so great in the history of the world that it may not be equaled by another.

But when we mention Jesus, there is no one to stand beside Him. He stands alone—august, unique, supreme. He is forever the great unlike. His name is above every name, and with Him no mortal can compare among the sons of men.

Charles Lamb was right who said: "If all the illustrious men were gathered together and Shakespeare should enter their shining company, they would all rise to do him honor. But if Jesus Christ should come, we would all kneel to WORSHIP Him."

"Who, being in the form of God, thought it not robbery to be equal with God: But made himself of no reputation, and took upon him the form of a servant, and was made in the likeness of men: And being found in fashion as a man, he humbled himself, and became obedient unto death, even the death of the cross. Wherefore God also hath highly exalted him, and given him a name which is above every name: That at the name of Jesus every knee should bow, of things in heaven, and things in earth, and things under the earth; And that every tongue should confess that Jesus Christ is Lord, to the glory of God the Father."— Phil. 2:6-11.

With these words on our tongues, with these and many other thoughts in our minds, let me ask how large a place you have given to this wonderful Christ in your own life. He **died** for you; do you *live* for Him? Love brought Jesus from the right hand of the eternal Father—love for us in the grips of the fell disease of sin, and took Him to the cross to pay the price for our redemption.

Christ was smitten; we are shielded. Christ was lacerated; we are liberated. Christ was slain; we are secured. Christ's was the judgment; ours is the joy. Christ's was the condemnation; ours is the justification.

Is it nothing to you that the Lord of life and glory should suffer all this for you? How can men have the heart to reject such a Lover of their souls? How can men and women treat with callousness the scenes of Christ's sacrifice on Calvary? How can men treat Calvary's sacrifice as if it were a secondary matter to be attended to or not according to their own convenience?

I pray you to seek the Lord while He may be found, and to settle the question of your salvation once and for all—before your chances be gone forever. Say to your soul, say to earth, say to Hell, say to Heaven, that for your weariest day, Christ shall be your stay—that for the darkest night Christ shall be your light—that for the weakest hour Christ shall be your power—that for each moment's call Christ shall be your all. Then in life and death, in time and eternity, no regrets will ever beset your heart.

(Sermon X from the book, GREAT SERMONS BY GREAT

RAYMOND W. BARBER
1932-

ABOUT THE MAN:

Dr. Barber has been pastor at Worth Baptist Church, Fort Worth, Texas, for some twenty-three years. The Sunday school averages over 800, and the church has a membership of over 2,000.

He is President of Independent Baptist Fellowship International, and an outstanding preacher of the Gospel whose message long remains in the minds and hearts of his congregation and all those who hear him in conferences and special meetings.

Dr. Barber is a member of the Cooperating Board of the Sword of the Lord Foundation, and he is a greatly respected man of God.

We certainly believe his great sermon, "The Deity of Christ," fits in a book on great preaching.

XVI.

The Deity of Christ: Is Jesus God?

RAYMOND W. BARBER

"And without controversy great is the mystery of godliness: God was manifest in the flesh, justified in the Spirit, seen of angels, preached unto the Gentiles, believed on in the world, received up into glory." —I Tim. 3:16.

This is the life of Christ in a nutshell.

ATTACKS UPON DEITY

Any attack upon the Bible, the Word of God, is an attack upon the deity of the Lord Jesus Christ. In John, chapter 14 and verse 9, Jesus said, "He that hath seen me hath seen the Father." Jesus said, "I and my Father are one."

When the liberals attack the inspiration of the Scriptures, they attack the deity of Jesus Christ.

When the atheists attack the existence of God, they attack the deity of Jesus Christ.

When the evolutionists attack the Genesis account of creation, they attack the deity of Jesus Christ.

When the skeptics attack the miracles in the Bible, they attack the deity of the Lord Jesus Christ.

When the infidels attack the virgin birth of Jesus, they attack the deity of the Lord.

NOTHING NEW

The war of attempted annihilation against Jesus Christ is not new.

It began in the long ago. Satan himself launched the first campaign in the Garden of Eden when he lied to our first parents, Adam and Eve.

Pharaoh launched a campaign in Egypt when he attempted to destroy all the male children of Israel.

Nebuchadnezzar launched a campaign in Jerusalem when he attempted to wipe out Judah, the tribe that was prophesied to bring into the world in the flesh the Lord Jesus Christ.

Herod the Great launched an attack in his campaign in Bethlehem when he issued a decree for the slaughter of all the infants.

In the Twentieth Century the battle rages on.

It is fought by professors in the classroom.

It is fought by preachers in the pulpit.

It is fought by profaners in the street.

Permit me to read to you from a book entitled *In Defense of the Faith* by the famed pastor of the First Baptist Church of Dallas, Texas. Dr. Criswell writes concerning some of the liberals and infidels in so-called Christian schools and seminaries. I quote Dr. Criswell who quotes another source, *The Leaven of the Sadducees*, by Ernest Gordon.

> One of our noble Christian seminaries had a professor who said, "An intelligent man who now affirms his faith in miracles can hardly know what intellectual honesty means. The hypothesis of God has become superfluous in religion. Jesus did not transcend the limits of purely human."
>
> Another great Christian theological school had a professor who said, "We shall hardly bandy words about the finality of Christ. The field is open for anyone at any time to mean more to men than Jesus has meant. He was a mere human being. He was the child of his people and of his time."
>
> A far-famed Christian college had a professor who wrote, "Whether Jesus ever lived is a historical question that is interesting, but it is not fundamental to religion, and if it be suggested in criticism that you then have a Christian religion without a historic Jesus, may I suggest that if Jesus was all that he so generously claimed, or that is so generously claimed of him, he ought not to be so sensitive about his own name or himself."
>
> A great seminary had a professor who said, "I believe that the whole view of the Bible with its theory of a chosen people, special revelation, and prophecies is utterly unconvincing and basically vicious."
>
> Possibly the most famous seminary in America had a professor who said, "I do not believe that the religion of tomorrow will have

any more place for prayer than it will have for any other form of magic."

Another who said, "As far as I am concerned, the idea of God plays no part in my religion."

Another who added, "Where the old religion made the supreme object God, the new religion makes it humanity. Sociology takes the place of theology, and an improved social order replaces the belief in immortality."

The editor of the *Chicago Daily News* wrote in an editorial:

> We are stuck with the hypocrisy and the treachery and the attacks on Christianity. This is a free country and a free age, and men can say what they choose about religion, but this is not what we arraigned these divinity professors for. Is there no place to assail Christianity but a divinity school? Is there no one to write infidel books but professors of Christian theology? Is a theological seminary an appropriate place for a general massacre of Christian doctrines? We are not championing either Christianity or infidelity, but only condemning infidels masquerading as men of God and Christian teachers.

DENYING THE FAITH

I heard an outstanding man of God and pastor of long standing say not long ago that he could count on one hand the seminaries in the United States that are still true to the inspired Word of God.

We're living in an hour when the professors are fighting in the classroom against the deity of the Lord Jesus. As I stated earlier, any attack against the Bible, any attack against the creation, any attack against inspiration, and any attack against miracles is an attack directly against the Lord Jesus Christ. Preachers in the pulpits are doing the same.

The name Bob Ingersoll will register with some of you. Bob Ingersoll was one of the most infamous infidels this country has ever known. He made it his business to go up and down the length and breadth of this nation denouncing the Bible, denouncing inspiration, denouncing the virgin birth, and denouncing the deity of the Lord Jesus Christ.

One day someone asked him after he had quit doing that, "Why, Mr. Ingersoll, have you quit going across the country denouncing the Bible and denouncing the Faith and denouncing Christ?" And his answer was, "The divinity professors in the classrooms and the preachers in the pulpits are doing a fine job without my help. I need no longer denounce the Faith."

The danger of denouncing the Faith is the fact that it is coming from so-called scholasticism—the so-called intellectuals of our day.

If some bum who just jumped off a railroad car would come up to you and say, "I don't believe God exists," that wouldn't disturb you.

If some long-haired hippie trying to find his way would come to you and say, "Christ was not the Son of God," that wouldn't disturb you.

But when a man of the cloth, when a man in high divinical circles stands in the pulpit or in a classroom and denies the inspiration of the Bible, denies the virgin birth of Christ and denies the deity of the Lord, that should cause you concern. And that's what is happening all over the world. It is difficult to choose a college in our day where you can trust the theology department or the department of religion.

God help us to come back to the hour when we make our stand for the blessed old Book, the Book that men have lived by and died by. This is our creed. This is our only and final rule of authority, and this is the blessed Book of God, and it tells us about the blessed Christ of God.

IS CHRIST GOD?

The crux of the whole matter is this: Jesus Christ is either God or He is not God. He is either right or wrong. He is either good or evil. He is either true of false.

Is Christ an impostor?

Is Christ an impersonator?

Is Christ a usurper?

Is Christ an imitator?

Is Christ a blasphemer?

Is Christ a fraud?

Is Christ a paranoid?

Is Christ a pretender?

If He is not the Son of God, He is all this and much more. If Jesus Christ is not the Son of God . . . He has deceived countless millions; He has blasphemed the Almighty; He has desecrated all that is sacred; He has made a laughingstock of multiplied countless millions of believers; He has falsely represented God; He has nullified the doctrine of the Trinity; He has scandalized the truth of God; He has invalidated the writings of the prophets.

To deny the deity of the Lord Jesus is to deny the ability of God, the truth of God, the creation of God, the worship of God, the power of God, the Word of God, the salvation of God, the mercy of God, the wisdom of God, the grace of God, and the love of God.

To strip Christ of His deity would be to put the demons back into the demoniac. It would mean to put the fever back into the sick. It would mean to put blindness back into the beggar. It would mean to put Lazarus back at the rich man's gate. It would mean to put the dead back into their graves, never to live again.

To take the deity away from Christ would be to take the wine out of the waterpots in Cana of Galilee. It would be to take the fish and loaves out of the boy's basket. It would be to take the fish out of the fisherman's net, the brightness out of the sun, the reflection out of the moon, the fragrance out of the flowers, and the light out of all the stars.

To erase the deity of Christ would be to erase all rhythm from all poetry. It would erase the music from all songs. It would erase the beauty from all art. It would erase the name of every born-again, blood-washed, redeemed soul whose name is recorded in the Lamb's Book of Life.

To destroy His deity means you will have to destroy the Bible. You will have to destroy the church. You will have to destroy the home. You will have to destroy government. You will have to destroy civilization. You would have to destroy history. You would have to destroy prophecy.

To eradicate His deity, you would have to uproot all the trees, dry up all the rivers, evaporate all oceans, eliminate all the elements, dissolve all matter, eradicate all energy, destroy all life, disintegrate the earth, darken the sun, denounce the truth, deny the miracles, desecrate the Faith, and ultimately dethrone God.

If you were to rob Jesus Christ of His deity, you would have to break up all the homes He has salvaged. You would have to disease all the bodies He has healed. You would have to kill all the dead He has raised from the grave. You would have to disease and twist the limbs of all those whom He hath straightened out. You would have to inebriate all the drunkards He has sobered. You would have to emaciate all the weaklings He has strengthened. You would have to shatter all the dreams He has fulfilled. You would have to break all the hearts He has mended. You would have to tear-stain all the eyes He has dried. You would have to unsave all the souls He has saved.

If you dissolve His deity, you would have to divorce all the couples who have married in His name. You would have to destroy all the documents that have been dated from His birth. You would have to denounce all the doctrines taught in His Book. You would have to defrock all the preachers who have been ordained to His Gospel. You would have to de-church all the people who have been added to His blessed body.

Ladies and gentlemen, none of this is necessary. None of this is possible. None of this can be done, nor should it even be attempted because Jesus Christ is the Son of the Living God. Peter said, "Thou art the Christ, the Son of the living God." And Jesus said to him, "Blessed art thou, Simon Bar-jona: for flesh and blood hath not revealed it unto thee, but my Father which is in heaven."

What I am giving you does not come out of the books of science. It does not come out of the books of knowledge. It does not come out of the books of learning. It comes out of the Book of God. Jesus Christ is God in the flesh. What a Saviour is our Saviour!

You need not blush to speak His name. You need not stutter or stammer to praise His wonderful Word. His story is written on every page of human history. His image is stamped on every member of Adam's race. His power is manifest in every motion of the universe. Jesus Christ is God! It is declared in John chapter 1, verses 1, 2, and 14:

"In the beginning was the Word, and the Word was with God, and the Word was God. The same was in the beginning with God . . . And the Word was made flesh, and dwelt among us, (and we beheld his glory, the glory as of the only begotten of the Father,) full of grace and truth."

It is written in Colossians 2:9, "For in him dwelleth all the fullness of the Godhead bodily" — God the Father, God the Son, and God the blessed Spirit. In the name of the thrice holy God, I declare to you that Jesus Christ is God.

JESUS IS GOD

He always has been God.

He always shall be God.

God never changes.

God never diminishes.

He will always be the same.

Jesus Christ was God in the world above.

He was God on the plains of Mamre as He spoke to Abraham.

He was God on Mount Sinai when He gave the commandments and the law to Moses.

He was God in the womb of the virgin Mary.

He was God in the manger at Bethlehem.

He was God in the carpenter's shop at Nazareth.

He was God in the boat at Lake Galilee.

He was God in the Temple at Jerusalem.

He was God on the Mount of Transfiguration.

He was God in the Garden of Gethsemane as He prayed, "Let this cup pass from me, nevertheless, not my will, but thy will be done."

He was God on the cross as He cried out, "It is finished."

He was God in the tomb of Joseph as He lay still in death.

He was God on the morning of the resurrection as He broke asunder the bands of death and came out triumphantly over death, the grave and Hell.

He was God on the Mount of Olives as His feet left that sacred spot.

He was God in the cloud of ascension as He went away.

He is God at the right hand of the throne now.

He will be God coming again as He comes in flaming fire to take vengeance upon all who know not Him and who have never trusted Him as Saviour.

UNMISTAKABLY DIVINE

History declares His deity. Prophecy accents His deity. Christianity testifies of His deity. Philosophy reasons of His deity. Literature writes about His deity. And music sings of His deity.

To explain Him is impossible. To ignore Him is disastrous. To reject Him is fatal. But to know Him is to love Him, and to love Him is to believe Him, and to believe Him is to be saved. Human speech is too limited to describe Him. The human mind is too finite to comprehend Him. The human heart is too small to contain Him.

He was God in the flesh during His days upon earth. When He worked, God labored with human hands. When He walked, God traveled on human feet. Jesus Christ is God! The deity of the Lord Jesus Christ is the one doctrine upon which all the other doctrines of the Bible either stand or fall.

I repeat, if He be not the Son of God, He is the greatest impostor and blasphemer the world has ever known. He surely was a man suffering under great delusions if He were not God.

Who else but God could say, "Thy sins be forgiven thee"? Who else but God could say, "Go thy way and sin no more"? Who else but God could say, "I am the way, the truth, and the life"? Who else but God could say, "I am Alpha and Omega"? About whom else could it be said, "Neither is there salvation in any other: for there is none other name under heaven given among men, whereby we must be saved"? Who else could claim to be the light of the world but God? Who else could be the bread of life but God? Who else could be the water of life but God?

Who else could say, "I am the resurrection, and the life: he that believeth in me, though he were dead, yet shall he live: And whosoever liveth and believeth in me shall never die"? Who else could say, "Come unto me, all ye that labour and are heavy laden, and I will give you rest"? Who else could say, "Take my yoke upon you, and learn of me; for I am meek and lowly in heart: and ye shall find rest unto your souls"? Who else could say, "Behold, I come quickly; and my reward is with me"? None but God! None but God in the flesh, and Jesus Christ was just as much God as though He had never been man, and just as much man as though He had never been God.

DEITY CONFIRMED

The deity of Christ is confirmed in seven basic ways. First, **His deity is confirmed by the _names_ given Him.** He is called "God" in Hebrews 1:8. He is called the "Son of God" in Matthew 16:16. He is called the "Lord" in Acts 16:31.

Second, **His deity is confirmed by the _worship_ that is ascribed to Him.** Men and angels worship Him. Let me read it to you from the Revelation, chapter 5, beginning at verse 11:

"And I beheld, and I heard the voice of many angels round about the throne and the beasts and the elders: and the number of them was ten thousand times ten thousand, and thousands of thousands; Saying with a loud voice, Worthy is the Lamb that was slain to receive power, and riches, and wisdom, and strength, and honour, and glory, and blessing."

And I read in Philippians, chapter 2:

"Let this mind be in you, which was also in Christ Jesus: Who, being in the form of God, thought it not robbery to be equal with God: But made himself of no reputation, and took upon him the form of a servant, and was made in the likeness of men: And being found in fashion as a man, he humbled himself, and became obedient unto death, even the death of the cross. Wherefore God also hath highly exalted him, and given him a name which is above every name: That at the name

*of Jesus every knee should bow, of things in heaven, and things in earth,
and things under the earth; And that every tongue should confess that
Jesus Christ is Lord, to the glory of God the Father."*

Men everywhere one day shall worship Him when the angels fall down
before Him ascribing to Him all majesty and glory and might and power
and wisdom from every tribe on this terrestrial globe. Out of every kin-
dred on the earth shall men come to pay honor to Him. Bless His
wonderful name! Love Him? Yes! Adore Him? Yes! Worship Him? Yes!
Crown Him Lord of all? Yes! Bring forth the royal diadem, and crown
Him Lord of all!

**The third fact that confirms His deity is His *equality* with the
Father.** In John, chapter 5, He is seen as being equal with the Father
in working, in wisdom, in His power to resurrect the dead, in His authority
to judge, in His position of honor, and in His ability to give life. He is
equal with the Father.

The fourth great fact that confirms His deity is His *virgin birth*.
In Genesis 3:15 it is prophesied that the seed of the woman would bruise
the head of Satan, the serpent. The old rabbi used to wonder about
that verse. The seed of the woman? Unheard of! The seed comes from
the man. But then 750 years before Christ was born, Isaiah took the
prophetic pen in hand and wrote, "The Lord himself shall give you a
sign; Behold, a virgin shall conceive, and bear a son, and shall call his
name Immanuel," which means "God with us." In Luke 1:35 when the
angel made the announcement to Mary, he said,

*"The Holy Ghost shall come upon thee, and the power of the Highest
shall overshadow thee: therefore also that holy thing which shall be born
of thee shall be called the Son of God."*

The virgin birth is the most important doctrine that supports the deity of the Lord Jesus Christ upon which all other doctrines fall or stand.

If Jesus Christ be not born of a virgin, there is no Trinity; for He is
the second person of the Trinity. If Jesus Christ be not born of a virgin,
there is no resurrection; for He is the resurrection. If Jesus Christ be
not born of a virgin, Christianity is only a myth that will in the end suc-
cumb to its own deception and be buried beneath the ashes of its own
presumption.

Jesus Christ was virgin-born. It matters not what all the infidels and
agnostics and unbelievers and college professors and "baboon chasers"
and D. D.'s and PH. D.'s and everybody else say, I believe He was born

of a virgin because the Bible says so. I believe He was born of a virgin because He lives in my heart. I believe! I believe! I believe that Christ is the virgin-born, sinless, perfect Son of the living God.

The fifth fact that confirms His deity is His *sacrificial death* upon the cross. I read in I Corinthians, chapter 15 and verse 3: "He died for our sins." If He were not the divine Son of God, His death would be meaningless. His death would mean no more than your death. He must be, and He *is*, the Son of God because He died a sacrificial death upon the cross. Peter said in his first epistle, chapter 2, "Who his own self bare our sins in his own body on the tree, that we, being dead to sins, should live unto righteousness: by whose stripes ye were healed."

The sixth outstanding fact that confirms His deity is His glorious *resurrection* from among the dead. I read in Romans 1:4 that He is declared to be the Son of God by the resurrection from the dead. Before Christ there was no resurrection. Until Christ comes again, there shall not be any resurrection; for He *is* the resurrection and the life.

The seventh fact that confirms His deity is His triumphant *return*. Sweeter words were never spoken than these from John's Gospel, chapter 14:

"Let not your heart be troubled: ye believe in God, believe also in me. In my Father's house are many mansions: if it were not so, I would have told you. I go to prepare a place for you. And if I go and prepare a place for you, I will come again, and receive you unto myself; that were I am, there ye may be also."

The deity of the Lord Jesus Christ is the central thought and the central fiber and the central doctrine of the Bible.

FOOTNOTE

I have a footnote and I am through: The deity of Christ is confirmed by the *testimony of men who died clinging to the belief that Jesus Christ is the Saviour.*

Mr. Pat Zondervan of the Zondervan Publishing House in Michigan often goes across the country making an appeal for the Gideons International, placing Bibles all over the world. In one of his recent presentations of the ministry of the Gideons, he held up a little Testament that had been taken off the body of a dead soldier in Vietnam—a marine from the state of Georgia. When he held it up, everybody noticed that there was a hole all the way through the little Testament. There was blood on every page—the blood of a soldier fallen in battle. And when he turned to the last page, there was written in the trembling handwriting of a dying soldier these words: *"I, Wilton Thomas, take Jesus Christ as my personal Saviour."* He signed his name, Wilton Thomas, and died clinging to the belief that Jesus Christ is the divine Son of God.

I believe it! It's in the Book!

GEORGE W. TRUETT
1867-1944

ABOUT THE MAN:

North Carolina was George Washington Truett's birthplace. By the time he was 18, he was educated well enough to begin teaching in a one-room public school on Crooked Creek in nearby Towns County, Georgia. It was during that two-year apprenticeship that George was converted. Then he established an academy at Hiawassee, Georgia, in 1887. The student body eventually numbered over 300.

When the Truett family moved to Texas in 1889, George went to college—Baylor University—though not as a student. He was offered the position of financial secretary and was instrumental in saving Baylor from bankruptcy. Afterward he became a student, graduated, and unbelievably was elected to become Baylor's president!

But the same year of his graduation he was called to the First Baptist Church of Dallas, remaining there for 47 years, or until his death in 1944. Under his leadership the church grew into the largest church in the world at that time, with 18,124 additions and 5,337 baptisms.

But Dr. Truett had many pulpits besides the pulpit at First Baptist Church. He instituted the Palace Theatre services, held each noon the week before Easter, with nearly 2,000 attending. He preached out in the country churches all across the South, and the common folk heard him gladly. He preached from the steps of our nation's Capitol, and in world centers in London, Stockholm, Paris, Berlin, Jerusalem, etc. Everywhere Truett's preaching produced souls for Christ.

In 1927 he was elected president of the Southern Baptist Convention, which office he served for three terms.

By any standard, he ranks as one of the most popular and influential preachers in America in the first half of the 20th century. He was a world figure; was on close terms with presidents, senators and governors.

Dr. Truett was a great man, a great leader, and a great preacher of the Gospel. His biographers knew whereof they spoke when they explained the man and his ministry in two well-defined words: "heart-power."

XVII.

Whom Say Ye That I Am?

GEORGE W. TRUETT

"Whom say ye that I am?"—Matt. 16:15.

The right views of Christ are necessary. Right relations toward Him and the right service for Him are necessary. The question, therefore, that Christ asked His disciples when He was here in the flesh nineteen hundred years ago is the supreme question to be faced by every rational human being: "Whom say ye that I am?"

His previous question to these same disciples a moment before was, "Whom do men say that I the Son of man am?" And they said, "Some say that thou art John the Baptist; some, Elias; and others, Jeremias, or one of the prophets." And then quickly he put to them the probing question, "Whom say ye that I am?" And one of the men, Simon Peter, made answer, and it was an inspired reply: "Thou art the Christ, the Son of the living God." To which Jesus replied, "Blessed art thou, Simon Bar-jona: for flesh and blood hath not revealed it unto thee, but my Father which is in heaven."

That same question, "Whom say ye that I am?" comes echoing its way all down the centuries. And the question will not be downed, for Christ crosses the threshold of every rational life and puts to every one the probing inquiry, "Whom say ye that I am?" And the sincere, the serious and the earnest seeker after the truth will at last come to say what Simon here said: "Thou art the Christ, the Son of the living God."

Let us make this question the theme for our meditation this morning hour. Who is Christ Jesus? Whom do you say that He is? "Whom say ye that I am?" is the probing question of Jesus. This question related directly to the person of Christ. Christianity stands or falls with the person of Christ. Historic, apostolic, supernatural Christianity stands or falls with the person of Christ.

There have been three views in this world about Christ: one that He was wicked; another that He was good, but mistaken about His claims; and the other that He was God—God manifest in the flesh—the Redeemer who came to save a needy world which was estranged from God and lost in sin.

Concerning this first view, one would go a long way before hearing any derisive word concerning Jesus. In all my lifetime I have had only one bad letter deriding Jesus, the writer using epithets which I shall not quote. I wonder if the man were not crazy. Thoughtful and candid men, whatever may be their unbelief, look at Jesus and say, "He is the fairest among ten thousand, and the One altogether lovely." Many who do not accept the higher claims concerning Him do not hesitate to say that Jesus was the best man who ever lived.

Another view concerning Christ was that He was good but mistaken in His claims: that He was earth's highest and best but mistaken in His own claims and assumptions. Edward Everett Hale held this view. Some clever men hold that view today. One wonders how on earth they can believe that Jesus, who made such astounding claims concerning Himself, could be good, wise or sane, if He was nothing more than man. They well know that nothing short of deity can satisfy the claims which Jesus made for Himself.

The theory that Christ was only a man reduces Him to a mere physical being. And this theory, no matter how beautiful, is lacking in that dynamic needed to lift men out of the mire. Men need a power above themselves. Every man needs a power to come into his life above himself. Mere ethics will not do. Beautiful theories will not do and dainty, perfumed philosophies will not do. If Christ be only a man, He cannot lift men out of the quagmire of sin, guilt and death.

The other view is the one held by you and me. That is the New Testament view that Jesus was just what He claimed to be: God manifest in the flesh. I stake my all on it. I have not the remotest semblance of a question in my mind concerning this other view—that Christ was more than man; that Christ was God and Man in one personality—the God-Man. That hyphen both joins and divides. That hyphen marks a distinction as though He were God and not man at all, and as though He were man and not God at all.

John describes Jesus in five little words, "The Word was made flesh."

Paul, speaking of Jesus, said, "Great is the mystery of godliness: God was manifest in the flesh, justified in the Spirit, seen of angels, preached unto the Gentiles, believed on in the world, received up into glory." That is Paul's majestic description of the person and worth of Christ.

Victor Hugo states the case—the universal verdict, almost—when he said that Jesus was the "ultimate in all life." Even Lord Byron rose up and said, "If ever man was God, and if ever God was man, this Jesus Christ is both." And Browning said, "The acceptance of God in Christ solves for us all problems in the world and the next."

Charles Lamb once said that he was at a luncheon with a group of brilliant men and women and their subject that evening was, "The Person I Would Like Best to Have Seen." A great array of brilliant personages was passed in review that evening. One said he would like to have seen Chaucer; another said John Milton; another said John Bunyan; another said Shakespeare. On and on they talked. Presently, Charles Lamb said, "If Shakespeare were to come into this room, we would all rise and bow to him; but I am thinking of One other whose name has not been called. If HE were to come into this room now, all of us here would fall down on our kness and cry out with Thomas of old, 'My Lord and my God!'"

Christ stands forth, unapproached and unapproachable, incomparable. Indeed, never was there another person like unto Him in all the annals of time and never will there be another like Him—Christ, the divine Son of God. Born nineteen hundred years ago in a stable and laid in a manger because there was no room for the mother in the inn, in that crisis hour of her life. Born in a stable, yet about that humble place there gathers more interest than about all the other treasure-houses of the great, from the first man until the last.

His name is the most potent, the most inspiring, the most majestic in all the world. His is the name which is above every name. "Thou shalt call his name JESUS: for he shall save his people from their sins." He is the One who stirs our hearts, who shares our sorrows, who gives us life, love, peace and joy.

We unwaveringly subscribe to the declaration made by Simon Peter when he said to Jesus, "Thou art the Christ, the Son of the living God." Without hesitation or any semblance of doubt, I declare my belief that Christ is the divine Son of God; that He is unlike any other being the universe has ever known, or ever shall know; that He is the Way, the Truth, the Life, the Pilot, the older Brother, the Guide who came to bring be-darkened, sinning men and women home to God. I believe

Him to be the one Mediator between God and man; the One by whom alone we can gain access to the Father and receive His forgiving and unfailing love.

Now, why do we hold unwaveringly to this higher view of Christ? The reasons are varied, but I think they are valid. Let us hurriedly look at some of them.

The Life of Christ Is the Answer to All Contentions As to Himself

He flings out the challenge, 'Who of you can convict Me of sin?' We can convict all others of sin. We can find defects in any other who ever walked the paths of earth. The founders of great religions, like Mohammed and Buddha, were wretchedly wrong in their own lives in many respects, which fact they did not disguise or deny. But Christ flings out the challenge to the whole world: 'Which of you can convict Me of sin?'

Is there one ill-advised word that He ever spoke? Is there one selfish deed that He ever did? Who of all the world can convict Him of sin? There He stands against the horizon: "THE Son of Man" —not a son of man, but THE Son of Man—for all humanity is summed up in Him. THE Son of Man, yet the sinless Son of Man!

If you look for the highest example of meekness that the world has ever known, you will not turn to Moses, called the "meekest man," but to Christ, unprecedently meek and lowly in heart.

If you look for the highest example of patience, you do not turn to Job, called the "most patient man," but to Christ who, when He was reviled, reviled not again.

If you ask for the highest example of wisdom, you do not turn to Solomon, called "the wisest man," but to Christ, "who spake as never man spake."

For the highest example of zeal, you do not turn to Paul but to Christ, concerning whom it is written, "The zeal of thine house hath eaten me up."

For the highest example of love, you do not turn to John, gentle John, but to Christ who so loved us that He left His Father's house and came down to earth, and lived His life of unselfishness, climbed His cross and died thereon, out of pure love for you and me and for all our broken, sinning fellow-humanity.

The life of Christ is the answer to His own divine claim.

Not even Pilate could find fault in Him. The searchlight of criticism, both from His friends and His foes, has been focused on Jesus for over nineteen hundred years, yet there He stands, flawless, spotless, sinless! You cannot say that about anyone else. You can find faults with Moses, with Abram, with Job, with Isaiah, with David, with Paul and Barnabas. You can put your finger on the defects of men up and down the world, without any exception; but Christ alone stands, flawless, spotless and without sin. You cannot say that about any other life. His life attests His divine claims.

His Teaching Gives Added Attestation

May we look at His teachings? Christ is the One universal Teacher. You see, sometimes, a picture on the wall, and no matter where you are, those eyes look right at you. You may change your place wherever you will, and those eyes follow you no matter where you go.

So it is with the teachings of Christ. They find universal humanity. He is the universal Teacher and His words are equally adapted to men of all races and all countries and all centuries; to the white man, the black man, the brown man, the red man, every man of every color. His teachings are for all men.

He is the One we want to hear about. Jesus, born in the first century, belongs to the twentieth century even as He did to the first. Born a Jew, He belongs to all races. Born in the little country of Palestine, He is now the universal Teacher of all men. The wise and the ignorant, the high and the low are probed alike by His questions and by His teachings. They find universal humanity.

Shakespeare, the very flower of the Elizabethan era, was marvelous in the eyes of the English people, but not so in the eyes of the French people.

Victor Hugo was marvelous as a literary leader with the French people, but not so with the English people.

And Napoleon, that military genius, swayed France in an amazing way, yet he was altogether undesirable and repellent in the eyes of the English people.

Oliver Cromwell deeply impressed England, but he was abhorred and abominated by France.

But Jesus belongs to all people. He spoke His first words and His last words, recorded in the New Testament, over nineteen centuries ago, and these words are not out of date today. Was there ever another lullaby sung by a mother to her child so haunting and so sweet as those words from the lips of Jesus: "Come unto me, all ye that labour and are heavy laden, and I will give you rest. Take my yoke upon you, and learn of me; for I am meek and lowly in heart: and ye shall find rest unto your souls. For my yoke is easy, and my burden is light"? Take these invitations from Christ and they are as honey out of the Rock of God. And He comes closer and closer, and more vitally, into relation with us every hour we live.

That saying of Jesus, "Render . . . unto Caesar the things that are Caesar's; and unto God the things that are God's," ushered in the sunrise of a new day. That was Christ's announcement of a principle designed for universal application. That saying of Jesus is the true Magna Carta of the doctrine of the separation of church and state, which doctrine someday, please God, will be embraced by all the nations of earth.

Christ is the only Person who can answer the big question that comes to us, "How can I make my peace with God, though I am broken by sin?" He said, "I am the way, the truth, and the life: no man cometh unto the Father, but by me."

How shall I treat my fellow-man? What are to be the relations of my race toward the other races of men? Jesus said, "Do unto others as you would have others do unto you." Jesus answered that by giving the Parable of the Good Samaritan, showing that the man of a hated race was neighbor to the Jew in need.

"Then, who is my neighbor?" we ask. Jesus tells us: Your neighbor is anybody on the face of the earth who needs you. Maybe he lives in Dallas; maybe he lives in the wilds of Africa and is the most ignorant creature walking on the earth today. Very well, wherever, under the whole heavens, there is a human being who needs you, he or she is your neighbor. Hasten to him and help him in every possible way.

In South America, North America, in Europe, in Asia, in Africa, people have heard the divine teachings of Jesus and have bowed before those teachings. Unparalleled among the religions of the earth are the words of Jesus, for Christ the Son of God 'taught as never man taught.'

Christ stands at the open grave, in the presence of darksome bereavement, telling us that death is not all. He cries, "I am the resurrection, and the life: he that believeth in me, though he were dead, yet shall he live: And whosoever liveth and believeth in me shall never die." "Because I live, ye shall live also." Be not afraid of this last and greatest enemy called Death, if your trust is in Christ.

What else? Not only does the life of Christ attest His divine claims, and not only does His teaching give added attestation, but . . .

His Death on the Cross Attests
His Divine Claims

The centurion, standing at the foot of that cross, seeing Jesus die and hearing Him as He prayed for His murderers, properly made the explanation when it was all over: "Truly, this was the Son of God."

The death of Christ was unique, substitutionary, redemptive. Wherever the facts concerning Christ's life and death are told throughout the world, men's hearts and consciences are stirred and they begin to ask, "What must we do to be saved?" And why?

Jesus tells us: "And I, if I be lifted up from the earth, will draw all men unto me. This he said, signifying by what death he should die."

The death of Christ was more than a dramatic example. It was a dynamic, sacrificial, substitutionary atonement for human sins. Verily He was the sacrificial Lamb of God which taketh away the sin of the world. The Scriptures tell us that He bore our sins in His own body on the tree; and that His blood cleanseth us from all sin.

John Newton was a notorious sinner—one of the world's most outstanding sinners, we are told; but when he had a full view of Christ dying on the cross, his heart was utterly broken and he made his surrender to Christ; and in the glow of that great surrender, he penned a hymn we often sing:

> In evil long I took delight,
>   Unawed by shame or fear,
> 'Til a new object struck my sight
>   And stopped my wild career.
>
> I saw One hanging on a tree,
>   In agony and blood—
> He fixed His languid eyes on me,
>   As near the cross I stood.
>
> Sure, never 'til my latest breath,
>   Can I forget that look.
> It seemed to charge me with His death,
>   Though not a word He spoke.
>
> My conscience felt and owned the guilt,
>   It plunged me in despair;
> I knew my sins His blood had spilt,
>   And helped to nail Him there.

A second look He gave, which said,
"I freely all forgive;
This blood is for thy ransom paid:
I die that thou mayest live."

This is the way home. The death of Christ attests His divine claims. No wonder it wins over legalism, over Judaism, over paganism. 'For every knee shall bow, and every tongue shall confess that Jesus Christ is Lord, to the glory of God the Father.'

Socrates died like a philosopher. Jesus died like a God. He was God. He died, "the just for the unjust, that he might bring us to God."

The Best Attested Fact — the Resurrection

Then again, let us look at the resurrection of Christ. Millions are thinking about that on this Sunday called Easter. They are thinking about it around the globe. They are thinking about it on the great ships in mid-ocean; they are thinking about it in churches, in hospitals; they are thinking about it in homes where life is about to be snuffed out by some fatal illness; they are thinking about it as they bend over the bodies of their dear, departed dead; they are thinking about it the world around. What shall I say about the fact of Christ's resurrection? Christ is not in the grave! He is risen! "Come, see the place where the Lord lay!" He is risen! He is alive from the dead! He is alive forevermore!

If your eyes and mine were not holden, we would see Him in this great throng. He is bringing to bear the resources of wisdom and mercy and power and love on us. Christ is alive from the dead! The grave was empty of its contents. That body carried to the grave came forth from the grave. Even now Christ is reigning yonder on high! And someday He is coming again to judge the world in truth and righteousness. And we believe that He will come with the same body that was put to death on the cross. We shall see that body glorified with the glorification which God will give to the redeemed in Christ who shall rise first to meet Him in the air on the resurrection morning.

Greenleaf, our greatest authority on evidence, says: "The best attested fact of all history is the fact that Jesus rose from the dead."

The Holy Scripture tells that Jesus was seen five times on the resurrection day. He was seen of Mary; He was seen of the women; He was seen of Simon Peter; He was seen by two disciples on the road to Emmaus; He was seen by the apostles as they sat at meat. Later, He was seen by seven apostles by the sea, and by above five hundred at another time. He was seen by James, and last of all, He was seen by Paul, earth's chiefest apostle.

The evidences external and internal that Christ rose from the grave are overwhelming. That is our hope in the face of broken humanity; that is our hope in the face of life; that is our hope in the face of death.

Christ went down into the grave and came up out of the grave, and He says to you and to me through His teachings, "You can trust Me, and when your time comes to die—no matter where, nor when, nor how—I will be there to pilot you through the dark waters and to take you Home on the other side, victorious, white robed and eternal conqueror over death and the grave."

What else? His influence is worldwide. Christ is cutting His way through all history, and His purposes are ripening with the rising and setting of every sun. We are in no losing battle. The hands of Christ's clock never turn back. The wheels of God's chariot never cease rolling. Here is His own great promise in the Bible: "HE MUST REIGN, till he hath put all enemies under his feet." It is a predestinated necessity. Christ MUST reign—not *may* reign—but HE MUST REIGN. Someday, "from the river unto the ends of the earth," Christ will be Lord of all, and even death shall be under His feet.

Behold! Christ comes to you and to me saying, "If you will put your trust in Me, I will show you the way. If you will decide for Me, cleave to Me, follow after Me, I will bring you out of the darkness; I will heal your broken heart; I will give you the joy of forgiveness; I will give you the sense of freedom; I will give you the spirit of triumph; I will put within you the power to overcome the temptations that assail you, and I will bring you out more than conqueror, when you come down to death, if you will put your trust in Me." Here is the crowning promise: "I will never leave thee nor forsake thee."

Christ puts Himself to the test by demonstration: "Come and see!" "Come and trust Me. Come and give up to Me. Come with your doubts! Come! I will dissolve them for you! Come with your fears! I will drive them back and dissipate them. Come with all your sins! Though you be marred and stained by sin; though your sins be red like crimson, come, yield to Me! With My own life, with My own atoning death, I will forgive you and I will set you free!" Will you come?

The Test of Personal Experience

Here is the real proof and demonstration, which should satisfy all

254 GREAT PREACHING ON THE DEITY OF CHRIST

science and all philosophy—a demonstration of experience.

A young man once asked an outstanding scientist what was his greatest discovery. The scientist waited a moment, then replied: "Young man, my greatest discovery of all is my discovery that Jesus Christ is my personal Saviour! I have trusted Him; He has saved me and I know it!"

Ah, here is the true test—the test of personal experience. "Therefore being justified by faith, we have peace with God through our Lord Jesus Christ," because our trust is in Him.

I saw a little boy trying to comfort his father. The father had lost his wife; the boy had lost his mother. The ten-year-old little fellow was a Christian. The big brawny man held the little sobbing boy against his own heart. The lad put his arms around his father's neck and said, "Daddy, it will not be long until we go Home. You won't cry like that anymore, will you? You and I love Jesus like Mama did, and it will not be long until we go Home, too. You won't cry anymore, will you, Daddy?"

The big man straightened up and said, "My boy, you have said the right word. Certainly not. We will think of the time when we will all go Home."

Take all your bereavements, woes, losses, shadows, and every kind of grief to that wonderful Saviour.

'Tis the Saviour that can give
Sweetest pleasures while we live.
'Tis the Saviour must supply,
Solid comfort when we die.
After death my joy shall be
Lasting as eternity.
Be that Living Christ my Friend,
Then my joys shall never end.

Oh, my men and women, heavy-burdened men and women, needy men and women, busy, suffering, sinning men and women; oh, men and women making one quick passage through time into eternity— what have you done with Christ? Do you say, "Sir, I trust Him. I am leaning on Him. Other refuge have I none, nor do I want any other"? Can you say, "I know whom I have believed, and am persuaded that he is able to keep that which I have committed unto him against that day"? Does your heart say that? Then, go your way rejoicing!

But what of you who are not saved, dear men and women, boys and girls? You have heard about Jesus today. Will you not turn squarely and face Him as you hear Him ask, "Whom say ye that I am?" Is He what He claims to be? Is He the one Saviour for all mankind? Is He the

Arbitrator, the Mediator, the Pilot, the Guide, the Redeeming Saviour to bring you victoriously Home? Is He? And does your heart say, "Yes"? Then, give yourself to Him. Will you yield to Him? Will you decide for Him? Will you decide for Him NOW? Will you decide for Him before the sermon is over? Before the day is out? Before the dark night comes? Before the door of hope closes? Before the gate of opportunity slowly swings shut for the last time? Will you come now with a definite surrender to Christ? Why should you wait, since He saves, since He does it all; since waiting has in it all of peril? He asks for you in spite of your sins, your difficulties, your sorrows and your fears. And since He is the Saviour, and since He does it all, and since His time is now, will you let Him save you now?

Surely there are men and women, fathers and mothers, husbands and wives, young men and maidens, sons and daughters, happy boys and girls who will say to Jesus, "Today I bow to Thee, Lord; today I decide for Thee; today I respond to Thy call; today I say 'Yes.'" Since Jesus does all the saving—all of it—and His time is now, your time is now, too! Won't you take Him now?

**O happy day that fixed my choice
On Thee, my Saviour and my God!
Well may this glowing heart rejoice,
And tell its raptures all abroad.**

For a complete list of books available from the Sword of the Lord, write to Sword of the Lord Publishers, P. O. Box 1099, Murfreesboro, Tennessee 37133.